Norway's Response To The Holocaust

Samuel Abrahamsen

HOLOCAUST LIBRARY

New York, N.Y.

Copyright © 1991 by Samuel Abrahamsen

Library of Congress Cataloging-in-Publication Data

Abrahamsen, Samuel, 1917-
    Norway's response to the Holocaust / Samuel Abrahamsen.
        p.   cm.
    Includes bibliographical references (p.
    Includes index.
    ISBN 0-89604-116-6 (cloth) : $20.95. -- ISBN 0-89604-117-4 (pbk.)
 : $13.95
    1. Jews--Norway--Persecutions. 2. Holocaust, Jewish (1939-1945)-
-Norway. 3. Norway--Ethnic relations. I. Title.
DS135.N8A27 1990
948.1'004924--dc20   90-5207
                                                              CIP

Cover design by the Applebaum Company
Printed in the United States of America

Thanks To Scandinavia

Until the founding of Thanks To Scandinavia in June of 1963, America was unaware of the singular acts of humanity and bravery of Denmark, Finland, Norway and Sweden in rescuing persons of the Jewish faith from the Holocaust. During the war years, the mass media featured major battles and armed struggle; but there was no way that information about the Scandinavian Rescue could have filtered out of occupied Europe. When the war was over and we learned the full horror of Hitler's "final solution," we still knew very little about those quiet heroes of the Rescue.

Against the Nazis, who were the perpetrators of such incomprehensible evil, most of the world made no decisive effort to rescue the persecuted and doomed victims. Fear, complacency and disinterest outweighed the sense of responsibility.

Since 1963, in devoted effort to honor the people, the governments and the churches of Denmark, Finland, Norway and Sweden, Thanks To Scandinavia has been raising money to provide "thank you" scholarships and fellowships to Scandinavians at American universities and medical centers. Grants for the fiscal year 1986/87 will exceed $200,000 and efforts continue to enlarge our capital funds (now over $1,750,000) to extend these educational opportunities in perpetuity.

Since 1963, the rescue activities of Denmark have been the subject of books (three funded by Thanks To Scandinavia), magazine articles and film documentaries. However, with the exception of brief chapters in Philip Friedman's book "Their Brothers' Keepers" and the literature of Thanks To Scandinavia, little has been printed in the English language about the rescue activities in Finland, Norway and Sweden.

For historical purposes, and to provide long overdue recognition of the rescue efforts made by the citizens of the three overlooked Nordic countries during the Holocaust, Thanks To Scandinavia has undertaken to publish authoritative and fully documented books by Dr. Hannu Rautkallio on Finland, Professor Samuel Abrahamsen on Norway and Professor Steven Koblik on Sweden.

Inquiries concerning the scholarship fund may be addressed to Thanks To Scandinavia, 745 Fifth Avenue, New York, New York, 10151. Telephone: (212) 486-8600.

We will indeed appreciate support in this honorable endeavor.

RICHARD NETTER
President

VICTOR BORGE
National Chairman

THANKS TO SCANDINAVIA records its gratitude to the following whose significant financial contributions made possible the research, writing and publication of this work:

SANNA & VICTOR BORGE
THE CROWN FAMILY
ALAN C. GREENBERG
CHRIS & BERNARD MARDEN
ALICE & RICHARD NETTER
BARBARA & EDWARD NETTER
THE ROSENSTIEL FOUNDATION
NELL & HERBERT M. SINGER
MARIANNE & JOHN H. SLADE

and

Eleanor & Mel Dubin
in tribute to the name and memory of
NINA MICHELLE DUBIN

and

SAS
in tribute to the name and memory of
S. RALPH COHEN

Holocaust Library

Statement of Purpose

The Holocaust spread across the face of Europe almost fifty years ago. The brutality then unleashed is still nearly beyond comprehension. Millions of innocents, men, women and children, were consumed by its flames.

The goal of Holocaust Library, a non-profit organization founded by survivors, is to publish and disseminate works on the Holocaust. These will include survivors' accounts, testimonies and memoirs, historical and regional analyses, anthologies, archival and source documents and other relevant materials that will help shed light on this cataclysmic era.

These books and studies will be made available to the general public, scholars, researchers, historians, teachers and students. They will be used in Holocaust Resource Centers, libraries and schools, synagogues and churches. They will help foster an increased awareness of the Holocaust and its implications. They will help *to preserve the memory* for posterity and to enable this awesome time to be better understood and comprehended.

"The worst crime you can commit today, against yourself and society, is to forget what happened and sink back into indifference. What happened was worse than you have any idea of. And it was the indifference of mankind that let it take place."

Odd Nansen

"In Loving Memory of our daughter Judy ז״ל".

Norway's Response To The Holocaust

Samuel Abrahamsen

Norway's Response to the Holocaust

Table of Contents

Listing of Maps, Charts, Documents, and Photographs

Acknowledgments

It is my pleasure to express thanks to organizations and persons for making this volume possible. My research has been assisted by these institutions: The National Endowment for the Humanities; The American Council of Learned Societies; The Royal Norwegian Ministry of Foreign Affairs; The Memorial Foundation of Jewish Culture; The Professional Staff Congress Faculty Research Award of the City University of New York; and Yad Vashem, Jerusalem. At Brooklyn College, thanks go to President Robert L. Hess; Provost and Vice-President Ethyle R. Wolfe; and to members of staff and faculty of The Department of Judaic Studies; The Office of Grants and Research; Linda B. Sitea and Brian B. Schwartz.

I would like to express my gratitude to *"Thanks to Scandinavia"* for its support. This generous organization was established in 1963 by Victor Borge and Richard Netter with the purpose of honoring Denmark, Finland, Norway, and Sweden for their humanitarian efforts in rescuing Jews. A special "thank you" is due to the late Mr. S. Ralph Cohen, Vice President of "Thanks to Scandinavia," for having, commissioned me to undertake the research and writing of this book. Professor Leni Yahil of Haifa University and Yad Vashem read the first draft and offered valuable comments and advice for which I am very thankful. The National Archives, Washington, D.C.; Riksarkivet, Oslo; The University Library and Archives, Jerusalem; The Public Record Office, London; the Library, Hebrew Union College–Jewish Institute of Religion/Brookdale Center, New York; the archives of *Adresseavisen* (Trondheim), *Aftenposten* (Oslo), *Dagbladet* (Oslo), and *Verdens Gang* (Oslo); the Library of the Department of Foreign Affairs, Oslo, were all helpful in providing research material for which I am thankful. I would like to thank research assistants Karin Gordon, Joy S. Land, and Trond Vernegg, as well as the following individuals: Abel Abrahamsen, David Abrahamsen, M.D., Heiman Abrahamsen, Dina Abramowitz, Ora Alcalay, Yitzchak Arad, Torleiv Austad, Karsten Alnæs, Randolph L. Braham, Tordis Bornholdt, Arvid Brodersen, Jannicke Bye, Hans Fredrik Dahl, Lene Dragland, Leo Eitinger, Paul Engstad, Kai Feinberg, Ingebjørg Sletten Fosstvedt, Eva Fuksman, Yoav Gelber, Tore Gjelsvik, Gerd Gordon Strong, Norma

Greenstein, Ole Kristian Grimnes, Berthold Grünfeld, Esther Hacco, Sverre Hartmann, Kåre Haukaas, Sigrid Helliesen-Lund, John M. Hoberman, Oddvar Høidal, Bjørn Jensen, Jahn Otto Johansen, Per Ole Johansen, Harold Jones, Jann Erik Joreng, Jack Kahn, Simon Klein, Ole Kolsrud, Jacob Komissar, Harry Koritzinsky, Tor Kummen, Julian Y. Kramer, Shmuel Krakowski, Robert Levin, Ulf Lindström, Ole Jacob Malm, Hadassah Modlinger, E.W. Norman, Miriam Novitch, Orm Øverland, Helge Paulsen, Kuno Paltiel, Willy and Herta Retting, Bruce Roberts, Sverre Rødder, Robert Savosnick, Eva Scheer, Arnt Erik Selliaas, Sigurd Senje, Magne Skodvin, Herman Steinfeldt, Knut Dag Tangen, Stein Ugelvik-Larsen, Ragnar Ulstein, Yngvar Ustvedt, Arbjørn and Sara Uthaug, Johan Vogt, Elie Wiesel, John Alexander Williams, Leiba Wolfberg, and Robert Wolfe. The late Tim Greve was of inestimable help. I especially want to thank Erik J. Friis for his editing of the manuscript and for his great interest in this work.

A heartfelt thanks to Evelyn Fachler, Diane Brenner, and Jan Roby for their careful manuscript typing. Above all, I extend my thanks to my wife who gave me the encouragement and strength to complete this work.

I.

Introduction

In the voluminous Holocaust literature in English, only scant attention has been paid to the fate of Norway's Jews during World War II. The reason may be attributed to the small Jewish population of about 1,600 in 1940, but the percentage of Jews murdered (about 45 percent) was much higher than that of France (26 percent) Bulgaria (22 percent) or Italy (20 percent).[1] Norway lies at the northernmost limit of the Jewish diaspora, in a region, Scandinavia, which displays a common culture and a pattern of social organization based on democracy within the pan-Scandinavian concept of the welfare state. The countries of Denmark, Norway, Sweden, Iceland, and Finland constitute *Norden* (The North) or *De Nordiske Land* (The Northern Countries). The total population of *Norden* in 1984 was about 22 million people. Among them live approximately 23,000 Jews, i.e., 15,000 in Sweden, 6,800 in Denmark, 1,000 each in Finland and Norway.[2] In Iceland there are no Jewish communities, only a few individuals, and Jews do not show up in any Icelandic statistics.

Having developed along parallel lines in many areas, the Nordic countries may appear as an entity instead of as separate, sovereign countries. The differences of the nations, however, show up clearly when one investigates the fates of the Jewish populations in the respective countries during World War II. For instance, none of the other Scandinavian Jewish communities suffered such staggering losses during World War II as did the Jews of Norway. It is against this background that the rescue of

1. Lucy B. Davidowicz, *A Holocaust Reader.* New York: Behrman House, 1976, p. 381.
2. *The American Jewish Year Book, 1986.* New York: The American Jewish Committee and The Jewish Publication Society of America, Philadelphia, 1986, p. 357.

almost half Norway's Jewish population, being brought from occupied Norway to Sweden largely by people of the Norwegian Resistance, takes on added significance.

This book attempts to give a truly balanced and factual account of the fate of the Norwegian Jews during the Second World War (1940-1945) as to the positive actions of thousands of brave Norwegian rescuing Jews from the claws of GESTAPO and the quislings. The negative aspects inherent in Norway's historical relationship to her Jews culminated in the tragic loss of close to half of its Jewish population. However, the stress of the book is on the cooperation between the Resistence Movement (i.e. The Home Front) and the local populations in their efforts to rescue Jews under the most difficult and perilous circumstances during the German occupation. Every escape demanded careful and extensive preparations to succeed: locating those in need of rescue; finding suitable cover places; using code names to avoid revealing information if caught by GESTAPO; obtaining services from trustworthy taxi and truck drivers; locating reliable border pilots; briefing the escapees as to what to tell Swedish authorities when crossing the border. During the years 1940 to 1945 it is estimated that about fifty thousand Norwegians escaped to Sweden among them 925 Jews.

This presentation traces the history of Norway's Jews; the effects of the brutal German occupation on both Jews and non-Jews; the rise and rule of the insignificant Quisling party, *Nasjonal Samling* (National Union) which never in free elections had obtained a single representatives to the Norwegian *Storting* (Parliament). At the last free elections in 1936 Quisling obtained 26,567 votes i.e. 1.84 per cent of the electorate. Furthermore, the book deals with Norway's Jews during the period of emancipation; the rise of anti-Semitism; stages of discrimination; mass arrests and deportations to Auschwitz. The last chapter, "In Retrospect" assesses the reactions and protests against Jewish persecutions, especially the vigorous protests by the Luthern and other churches; the return of the few who survived, and Norway's generous offer to resettle about seven hundred "hard core" central-European concentration camp survivors from tuberoulosis or other physical or mental diseases. In this way Norway confirmed her commitment to international human rights by rehabilitating seriously ill persons of many nationalities who had been denied admission to other countries.

At the time of the German invasion on April 9, 1940, Norway had a population of 2,810,000; out of this total approximately 0.05 percent or fourteen hundred were Jews.[3] In addition, about 200 Jewish refugees from Central Europe were living in Norway at the time,[4] the small number owing to severe immigration restrictions.[5] The chief officer in charge of *Statens Utlendingskontor* (The Norwegian Immigration and Naturalization Authority), Leif Ragnvald Konstad, was a pro-Nazi who had stated that "not a single Jew would be admitted into Norway no matter what the pretext."[6] He regarded Jews as a foreign element "which we ought not to admit into the country," a view which he felt was "probably shared by the entire Norwegian people."[7] Reporting from Bern, Switzerland, September 23, 1942, Norwegian Chargé d'Affaires Ove C. L. Vangenstein wrote to the Royal Norwegian Ministry of Foreign Affairs in London regarding Jewish persecution in Europe and the right to obtain asylum. Switzerland had, however, at that time instituted extraordinary measures not only to return refugees who tried to cross the

3. *Blackbook of Localities Whose Jewish Population was Exterminated by the Nazis*, Jerusalem: Yad Vashem Martyrs' and Heroes' Remembrance Authority, Jerusalem 1965, pp. 410–411: "The list of localities is based on the official publications of the Norwegian Central Bureau of Statistics (*Statistisk Sentralbyrå*)." See also Martin Gilbert, *Atlas of the Holocaust*, Jerusalem: Steimastsky, 1982. Map on p. 46: "The Jews of Norway at the Time of the German Invasion," lists the number of Jews living in fifteen of Norway's 19 *fylker* (provinces): Finnmark (7), Troms (22), Nordland (13), Nord-Trøndelag (1), Sør- Trøndelag (117), Møre og Romsdal (34), Opland (3), Hedemark (14), Buskerud (25), Telemark (5), Bergen (27), Rogaland (10), Oslo (749), Akershus (134), and Østfold (38): a total of 1364 persons. Cf. *Minutes of the Wannsee Conference*, June 20, 1942, listing 1,300 Jews, and "Jødene i Norge. Grafisk fremstilling av antall heljøder efter beskjeftigelse. Efter tellingen av heljøder, begynnelsen av 1942." (The Jews in Norway. Graphical representation of the number of full Jews according to occupations. According to census of full Jews in the beginning of 1942.) *NS Statistiske Kontor.* The National Union Statistical Office gave a total of 1,418 full Jews at that time. See also Carl J. Hambro, *I Saw It Happen in Norway*, New York/London: Appleton-Century Co., 1940, p. 67: "The total number of Jews in Norway never exceeded 1,500 (at the census of 1930, 1359), and of those, none have been very prominent or very rich. There is not a single Jewish banker or financier in Norway."
4. *Encyclopedia Judaica*, "Norway: Holocaust Period," Jerusalem-New York: MacMillan Publishing Co., 1971, Vol. 12, p. 1224.
5. Public Record Office, FO 371/3286, November 19, 1942, British Embassy to Norway, Part I, pp. 2–3.
6. Per Ole Johansen, *Oss selv nærmest. Norge og Jødene 1914–1943*. (Nearest to ourselves. Norway and the Jews 1914–1943) Oslo: Gyldendal Norsk Forlag, 1984, p. 117: "*Konstad . . . hadde sagt at ikke en eneste jøde slapp inn i Norge uansett påskudd.*"
7. *The Legal Accounting against Leif Ragnvald Konstad.* Letter of October 15, 1945, from Hans Heisten, Centralpasskontoret, Oslo, to Counsel Arne Vislie. *Riksarkivet, Oslo* (hereinafter referred to as RAO), p. 2: "*Siktede hadde det syn at jødene var et fremmedartet element som vi ikke burde slippe inn i landet. Personlig var jeg enig heri, og det samme gjaldt vel hele det norske folk.*" Konstad had been appointed to the nazified Norwegian Supreme Court during World War II. He was sentenced in 1946 to five years' imprisonment.

borders, but also to expel those who had slipped in. In this respect, Norway had very little to brag about "because there were not many countries in Europe which were more closed to political and Jewish refugees than Norway before the invasion."[8]

During the war, a total of 6,193 Norwegians were deported, among them 763 Jews. Out of the 5,431 non-Jews deported, 649 died (12 percent). Out of the 763 Jews who were deported, 739 were murdered (97 percent).[9] In addition to the 739 Norwegian Jews killed at Auschwitz and other death camps, 22 Jews perished as a result of war-related actions.[10] Altogether, 24 of the 763 deported Jews returned to Norway. Among the survivors of the deportation, 11 (1.7 percent) were Norwegian-born. Out of the approximately 200 Jewish refugees remaining in Norway after the occupation, 101 were deported and 13 (12 percent) survived.[11] The number of survivors had been "frighteningly low."[12] The Norwegian Jewish community had sustained a loss of "nearly half of its members . . . some families were wiped out entirely,"[13] such as the Shotland families living in Mosjøen, Harstad, and Tromsø.[14] One who returned and wrote a book about his experiences in Auschwitz, Herman Sachnowitz, whose

8. Ove C.L. Vangenstein, *Legation de Norvège*, Bern, September 23, 1942, No. 1398: "*Sveits, jødeforflgelsene og asylretten*," *p. 4*: "*Vi selv har neppe foranledning til å slå oss for brystet, for der var vel ikke mange land i Europa som var mere lukket for politiske og jødiske flyktninger enn Norge før invasjonen*."

9. Leo Eitinger, "On Being a Psychiatrist and a Survivor," in Alvin H. Rosenfeld and Irving Greenberg, eds., Confronting the Holocaust, the Impact of Elie Wiesel, Bloomington: Indiana University Press, 1978, p. 189.

10. Oskar Mendelsohn, "*Jødene i Norge*," in Egil A. Wyller and Terje Gudbrandson, eds., *Jødene og jødedommen. Fra det gamle testamente til Midt-Østen konflikten*, Oslo-Bergen-Tromsø: Universitetsforlaget, 1977, p. 84.

11. Leo Eitinger, "*Overlevende fra konsentraskonsleirer i judaistisk sikt*," *Nordisk Judaistik* (Scandinavian Jewish Studies), December 1975, Vol. I. No. 1, p. 45, Table 2: "*Jødiske overlevende*," (Jews who survived).

12. Leo Eitinger and Oskar Mendelsohn, "*Ni av 530 på 'Donau' overlevde*," (Nine out of 530 on board the *Donau* survived), *Aftenposten*, Oslo, May 8, 1985. See also *Bergens Tidende*, February 8, 1977, "Dystert 35 års minne," (Somber Reminiscence of 35 Years Ago).

13. Hugo Valentin, "Rescue and Relief Activities on Behalf of Jewish Victims of Nazism in Scandinavia," *YIVO Annual of Jewish Social Science*. New York, 1953, Vol. VIII, p. 234.

14. *Våre falne norske jøder, utarbeidet av Det Mosaiske Trossamfund, Oslo, (n.d.)* (Our fallen Norwegian Jews as listed by The Mosaic Religious Society of Oslo.) Yad Vashem Archives B/28-1, p. 36. (Hereinafter referred to as YVA.) The percentage of destruction of Norway's Jews was much higher than that of France (26%), Bulgaria (22%), or Italy (20%). See Lucy S. Dawidowicz, *The War Against the Jews 1933–1945*, New York and Philadelphia, Holt, Rinehart and Winston; Jewish Publication Society of America, 1975, p. 403.

mother had died in 1939, lost the rest of his nuclear family: his father, four brothers, and three sisters.[15]

How and why did these murderous attacks on Norway's Jews occur? The answer must be seen in a wider, European perspective.

The Wannsee Conference*, which took place on January 20, 1942 and had been called by Reinhard Heydrich, consisted of high-ranking German government and party officials. Adolf Eichmann, who took down the minutes, recorded that the Under-Secretary of State of the German Foreign Office, Martin Luther, warned of encountering difficulties in deporting the small Scandinavian Jewish populations.[16] This was especially true of Denmark, where the government, public opinion, the civil service, and the administration obstructed German plans.[17] The Nazi aim of making Europe *Judenrein* (clean of Jews) included Norway "no matter how high the cost, no matter how small the yield."[18]

The Nazi machinery of destruction was headed by *Reichsführer-SS und Chef der Deutchen Polizei* Heinrich Himmler and Reinhard Heydrich, *Chef der Sicherheitspolizei und des SD* (Chief of Security Police and Security Services). Its central office, known as *Reichssicherheitshauptamt* (RSHA, or Reich Security Main Office), with its regional and local branches, became the main implementing organization for the killing of Jews. One of these units, located in Norway, was headed by *Oberregierungsrat* and *SS-Oberführer* (Colonel) Franz Walter Stahlecker. He had been ordered on April 10, 1940 to act as Himmler's personal representative and to assume charge of the German police in Norway. The chief of the Gestapo from January 1942 to February 1945 was *SS-Sturmbannführer* (Major) Hellmuth Reinhard. Other high Gestapo officials involved with Jewish persecution in Norway were SS-

---

15. Herman Sachnowitz, *Det Angår også deg* (It Also Concerns You.) Oslo: J.W. Cappelens Forlag, 1976, pp. 6–9.

16. The approximate prewar Jewish populations were: Denmark, 6,500; Finland, 1,700 (1937); Norway, 1,359 (1930); Sweden, 6,653. *The Universal Jewish Encyclopedia*, New York, Vol. 3, p. 534; Vol. 4, p. 309; Vol. 8, p. 242; Vol. 10, p. 112 for the four countries respectively.

17. Michael R. Marrus and Robert O. Paxton, "The Nazis and the Jews in Occupied Western Europe, 1940–1944," *The Journal of Modern History*, 54:4 (December 1982), p. 688.

18. Raul Hilberg, *The Destruction of European Jews*. Chicago: Quadrangle Press, 1961, p. 355.

* On May 8, 1990 a group of 150 Jews from around the world gathered at Wannsee to commemorate the place where leaders of the Third Reich had met to plan the systematic *killing of European Jews. N.Y. Times* 5/9/90.

Oberführer Heinrich Fehlis and *Obersturmbannführer* (Lieutenant Colonel) Gerhard Friedrich Ernst Flesch who, in the fall of 1941, had been transferred as Gestapo chief from Bergen to Trondheim where the Jewish persecution began that same Fall. The person in charge of the RSHA Jewish Office in Norway, IVB4, was *Hauptsturmführer* (Captain) Wilhelm Constantin Wagner, who had arrived in Oslo from Berlin on February 13, 1941. He succeeded the Criminal Commissar, Wilhelm Esser, who had established lists of Jewish stores and of the members of the Jewish congregations.[19] The triumvirate of Helmuth Reinhard, *Reichskommissar* Josef Terboven, and *Obergruppenführer* (Lieutenant General) Rediess of the SS, with the close cooperation of the Norwegian state police, the regular police, and Vidkun Quisling with his party *Nasjonal Samling* (National Union), set the stage for the identification, registration, roundup, arrest, property confiscation, and deportation of Jews from Norway.

Did racial theories play a role in the registration, arrest, and deportation of Jews by Quisling or non-Quisling participants? In his book, *From Day to Day*, Odd Nansen wrote:

> We are guilty of a disgraceful action. We are accepting the German division of mankind into two classes, Jews and scoundrels in one, the rest, in the other.[20]

A prominent Norwegian social scientist, Dr. Johan Galtung, maintained that the catastrophe that befell the Norwegian Jews had some connection with the national rejection of Jews and dissenters in general.[21]

Was a lack of cultural and social integration of Jews in a non-pluralistic society a factor in the victimization of Norway's Jews, based on a concept that Norwegians "have a profound sense of community feeling" as expressed by Harry Eckstein in his well-received study on Norway?[22] Does his theory signify that the Norwegian community feeling did not include Jews, as implied by the Norwegian historian Haakon Holmboe

---

19. Ole Kolsrud, *"For 40 år siden — Da nordmenn jaget jøder: Rød "J" i alle pass,"* (Forty years ago — when Norwegians Persecuted Jews: Red "J" in all Passports) *Dagbladet*, Oslo, October 16, 1982, p. 19.

20. Odd Nansen, *From Day to Day*, New York: Putnam, 1947, p. 171.

21. Gerd Gordon, *The Norwegian Resistance During the German Occupation, 1940–1945; Repression, Terror and Resistance: The West Coast of Norway*, Ann Arbor: University Microfilms International, 1981, p. 498.

22. Harry Eckstein, *Division and Cohesion in a Democracy: A Study of Norway*. Princeton: Princeton University Press, 1966, p. 79, footnote #2.

in his description of prisoners at the Grini Concentration Camp?[23] This
implication has been strengthened by Professor Johan Vogt's hypothesis,
in his book *Det store brennoffer* (The Holocaust), where he stated that
the fate of the Jews during World War II was for non-Jews only one of
the war's many problems and probably, for quite a few, one that was
mostly in the periphery. Dr. Vogt opined that most non-Jews, including
his countrymen, were "spectators and indifferent to the persecution of
the Jews in Norway."[24]

In view of the minuscule size of the Jewish minority one might expect
Norway to be free of anti-Semitism, but this was not the case. Article
2 of the Constitution of May 17, 1814, had forbidden Jews admission to
the Kingdom. A noted author asked: "Was our constitution perfect?
Keeping the Holocaust freshly in mind, Article 2 becomes exceedingly
painful."[25]

An example of xenophobia and dislike of Jews is found in Ragnar
Ulstein's *Svensketrafikken* (1974), a work on the rescue of Jews from Norway to Sweden. He relates an episode from a training camp for Norwegian police in Dalarna, Sweden, in 1944, where a film was to be
shown. The movie projectionist was "short and dark and reminded the
soldiers of a Jew. . . . When he entered the hall, one shouted and many
joined in: 'Get out that Jewish devil!' Another refugee who knew the projectionist well, shouted in despair, "You err, he is no Jew, he is one of
us!" The author added that "anti-Semitism was not dead among Norwegians."[26]

Even among the Norwegian police troops in Sweden (1943-1945),
anti-Semitism had become so marked that the Chief of Police Troops,

23. Haakon Holmboe, "*De som ble tatt,*" in Sverre Steen, ed., *Norges Krig,* Oslo:
Gyldendal Norsk Forlag, 1950, Vol. III, p. 480: "*Da den store deporteringen av jøder
foregikk på slutten av året 1942, ble det tilbake en del som var gift med 'ariske' kvinner
og som reddet livet på den måten. . . . Utenom disse ble det i alt vesentlig anbrakt
nordmenn der. . . .*" (When the large deportation of Jews took place towards the end of
1942 some of those who were married to "Aryan" women remained behind, and thus saved
their lives . . . Except for these, Norwegians were for the most part brought there.)

24. Johan Vogt, *Det store brennoffer. Jødenes skjebne under den annen verdenskrig,*
Oslo: Universitetsforlaget, 1966, pp. 14–15, 24.

25. Elizabeth Aasen, "*Er skolen kunnskapssentral eller kulturformidler?*" *Samtiden,*
Aschehoug, Oslo, Vol. 90, No. 1, 1981, p. 76: "*Vi skal nok huske 1814, men er alt verdt
å minnes med like stor jubel? . . . Var vår grunnlov perfekt? Med Holocaust i frisk
erindring blir paragraf 2 ekstra pinlig.*"

26. Ragnar Ulstein, *Svensketrafikken. I. Flyktningar til Sverige, 1940–43,* Oslo: Det
Norske Samlaget, 1974, p. 250.

Ove Gjedde, issued an announcement on August 7, 1944, warning about
the increase in anti-Jewish episodes, "which have also been present during programs of entertainment." He found it necessary to draw the attention of the various commanders to the growing anti-Semitism so that
they could "take the necessary measures preventing repetitions."[27]

A factor of great importance in analyzing the fate of Norway's Jews was
the attitude of the local population, which ranged from active sympathy
to apathy, indifference, and direct hostility leading to betrayal of Jews
in hiding or to direct participation in their destruction. The annihilation
of European Jewry could not have taken place without the active
participation of the local population. This collaboration and assistance
by the local population made possible the terrible effectiveness of the
machinery of destruction in countries allied with or occupied by Germany.[28] This destruction process took place not only under the auspices
of Gestapo, SS, and German armed forces, but with the cooperation of
European civil servants, engineeers, lawyers, physicians, professors,
diplomats, the transportation workers, local police, and labor unions.
The breakdown of moral and ethical values and the lack of integrity of
the professional elite allowed for its participation in the destruction of
Jews. In Norway, the identification, roundup, and arrests were carried
out by Norwegian police "who were not active Nazis. . . . It shows how
dangerous it is when a powerful force is combined with a totalitarian system, how easy it is to become a victim of this system."[29] Other factors
contributing to the annihilation of European Jews were the collaboration of local Nazi sympathizers, the coordination of bureaucracies to increase the efficiency of the murder machinery, the lure of enrichment
through confiscation of Jewish properties, as well as prospects of re-
wards and promotions. The swiftness of the German actions against the
Jews in October-November 1942 found both the Jews and their would-
be rescuers unprepared.

27. *Kunngjøring til Reservepolitiet, Nr. 222/1944, Stockholm, den 22. aug. 1944:* Fra
Sjefen for Reservepolitiet, *"Episoder overfor jødene.* Sjefen for Reservepolitiet har fått
melding om at der i enkelte leire har inntruffet episoder hvorunder mannskapene er
kommet i konflikt med de innkalte jøder. Tendenser til sjikanering av jødene har også vært
til stede i underholdingsprogrammene. Da episodene synes å øke, finner Sjefen for
Reservepolitiet å burde gjøre Leirkommandantene oppmerksomme på saken. En tør be
Leirkommandanten treffe de nødvendige forholdregler for å hindre gjentagelse."

28. Theodore S. Hamerow, "The Hidden Holocaust," *Commentary,* 79, 3, 1985, p. 34.

29. Stein Ugelvik Larsen, "Det angår også Norge: Vanlige politifolk offer for farlig
kobling," *Bergens Tidende,* March 31, 1979.

On the other hand, threats of severe punishment by the occupying power for assisting Jews did not prevent rescue operations. It has been established that the earlier public protests took place, the greater their influence in diminishing the victimization of Jews.* This holds true also for the national leadership. There were far more survivors when a clear stand on attacks against Jews was taken at an early stage. When there was a lack of national direction, the local bureaucracy obediently implemented German requests and instructions, increasing the number of victims.[30]

The first example of obedient compliance with German demands took place on May 10 and 11, 1940, when Norwegian police confiscated radios belonging to Jews. The highest Norwegian civil authority at that time, *Administrasjonrådet* (The Administrative Council), made no protest against this discriminatory action. By October 1942, when the decisive action against the Norwegian Jews took place, effective means had been developed by the Home Front leadership to alert the general Norwegian population to impending arrests of other groups, such as union members, teachers, students, clergymen, etc. This was done through the use of *paroles*, that is, directives on civil resistance during a period of *holdingskamp* (steadfast moral struggle) against Nazification. The *parole* had gradually assumed the status of a directive, to be observed by all loyal citizens. Whenever a group was threatened with encroachment of civil or judicial rights, a massive machinery went into effect to thwart such persons' arrests and, if arrested, to secure release or prevent deportation. These civil protests reached a climax in May 1941, when 43 professional organizations in Norway, representing more than 750,000 individuals, delivered a formal protest to Reichskommissar Josef Terboven against the intense attempts at Nazification of these organizations.[31]

No nationwide directive was ever issued warning the Norwegian population against cooperation in any aspect of the Jewish persecutions: the registering of Jews; stamping of "J" on identity cards and sale of Jew-

---

* "Victimization" in this context is defined as the percentage of the total Jewish population declared by the Nazi-Quisling ideology as "Jews" and "*Mischlinge*" who were arrested, deported, murdered, or Jews who succumbed as a result of war-related actions (1940–45).

30. Aharon Weis, "Quantitative Measurement of Features of the Holocaust: Notes on the Book by Helen Fein," *Yad Vashem Studies*, Vol. XIV, Jerusalem: Yad Vashem, 1981, p. 328.

31. Johs. Andenæs, O. Riste and M. Skodvin, *Norway and the Second World War*, Oslo: Johan Grundt Tanum Forlag, 1966, p. 68.

ish properties; roundup and arrest; and, finally, deportation. Jews were the only ethnic group destined for destruction that did not receive the support and potential protection afforded through the *parole*, a directive which Tore Gjelsvik, an authority on the civil resistance, called an "effective and distinctive instrument of warfare in the resistance against Nazification."[32] Written directives as to arrests and deportations of Norwegians, however, were not used until 1943.[33]

The official reaction of the Norwegian Government-in-Exile to the deportation of Norway's Jews, contained in a letter of December 1, 1942, from Trygve Lie, Norway's Minister for Foreign Affairs, to the British Section of the World Jewish Congress, stated that:[34]

> ". . . it has never been found necessary for the Norwegian Government to appeal to the people of Norway to assist and to protect other individuals or classes in Norway, who have been selected for persecution by the German aggressors, and I feel convinced that such an appeal is not needed in order to urge the population to fulfill their human duty towards the Jews of Norway."

In the Nazi ideology, however, Jews differed from non-Jews in many fundamental respects. The war against the Jews aimed at the total destruction of *all* Jewish children, women, and men, regardless of age or status in life. Furthermore, the "Final Solution" had to be accomplished while World War II was still on. Destruction of other "inferior races" could wait until after the war. No economic considerations or ethical and moral principles would stand in the way of completing the "Final Solution." It is against this background that the rescue of nearly half of Norway's Jews must be seen. Hundreds of would-be rescuers did not wait for any directive to assist their Jewish countrymen *in extremis*. These rescuers followed their own conscience and went forth to perform magnificent deeds against heavy odds, including risking their own lives. A spontaneous outburst of active helpfulness provided aid to hundreds of endangered Jews, enabling them to reach Sweden through improvised and often difficult rescue operations. Some of the rescuers were killed, others committed suicide, or were themselves forced to flee to Sweden

---

32. Tore Gjelsvik, *Norwegian Resistance, 1940–45*, London: C. Hurst and Co., 1979, p. 31.

33. Letter from Tore Gjelsvik to author, June 28, 1983.

34. Trygve Lie to A.I. Easterman, Political Secretary, British Section, World Jewish Congress, London, *Utenriksdepartementets arkiv*, Oslo (Archives of the Ministry of Foreign Affairs), #24373, 1/12/42.

to avoid being arrested by the Gestapo.[35] These were individuals whose courage and moral strength made them protect and hide Jews, sometimes in hospitals, providing them with food, clothing, and false identification cards for illegal border crossings over treacherous terrain. For such courageous acts, Yad Vashem of Jerusalem gave recognition on March 21, 1967 to Ingebjørg Sletten Fosstvedt for her singular rescue achievements. For their heroic rescue of endangered Jews group recognition was given to the Norwegian Resistance Movement on October 30, 1977, with the "Yad Vashem Medal" naming Norway as "one of the Righteous among Nations."[36] On this occasion Israel's ambassador to Norway, the Hon. David Rivlin, spoke on behalf of Yad Vashem:[37]

> The Norwegian Resistance, in the dark years of the Nazi occupation, added a golden chapter to the book of heroism of patriots, warriors and lovers of freedom, sons and daughters of occupied Europe who fought the enemy of mankind for their countries and for the freedom of Europe. Members of the Norwegian Resistance also inscribed themselves in the hearts of the Jewish people for what they had done to save Jews of this small community, which lost half of its members in the extermination process.

A report from the U.S. Office of Strategic Services of December 29, 1942, gave some details of the many seemingly insurmountable difficulties encountered by rescuers. It stated that on December 21, 1942, thirty-four Norwegian refugees crossed into Sweden. In all cases the refugees were aided and assisted by Norwegians, who furnished them food and clothing and oftentimes money. "The Norse are infuriated by the anti-Jewish attitude of the Germans and Quislings, and in order to frustrate the maltreatment of Jews risk their own lives. In one case, that of Dr. Henri Zellner, 74-year old escapee, he stated that his wife, who was paralyzed, refused to leave Norway, and she was carried across the border bodily by the Norwegians."[38] Gideon Hausner, Chief Prosecutor at

---

35. Arvid Brodersen, *Mellom Frontene* (Between the Fronts), Oslo: Cappelens Forlag, 1979, p. 67.

36. *Jødisk Menighetsblad for Det Mosaiske Trossamfund, Oslo og Trondheim* (Jewish Journal for the Mosaic Religious Community, Oslo and Trondheim), Vol. 2, No. 3, December 1977, pp. 13–32: "*Yad Vashem-medalje til våre redningsmenn*" (Yad Vashem Medal to our Rescuers). The Yad Vashem medal is given to non-Jews who endangered their own lives to save Jews from Nazi persecutions.

37. *Særtrykk av Jødisk Menighetsblad*, vol. 2, No. 3, 1977. *Talene ved overrekkelsen av medaljen fra Yad Vashem til Norges Hjemmefrontmuseum 30. oktober 1977, p. 27.* (Speeches at Presentation of Medal to Norway's Home Front Museum from Yad Vashem, October 30, 1977).

38. Office of Strategic Services, Washington D.C., CD 11880, declassified N7750140,

the 1961 trial of Adolf Eichmann, stated in *Justice in Jerusalem* that "the
Norwegian underground transported eight hundred Jews across the
country to safety in Sweden under especially perilous circumstances."[39]
Sweden was not easily accessible on foot. The border zone patrolled by
German troops was an area of thick forest, mountainous terrain, difficult
to cross in snow and frost.

Compared with the well-organized Nazi machinery of destruction in
Norway no comparable organized force for rescue existed. However, the
Norwegian Resistance Movement rose to the occasion by improvising
and later organizing the rescue of most of Norway's Jews coming to Sweden between the years 1941 and 1944. Warnings of impending roundups
and arrests of Jews had been given, only to be met with disbelief, even
by many Jews themselves.

A closer look at the development of anti-Semitism, emancipation, and
counter-emancipation in Norway will clarify the position of Jews in Norway and throw light on the various events and policies leading on the
one hand to the murder of close to half of Norway's Jewish population
and, on the other, to the successful rescue and escape of hundreds of
Norway's Jews to Sweden. During 1941, however, there were inci-
dences of Jews from Norway being denied asylum in Sweden. This policy was changed in November 1942. At that time, the Swedish Red Cross
informed the Reichskommissariat in Oslo through the president of Norway's Red Cross, that Sweden was prepared to accept all Jews who were
going to be deported. On December 15, 1942, a written objection was
received stating that the removal of Norway's Jews to Sweden was not
in accord with the objectives of the government of Germany.[40] In looking at these events, it is important to keep in mind the political, military,
economic, and social control exercised by the occupying power in Norway during the occupation.

dated December 29, 1942: "From a confidential source in Stockholm this Agency has received a report, dated December 29, 1942, based on reliable information as of December
22."

39. Gideon Hausner, *Justice in Jerusalem*, New York: Harper & Row Publishers, 1966,
p. 256.

40. *Norge och den norska exilregeringen under andra världskriget* (Norway and the
Norwegian Government-in-Exile During the Second World War), Statens öffentliga
utredningar 1972. The Department of Justice, Stockholm: Justitiedepartementet, 1972,
p. 133: "*judarnas överflytting til Sverige ej överensstämde med den tyska regeringens
syften.*"

כל המקיים נפש אחה כאילו קיים עולם QUICONQUE SAUVE UNE VIE SAUVE L'UNIVERS

תעודת כבוד
ATTESTATION

Le présent Diplôme atteste qu'en sa séance du 26 Juin 1977 la Commission des Justes près l'Institut Commémoratif des Martyrs et des Héros Yad Vashem a décidé sur foi de témoignages recueillis par elle, de rendre hommage aux SAUVETEURS DES JUIFS DANS LA RESISTANCE NORVEGIENNE qui au péril de leur vie ont sauvé des Juifs pendant l'époque d'extermination, de leur décerner la Médaille des Justes et de les autoriser à planter un arbre en leur nom dans l'Allée des Justes sur le Mont du Souvenir à Jérusalem.

Fait à Jérusalem, Israël, le 31 juillet 1977

POUR L'INSTITUT YAD VASHEM POUR LA COMMISSION DES JUSTES

Translation of Diploma Presented to the Norwegian Resistance Movement by Yad Vashem:

ATTESTATION

This diploma confirms that at its meeting on June 26, 1977, the Commission of the Just of The Holocaust Martyrs' and Heroes' Remembrance Authority of Yad Vashem decided, having received verified witnesses to honor the Rescuers of Jews by the Norwegian Resistance Movement which with danger for their own lives saved Jews during the period of annihilation, and to present THE MEDAL OF THE RIGHTEOUS and to plant a tree in their honor in the Avenue of the Righteous on The Memorial Hill in Jerusalem.

Jerusalem, July 31, 1977

The sentence surrounding the diploma like a wreath reads:
"THE ONE WHO SAVES ONE LIFE, SAVES THE WHOLE WORLD."

II.

RESCUE

At the Eichmann Trial in Jerusalem in 1961, Mrs. Henrietta Samuel, the wife of Norway's rabbi, explained how she and her three children were brought safely to Sweden by members of the Resistance Movement. Hours before the arrest of women and children on November 26, 1942, Mrs. Samuel received a call from "Inge" (i.e., Ingebjørg Fosstvedt Sletten) who said: "It is very cold tonight. Please dress your children warmly." Mrs. Samuel understood the warning and dressed the children immediately.* An hour later "Inge came and took us, my sister-in-law and her two children to a neighboring house where we could stay only for one day." Then the group was taken to an empty house in the outskirts of Oslo. Mrs. Samuel's ten-year-old son saw a radio and was frightened that it might be a Nazi house, since loyal Norwegians had been ordered to turn in their radios early in the occupation. Mrs. Samuel calmed down her son by saying, "If Inge sent us here, the place is safe."[1] The Samuel family stayed there for about one week before joining a group of about forty persons at a collecting point on Meltzer's Street for transportation by truck to the Swedish border.[2]

Rabbi Elchanan Samuel related in an interview in 1979 that he escaped in a truck "hauling potatoes to a village near the Swedish border ... so we were a cargo of potatoes. We travelled about two hours from Oslo, walked another half hour or three quarters of an hour in cold

---

* It should be noted that telephones were tapped.

1. "Norse Underground Saved Many Jews, Israel Trial Told," *The New York World Telegram*, Vol. 128 No. 211, May 11, 1961 pp. 1,2.

2. *"Hjelpen til jødene i Norge et lyspunkt i Eichmannsaken,"* ("Assistance to the Jews in Norway a Ray of Light in the Eichmann Process"), *Aftenposten*, Oslo, May 12, 1961, pp. 1;11.

16 SAMUEL ABRAHAMSEN

weather — 4 degrees below zero Fahrenheit ... until we crossed the Swedish border, thank God, and we were saved. The Swedish police welcomed us, it was the night of December 4 and 5th, the first night of Hanukkah. The Swedish police greeted us, questioned us about why we crossed the border. We said we were Jews. They let us travel to a refugee camp in Alingås, east of Gothenburg, where we spent the first few days in Sweden. The Jewish community had established a children's home there with Nina Hasvold in charge."[3]

The Samuels were among the many Jews who escaped to Sweden from Norway during the years 1942-1943, as stated in a Swedish report:[4]

"Altogether, about 700 persons of Jewish descent arrived from Norway during the year 1942. About 500 of these have Norwegian citizenship. Among the refugees who arrived during the year [1943], about 150 are made up of Norwegians and those stateless Jews living in Norway. The majority of these arrived in Sweden in the beginning of the year 1943."

These rescuers did not wait for directives from any organization to help their Jewish countrymen in extremis. They went forth to perform humanitarian deeds against heavy odds. Some of the rescuers were killed, others committed suicide or were themselves forced to flee to avoid being arrested by the Gestapo.[5] They demonstrated moral courage under severe mental and physical stress, and risked their lives in providing Jews with food, clothing, false identity and ration cards, and transportation across the Swedish border. The rescue actions followed various patterns, both organized and spontaneous. Many Norwegians who otherwise would not have taken part in clandestine operations became actively involved in rescuing Jews, thereby lending support to the Resistance.

One of the most extraordinary achievements was the rescue of fourteen children who in 1938 and 1939 had been brought to Norway from

3. Rabbi Elchanan Samuel, interviewed by Bonnie Gurewitsch. Tape No. OH 79-15 SuC Rg 546, February 1, 1979, Center for Holocaust Studies, Brooklyn, N.Y. pp. 10-11.
4. Sveriges Förhållande till Danmark och Norge under krigsåren, Redogörelser avgivna til den svenska utrikesnämnden av ministern för utrikesärendena 1941-1945 (Stockholm: Nordstedts och Söner, 1945), P. 149. "Sammanlagt hava under år 1942 omkring 700 personer av judisk börd inkommit från Norge. Omkring 500 av dessa hava norskt medborgarskap. Av de flyktninger, som anlänt under året, (1943) utgjördes omkring 150 av norska och i Norge bosatta, stastlösa judar. De flesta av dessa inkommo til Sverige i början av år 1943 ...".
5. Arvid Brodersen, Mellom Frontene (Between the Fronts) Oslo: J.W. Cappelens Forlag, 1979, pp. 67-68.

Austria and Czechoslovakia and resided at the Oslo Jewish Children's Home[6] in Holberg's Street. One of the Norwegian women who had worked indefatigably to bring Jewish children from Central Europe to Norway was Sigrid Helliesen Lund, a member of the governing council of the "Nansen Help." Her main job was to take care of the children who came to Norway through this refugee organization. During the month of October 1939, she and her assistants travelled to Czechoslovakia to transport to Norway 37 children from 5 to 13 years of age from Prague through Germany and Sweden to Norway. Most of them were placed with foster parents in southern Norway. Mrs. Lund related:[7] "Together with two nurses we left Praha for Sassnitz . . . The journey through Germany had been very uncomfortable. For instance, in Berlin we had to walk from one railroad station to another since no transportation would take us along either by bus or by car. We were on our way to the synagogue for a meal. While walking there, quite a few persons spit at the children. One of the boys asked in German: "Why do people in Berlin spit at us?" I tried to explain to him that they probably had a cold, or that it possibly was just a manner they had, and that he should not concern himself about it. This was a consolation for him — but not for me."

During the night of November 25, 1942 Nina Haslund, the administrator of the Oslo Jewish Children's Home received a warning about impending arrest of children and women. She immediately contacted other members of the Resistance Movement, among them Ingebjørg Fosstvedt Sletten and Tove Filseth Tau. The children were transported across the Swedish border to Alingås, where they remained until the end of the war. Several official rescue organizations participated in the various missions, most notably *Nasenhjelpen* (The Nansen Aid) led by Odd Nansen, son of the noted explorer and humanitarian, Fridjof Nansen. Odd Nansen was arrested in early 1942, incarcerated at Grini and depoted to Sachsenhausen, but survived. Other members oo the Nansen Aid were professors Fredrik Paasche, Georg Morgenstierne, Fredrik Winsnes and Mrs. Sigrid Helliesen Lund.

One of the "Nansen Children," as they were called, Berthold Grünfeld from Bratislav, Czechoslovakia, had arrived in Norway during

6. Arieh L. Bauminger, *Roll of Honor*, Tel Aviv: Hamenorah Publishing House, 1971, p.66.

7. Celine Wormdal, *Kvinner i krig. Gløtt inn i en forsømt samtidshistorie* (Women at War. Glimpses from Forgotten Contemporary History), Oslo: A. Ashehoug and Co., 1979, pp. 10-11.

the fall of 1939 through the Nansen Aid. He travelled together with a
group of 42 Jewish children through Europe[8] "in the firm belief that we
were going on vacation to Norway. When we passed through Berlin, the
victorious German troops had just returned from the war against Poland. The illusion about vacation was emphatically broken soon after our
arrival in Norway. We were told that we would not see our parents again,
which was a shock for us, but proved to be true." His parents, fearing
for the children's lives under Nazi rule, sent them away to a safe place.[9]
With the occupation of Norway in April, 1940, and the subsequent Jewish persecutions in October, 1942, the children's lives were endangered.
Sigrid Helliesen Lund has given this description.[10]

> On October 25th, the phone rang. A male voice said: 'It will be a large
> party tonight. But we only want to have the large packages.' Then he hung
> up. At first I was in doubt as to what it meant. Myrtle and I spoke about
> it for quite some time. Then we said almost simultaneously: 'This must
> be about the Jews. And the large packages must be the men.' They were
> at risk of being arrested immediately.

It was agreed to warn as many men as possible without daring to use
the telephone. The problems were how to locate the men and obtain access to their homes. Many Jews were warned but did not believe persecutions could happen in Norway on any large scale. For others the
warning came too late. The Norwegian police had already been there.
On the other hand, when women and children were being arrested in
November, 1942, many had received warnings by the Norwegian State
Police, which had been infiltrated by the Resistance.[11] Such rescue efforts succeeded in bringing about 850 Jews to Sweden, which had no
policy to permit large-scale Jewish immigration. Only after 1942 did
Sweden "seriously begin to seek ways to help Jews, but it was "late . . .
very late."[12] The official documents from the Norwegian Charge

8. "*Nansenbarnet-tretti år etter,* (The Nansen Child — Thirty Years Later), *Dagbladet,*
Oslo, June 2, 1971.
9. "*Nansenbarn med seksualliv som fag,*" (Nansen Child With Sexuality as Profession),
Aftenposten, Oslo, February 3, 1973.
10. Sigrid Helliesen Lund, *Alltid Underveis. I samarbeid med Celine Wormdal.* (Always on the Road. In Cooperation with Celine Wormdal), Oslo: Tiden Norsk Forlag, 1981,
p. 96.
11. Per Ole Johansen, *Oss selv nærmest. Norge og jødene 1914-1943,* Oslo: Gyldendal
Norsk Forlag, p. 151.
12. Steven Koblic, "Sweden's Attempts to Aid Jews, 1939-1945," *Scandinavian Studies,*
Vol. 56, No. 2, Spring 1984, pp. 92-93.

d'Affairs in Stockholm related several instances of entry being refused by the local *landsfiskal* (rural sheriff) during the years 1941-1942, such as the author's mother and three of her sons. But the rescue efforts of Norway's Jews continued unabated. From 1938 to 1940 Sweden granted permission to some three thousand Jews to remain in the country. The Swedish consul in Oslo, Leif H. Øhrvall worked tirelessly for rescuing Norwegian Jews to Sweden.

The escape routes from Norway had been extended across the North Sea to the Shetland Islands and Northern Scotland. Among those who escaped with the help of the local Resistance was a business man from Bergen, Alexander Eidenbom. It was logical that persons on the west coast would rather try to escape by boat to England than to travel the long way across Norway to reach the Swedish border. Such was the case of Eidenbom who, having been warned about his imminent arrest because he was a Jew,[13] escaped aboard the M.B. Stølegut, which docked in October, 1942, in Lerwick, the Shetland Islands, after a stormy crossing.[14]

Other Jews crossed by boat to Iddefjord in sourtheastern Norway. Jo Benkow, who later (1985) became president of the Norwegian *Storting* (Parliament), related his escape together with his uncle Herman Florence:[15]

"Together with a border pilot, Uncle Herman and I travelled to Berg station outside of Halden. We went into town and had dinner at a hotel. After dark we walked towards the Iddefjord, where the border pilot had arranged for a row boat. We said good-bye to our helper. I was given permission to row. I can't deny that my heart was hammering in my chest. I did not actually panic, but I was afraid. As far as I could understand, it was not in in the least difficult to discover us, although it was total darkness.

"We arrived safely [in Sweden]. Three weeks later we were informed that my brother [Harry] had arrived safely. Right afterwards, my father and my brother's family arrived. The others never arrived. . . . all women in the family were killed at Auschwitz. My mother was 47 years old

---

13. Ragnar Ulstein, *Englandsfarten*. Band II. *Søkelys mot Bergen* (The Voyage Towards England. Vol. II. Spotlight on Bergen), Oslo: Det Norske Samlaget, 1962. p. 162.

14. Ulstein, op.cit., pp. 352-353.

15. Jo Benkow, *Fra Synagogen til Løvebakken* (From the Synagogue to the Lion's Hill), Oslo: Gyldendal Norsk Forlag, 1985, p. 180.

and my sister 28. Aunt Solveig was 38 and Cecilie 42. Her daughter was only four years old."

Another successful escape route across the Iddefjord was related by Mr. Harry Koritzinski, President of the Oslo Jewish congregation from 1921 to 1941. In an interview in the Oslo *Dagbladet* (The Saily Journal) of July 25, 1970 by Olav T. Storvik Mr. Koritzinski told about his own escape:

> "I went into hiding during the fall of 1942 until I managed to escape through the help of Marine Captain Holter, Secretary General of *Norsk redningsselskap* (Norwegian Rescue Organization at Sea). He brought my family and myself by boat to Sweden."

The rescue of individuals and their families called upon great courage and resourcefulness in view of the harsh reprisals introduced by the occupying authorities to prevent escape. A decree, issued on October 12, 1942, by Reich Commissar Terboven, made the following offenses punishable with death sentences or penal servitude:[16]

> Entering or leaving Norway without permission; associating in any way or giving any aid to prisoners of war or political prisoners, or to any person working for an enemy power spreading propaganda hostile to German interests; listening to radio broadcasts other than German-controlled; acting in any way against German interests in favor of the enemy or committing acts of violence against representatives of the occupying Power.

When the need for mass rescue of Norway's Jews became apparent, a special transport organization was formed under the code name "The Carl Fredriksen Transport Organization," which worked closely with the Resistance in the rescue operation. In charge were a former policemen, Alf Tollef Pettersen and Rolf Syversen, who owned a gardening property at the Sukkertop Road, which became the collecting point for the refugees to be ferried by trucks to the Swedish border.[17]

Leon Bodd of Oslo, one of those rescued by the Frediksen Transport Organization, recounted his escape:[18]

> My family lived in Trondheim. I spent my childhood there and attended

---

16. *Public Record Office*, (London) FO 371 36877, p.8; "Reprisals."
17. "The Border Pilot," (Grenselosen), *Nordisk Kriminalkrønike i Samarbeid med Nordisk Politiidrettsforbund* (Nordic Criminal Chronicle in Cooperation with Nordic Athletic Organizations), Oslo: *Nordisk Kriminalkrønike*. A/S, 1982, p. 386.
18. *Op. cit.*, pp. 388-389.

the grammar school. It was a happy and sorrowless existence, and I gained some very good friends. The German invasion in 1940 changed all that. On October 28, 1942, the Gestapo started arresting all Jewish males over 15 years of age. At this time there was no school attendance, so we were sent to different farms in Trøndelag to assist with the harvest. When my mother heard about the anti-Jewish actions in Trondheim, she called me not to return to Trondheim; but I had to report to the local police at Steinkjer and show my identity card, stamped with a "J." I was warned to escape immediately.

A new identity card was issued to him without a "J." He went by boat to be with his mother at Leksvik but soon decided to leave for Oslo to be with his father. He stayed with a classmate, Hans Petter Johnsen, but had to change lodgings because it was unsafe to stay too long in one place.

The Home Front hid Leon Bodd in the Lovisenbery Hospital, where the doctor in charge cooperated with MILORG (the military organization of the Home Front).[19] Hospitals had become centers for the hiding of Jews until rescue could be arranged. Doctors, nurses and hospital administrators falsified the records of these "patients" and failed to report the release of Jewish patients to the State Police, as ordered by the Quisling government. Even Jews who had been hospitalized with legitimate illnesses were spririted safely across the Swedish border on stretchers. The Carl Fredirksen Transport Organization" used two trucks five evenings weekly from October 1942 to January 1943, rescuing hundreds of Jews.

The Resistance Movement drew heavily upon the many athletic organizations, constituting more than three hundred thousand young men and women who had, early in the occupation, been subjected to intense nazification.[20] Nevertheless, they remained committed to humanitarian ideals as evidenced by their courageous efforts in rescuing Norway's Jews. Sigrid Helliesen Lund, Alf and Gerd Pettersen, as representatives of the Norwegian Resistance Movement, were honored at Yad Vashem, Jersualem, on March 20, 1978 as *The Righteous Among Nations.*

19. MILOG, i.e., Military Resistance Organization, called Home Front from 1944. See, Tore Gjelsvik, *Hjemmefronten. den sivile motstand under okkupasjonon 1940-45.* Oslo: J.W. Cappelens Forlag, p. 238.

20. Sverre Kjellstadli, *Hjemmestyrkene. Hovedtrekk av den militære motstanden under okkupasjonen* (The Home Forces. Main Account of the Military Resistancce during the Occupation). Oslo: H. Aschehoug and Co. (W. Nygaard), 1959, Vol. I, p. 73.

Tragically, some of the rescuers sacrificed their lives. One of them, Supreme Court Justice Erling Malm, had been very active in hiding Jews in his home and in assisting their escape. When arrested by the Gestapo, he took his own life rather than face torture. He knew too much about the rescue operations and the leaders of the Home Front, which included his son, Dr. Ole Jakob Malm, who had to escape to safety in Sweden,[21] where Norwegian refugees received good assistance. The two Swedish customs supervisors, Vidar Hed and Nils Sjöstedt at Töckfors have been singled out for their courage. They often crossed over the border to Norway to assist refugee needing help, or to gather information about the Norwegian border police.[22]

It took several years before the various resistance groups became organized into a Resistance Movement, although these forces had taken up the fight against the German occupiers as early as 1940. After the Norwegian military forces had left Norway in 1940 they continued the fight from abroad. The Norwegian Government in London, the Allies, and the Home Front were victorious in their ideological as well as their military battles against Nazism. The rescue of about half of Norway's Jews during World War II represented one of the failures in Nazi-Germany's diabolic plan to exterminate the Jews of Europe.

21. Brodersen, op. cit., pp. 67-68.
22. Ragnar Ulstein, *Svensketrafikken 1. Flyktningar til Sverige 1940-43 (The Sweedish Traffic. Refugees to Sweden 1940-43)*. Oslo: Det Norske Samlaget, 1974, p. 244.

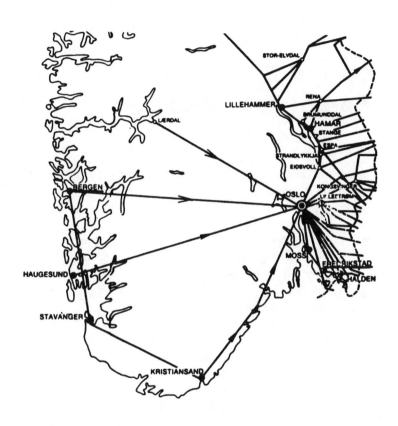

Escape Routes in Southern Norway to Sweden

Source: Ragnar Ulstein, Svensketrafikken. Flyktningar til Sverige 1940-43. Oslo: Det Norske Samlaget, vol. I, 1974.

III

Norway's Jews during the Period of Emancipation

In the history of emancipation of European Jewries the French Revolution constituted the great dividing line; that was the event that ushered in a new era for Jews to obtain social equality and civil rights. This emancipation, however, suffered serious setbacks in countries where the old restrictions were reimposed. The road to full emancipation for European Jews was opposed by strong, hostile forces, a development generally known as Counter-Emancipation, i.e., ". . . efforts to exclude or limit the participation of Jews in the life of the surrounding society or in the state."[1] One of these countries was Norway.

On May 14, 1814, the Norwegian Constituent Assembly at Eidsvold barred Jews from entering the country. The vote was 94 in favor, 7 opposed. This action falls within general definition of anti-Semitism, which authoritative sources describe as actions aimed at preventing religious and civil rights for Jews. These inimical actions take place, in the words of the eminent Swedish historian Hugo Valentin, "because it is not the Jew who is hated, but an imaginary picture of the Jew, which is confounded with reality."[2]

The Exclusion Clause was contained in the very last sentence of Arti-

---

1. Abraham G. Duker and Meir Ben-Horin, eds., *Emancipation and Counter- Emancipation*, New York, Ktav Publishing Co., 1974, p. 357.
2. Hugo Valentin, *Antisemitism Historically and Critically Examined*, London, 1936, p. 305. See also Nathan Ackerman and Marie Jahida, *Antisemitism and Emotional Disorder*, New York, 1950, p. 19: "Antisemitism is any expression of hostility, verbal or behavioral, mild or violent against Jews as a group or against an individual Jew because of his belonging to that group."

cle 2 of *Norway's Fundamental Act of May 17, 1814*, known an *Norges Grunnlov*. This clause states: "The Evangelical-Lutheran Religion shall be maintained and constitutes the established Church of the Kingdom. The inhabitants who profess the same religion are bound to educate their children in the same. Jesuits and Monastic orders shall not be tolerated. Jews are furthermore excluded from entering the Kingdom."[3]

Article 2 was adopted in a country with no professing Jews and with only a few having personal acquaintance with them. Furthermore the Norwegian Contitution of 1814 made no provisions for obtaining *Lejdebrev* (Letters of Safe Conduct) that would enable Jews to legally enter Norway for specific, limited purposes. Norway had been united with Denmark from the year 1397 to 1814, and safe conduct letters had been provided for in King Christian's Law for Denmark (1683) for those descended from Spanish and Portugese Jews. This provision was adopted for Norway in 1687. Moreover, there was a reward of half a hundred Rixdaler (fifty dollars) for anyone reporting illegal Jews in Norway, and a fine of one thousand dollars for Jews having illegally entered the Kingdom of Norway.[4] An amendment to affect a change would need a two-thirds majority in the Norwegian parliament (the Storting). The battle for a change had to go through four regular parliamentary sessions before its successful adoption in the year 1851.[5] The person who success-

---

3. *Kongeriget Norges Grundlov Given I Rigsforsamlingen paa Eidsvold den 17de mai 1814*, Oslo, H. Aschehoug & Co., 1964, p. 1. *"Den evangelisk-lutterske Religion forbliver Statens Offentlige Religion. De Indvaanere, der bekjende sig til den, ere forpligtigede til at opdrage sine Børn i samme. Jesuiter og Munkeordener maae ikke taales. Jøder ere fremdeles udelukkede fra Adgang til Riget."* This edition contains a facsimile of the May 17, 1814, Constitution, but the translations of Article 2 into English (p. 33) and French p. 49) are of the *amended version*, and do not therefore contain the sentences prohibiting admission of Jews.

4. *King Christian V Law of 1683*, Vol. 3 Chapter 20, Articles 1 and 2, *"Om Jøder og Tatere."* (Regarding Jews and Gypsies): *"Ingen Jøde maa sig her i Riget indbegive, eller sig finde lade, uden Kongens særdellis Lejdebrev under tusinde Rix Dalers Straf af hver Person, som uden foreskrefven Lejdebrev betrædis. Hvo, som nogen Jøde angiver og Kongens Ampt-Mand anviser, skal derfor hver Gang have et halv hundred Rix Daler."* (No Jew must enter this country, or stay here, without a special Letter-of-Safe-Conduct from the King under penalty of one thousand dollars for each person who enters without the authorized Letter-of-Safe-Conduct. Any one who informs against a Jew to the King's County Sheriff shall receive each time fifty dollars. See, also, Sverre M. Nyrønning, *"50 riks-daler for å angi en jøde,"* (50 dollar to denounce a Jew), Trondheim, *Adresseavisen*; November 20, 1982.

5. Article 110 of the constitution contains details regarding amendments. See: *Kongeriget Norges Grundlov,*, op. cit., p. 12. The amendment for changing Article 2 needed a 2/3 majority. It was defeated by the Norwegian Parliament three times: in 1842 with

fully led the fight for admission of Jews into Norway was the poet Henrik Arnold Wergeland (1808–1845), who worked indefatigably for an amendment to the Constitution.

The arguments for prohibiting the entry of Jews to Norway had been articulated in 1817 in the Bergen newspaper *Den Norske Tilskuer* (The Norwegian Spectator) by the noted political leader Christian Magnus Falsen (1782–1830) also known as "the Father of Constitution." He had voted against admission of Jews because he was convinced that Jews could never become reliable citizens in a state where they did not rule. Neither could the Jewish faith "harmonize with our form of government. It is as a Jew, not as a human being" that Jews were excluded.[6] Wergeland fought with all the means at his disposal against the restriction. As a practical politician, theologian, publicist, and poet he agitated through the latter part of his life to win admission for the Jewish people to Norway. On his visit to Paris in 1831, he had, for the first time, met Jews and described in his memoirs in 1839 that he felt "humbled in front of them as if I stood confronted with two ancestors of humanity, or in front of Abraham and Melchizedek, in whose tent the only true God was being worshiped."[7] Wergeland heaped scorn upon his countrymen who were so proud of having enacted a liberal Constitution, and pointed out that only Spain and Norway had enacted legislation to bar Jews from entering their respective countries.[8] Norway had, in fact, become "a Protestant Spain in intolerance."

On June 28, 1839, Wergeland sent a proposal to amend the last sentence of Article 2 via a member of the Norwegian Parliament, Søren Anker Wilhelm Sørensen (1793–1853). The compelling arguments for lifting the ban were primarily based on moral grounds: Can a Christian

---

51 votes for and 43 against; in 1845 with 45 for and 54 against; and in 1848, when there were 43 in favor and 59 against. On June 13, 1851, the amendment was finally adopted with 93 in favor and 10 against admission of Jews to Norway.

6. *Den Norske Tilskuer*, (The Norwegian Observer), October 8, 1817, nos. 41, 42, pp. 334–336. For further details, see the author's article, "The Exclusion Clause of Jews in the Norwegian Constitution of May 17, 1814, "*Jewish Social Studies*, Vol. XXX, No. 2 (1968): 67–88.

7. *Henrik Wergelands Samlede Skrifter*, Kristiania, Chr. Tønsbergs Forlag, 1857, Vol. 8, p. 571.

8. In respect to Spain, Wergeland was in error since there was no ban in the Spanish constitution against the entry of Jews. See Caesar C. Aronsfeld, *The Ghosts of 1492 — Jewish Aspects of the Struggle for Religious Freedom in Spain 1848–1976, New York, Jewish Social Studies Monograph Series Number 1, Columbia University Press, 1979, pp. 2, 12.*

state exclude other human beings whose family life is beyond reproach and whose life style is worthy of emulation? Shall a people whose history abounds in spiritual giants, mighty law-givers, great scientists and humanitarians, as well as being intellectual leaders in ethics, arts, music, literature and philosophy, forever be banned from Norway? These questions preoccupied Wergeland while he prepared a document in 1841 entitled *Indlæg i Jødesagen til Understøttelse for Forslaget om Ophævelse af Norges Grundlovs Paragraph 2, sidste Passus* (Plea for the Jewish Cause to support the Proposal to amend the last sentence of Article 2 of the Norwegian Constitution.)

Professor Halvdan Koht in his book on Wergeland[9] surmised that what impelled him to write "The Plea for the Jewish Cause" was the fact that on May 12, 1839, a Jew from Altona had arrived in Kristiania by ship. Since the latter did not know that Jews were barred from Norway, he returned immediately after having been warned not to disembark without at first obtaining a letter-of-safe-conduct. There is also the incident of 1817 on the West Coast, involving a shipwrecked crew with a Polish Jew, Michael Jonas, who arrived in Bergen on his way from Königsberg to London. Mr. Jonas was arrested and transported as a common criminal under police surveillance to Kristiania and from there over Svinesund to Sweden.[10] This shows that the exclusion clause was strictly enforced.[11]

One instance of legal admission of Jews to Norway involved an application fom the Department of Finance to the Department of Justice on July 17, 1834. It requested that a letter-of-safe-conduct be issued to Solomon Heine (uncle of Heinrich Heine) to complete a loan to the State of Norway on behalf of the banking firm of Hambro and Søn. The request was granted.

To further strengthen his case Wergeland published a sequence of

9. *Halvdan Koht, Henrik Wergeland. Ei Folkeskrift*, Kristiania, 1908, p. 140.

10. Henrik Jæger, *Illustrert Norsk Litteraturhistorie*, Kristiania, 1896, vol. II, p. 235: "*Den skibbrudne jøde var saaledes imod sin vilje nødt til at betræde norsk grunn. Følgen var at han øieblikkelig blev fakket av øvrigheten og som en forbryder under politieskorte transportert til Kristiania, og derfra over den svenske grense.*" (The shipwrecked Jew was thus against his will forced to step on Norwegian soil. As a consequence he was immediately captured by the authorities and like a criminal transported to Kristiania under police escort and from there across the Swedish border.)

11. *Storthingsforhandlinger* (Parliamentary Debates), 1842, pp. 270–274, contain detailed information regarding police enforcement of the constitutional prohibition of admitting Jews to Norway.

poems, *Jøden* (The Jew), which ranks as some of the most beloved poetry
in Norway, among them the poems "Sandhedens Armée" (The Army of
Truth), "Røst i Ørknen" (A Voice in the Desert) and "Juleaftenen"
(Christmas Eve). In the latter, the poet raises the fundamental ethical
question of right and wrong, when the peddler, "Old Jacob," is left out
in the snow to die in a blizzard while a dog is let in, "men ingen Jøde
i et kristent Huus" (but no Jew in a Christian house).[12]

In preparing Norwegian public opinion in 1842 for the parliamentary
debate regarding admission of Jews, Wergeland had to refute the many
false and baseless charges against their religion, their moral conduct,
and their responsibilities as citizens. Wergeland has given us a very vivid
and detailed account of what took place in the Norway Parliament of September 9, 1842.[13] He began by noting that there are times in the affairs
of any nation when there may be a lack of men willing to make difficult
decisions.[14] The poet added that Friday, the 9th of September 1842, had
been an important day in Norway's history since on that day the proposal
to rescind the constitutional prohibition for admission of Jews had been
defeated.[15]

Wergeland had prepared the way carefully, not only through prose
and poetry, but also by printing handbills. One of them had been printed
in such large type that they could be read from the gallery. They were
"meant for the farmers to enable them to read without glasses." This important handbill contained the following:[16]

"To Parliament.
What is morally right ought to happen. It is also morally necessary and
useful in our time although its utility may not be clear at the moment.
This is as certain as that which is morally wrong carries its own inner
punishment although it may be temporarily useful. This is the Constitution for the Government of God, for the moral order in the world, and
is recommended for serious reflection concerning today's question of Ar-

12. *Henrik Wergeland Samlede Skrifter* — *efter det norske Studentersamfunds
forvaltning udgivne af Hartvig Lassen. Kristiania: Chr. Tønbergs Forlag* (Nine Volumes:
1852–57), Vol. 3, pp. 316–322: *"Juleaftenen,"* (Christmas Eve). Hereinafter referred to as
Skrifter.
13. *Skrifter*, Vol. 8, *"Jødesaken i det norske Storting,"* pp. 435–439 (The Jewish Case
in the Norwegian Parliament).
14. Ibid., p. 437.
15. Loc. cit.
16. Ibid., pp. 454–455: see also, Hans Heiberg, *Så stort et hjerte* — *Henrik Wergeland,*
(Such a Big Heart), Oslo, Aschehoug & Co, 1972, p. 149 ff.

ticle 2, last paragraph, of *our* Constitution. In addition, there are many positive, unambiguous and religious commands for the Christians, from the mouth of Jesus Christ and his Apostles, such as Matth. 5, 44–45; 7, 12, 22, 39; Luke 6, 36; Hebr. 19, etc. all of which confirm the above.

Kristiania, September 9th, 1842
Respectfully,
Henrik Wergeland."

Wergeland represented the humanistic and democratic tradition of individual Norwegian fighting for Jews. He viewed admission of Jews as a moral issue of the highest order, and one which for him had become a question of conscience. It was his father, Nicolai Wergeland (1780–1848), an exponent of eighteenth-century humanism and rationalism,[17] who was his son's main source of influence and his best friend.[18] Nicolai Wergeland had been a member of the Constituent Assembly at Eidsvold in 1814, where he was one of the strongest opponents of the admission of Jews to Norway.[19] But his son took the opposite stand.

In his work *Norges Konstitutions Historie* (The History of Norway's Constitution) Henrik Wergeland included a report on the session that took place on April 16, 1814, at Eidsvold. The following additional anti-Semitic argument was expressed during the debate on the eighth "basic proposals" (Grundsætninger) by Professor Georg Sverdrup and Nicolai Wergeland: since it was alleged that the Jews regarded fraud against Christians, not only as permissible, but as meritorious, the Jews had themselves forfeited all rights to be admitted.[20] The comments by Wilhelm F. K. Christie, Secretary to the Constituent Assembly, revealed superstition and prejudice against Jews. It was his wording that was adopted for Article 2.[21]

---

17. Gunnar Christie Wasberg, *Historien om 1814. En beretning i dokumenter, sitater og illustrasjoner* (The History of 1814. A Descripton with Documents, Quotations and Illustrations), Oslo: Dreyers Forlag, 1964, p. 43.

18. Francis Bull and Fredrik Paasche, *Norsk Litteraturhistorie*, Oslo: H. Aschehoug & Co., 1959, Vol. III, p. 123.

19. Harald Beyer, *Henrik Wergeland*, Oslo, 1946, p. 364.

20. *Skrifter*, Vol. 9, Kristiania, 1857, p. 164: "Jøderne skulle anse Bedrageri mod Kristne for tilladt, ja forjenestefullldt, og maatte saaledes ansees for selv at have betaget sig al Ret til Optagelse. (Jews are supposed to consider fraud against Christians as permissible, yes, meritorious, and have thus to be regarded as having excluded themselves from all rights to admission.)

21. Nils Braunaas, "Jødehat på Eidsvold — og i København," (Jew-hatred at Eidsvold and in Copenhagen), "Dagbladets Kronikk," *Dagbladet* (Oslo), December 29, 1964, pp.

The debate also heard the views of Pastor Hans Jakob Grøgaard (from
Nedenæs Amt), who maintained that it would be considered neither intolerant nor illiberal to refuse admission to Jews since "the question was
not to expel the Jews from the country." The "foremost among the farmers,"[22] Teis Jakob Torkildsen Lundegaard (from Austad), made an abrupt
end to the discussion "by suddenly getting up and shouting: 'Stand up
all who do not want to have Jews in the country!' And everyone followed
as if hit by an electric shock."[23] The prohibition of the entry of Jews was
voted upon on Wednesday, May 4, 1814, with 94 in favor and 7 against.
Wergeland had completed his own studies which made it abundantly
clear that the anti-Jewish arguments were based on falsehood and ignorance. A survey made by Leiv Amundsen regarding Wergeland's read-
ings at the University Library in Oslo showed the poet's wide interest
in the Jewish problem.[24] He had assisted the Constitutional Committee
during the preceding years in preparing forty-seven important documents in six foreign languages: Danish, Dutch, English, French, German, and Swedish, not all of them favorable to the Jewish cause. Those
in the German language warned against admitting Jews.[25] Wergeland
had prepared primary source material to show how Jews were treated

---

3–4.
   22. Wasberg, op. cit., p. 50: "Den fremste bonden var likevel *Teis Lundegaard* fra
Austad."
   23. *Skrifter*, Vol. 9, pp. 164–165: Grøgaard fandt, at da Spørgsmaalet ikke var om at
udjage jøderne af Landet, kunde det ikke kaldes intolerant eller illiberalt at nekte dem
Adgangen; — Spindværingen Teis Lundegaard gjorde omsider en brad Ende på Debatten
ved raskt at rejse sig med Raabet: 'Staar op Alle, som ingen Jøder ville have i Landet!'
Og alle fulgte det som ved et elektrisk Stød." ("Grøgaard opined that since the question
was not to expel the Jews from the country, it could not be called intolerant or illiberal
to refuse them admission; Teis Lundegaard from Spindvær made at last an abrupt end of
the debate by suddenly getting up and shouting: 'Stand up all who do not wants to have
Jews in the country!' And everyone followed as if hit by an electric shock.") See also Bernt
A. Nissen, *Året 1814*, (A) Oslo: Aschehoug, 1964, pp. 96–97.
   24. Leiv Amundsen, "Henrik Wergeland og Universitetsbiblioteket," *Edda*, Vol. XLV
(1945), pp. 120–121, 131; among the books Wergeland borrowed in 1839 were: February
18 — Chr. Fr. Rühs, *Over Jødernes Fordringer på Tydsk Borgerret*, København, 1816,
and by the same author: *Christendommens og det Tydske Folks rettigheter Forsvarede mod
Jødernes Fordringer*, København, 1817; August 7, 1839 — N. Treschow, "Kultur forbinder
Nationer, men smelter dem ikke sammen. En Tale holden 18111 i den jøiske Frieskole,"
København, 1811. Also, April 24, 1844 — J.W. Gertz, *Det befriede Israel*, København,
1804.
   25. *Storthingsforhandlinger*, 1842, Vol. IX, "Stortinget den 9de September," p. 259:
"5 Exemplarer af et trykt Skrift under Titel: Beweis aus der jüdischen Religion, dass die
Juden in den christlichen Staaten nich emancipiert werden können, wenn die Christen
nicht dadurch sich ihnen zinsbar und unterthan machen wollen."

in France and Holland, in Catholic Belgium, and in North America, "which had offered the Jews a fatherland in the complete meaning of the word, and these have offered the country their best efforts, their property and their blood. In all the above countries no one regards the native Jew ("den i Landet Fødte Jøde) as a stranger."[26]

By the year 1841 Wergeland had become fully acquainted with foreign constitutions and their treatment of Jews. He found religious liberty flourishing in most countries — but not in Norway. He reported on England and France, where religious tolerance had been firmly established. He concluded that his native country was not a leader, but a laggard; a nation way behind most other countries in respect to emancipation of Jews.[27] For instance, in the same year, 1814, when Norway on May 4 enacted the constitutional ban on admitting Jews, the Danish Parliament had on March 29 enacted emancipatory legislation, i.e., giving Jews "equal access with other citizens to make a living in any legal way."[28]

The amendment to admit Jews was defeated, 51 in favor, 43 against, since a two-thirds majority was needed. The next day, September 10, 1842, Wergeland introduced a new proposal for consideration by the Storting in 1845. During this period he published poems advocating admission of Jews to Norway. At this time the poet was ill with tuberculosis, but his poem Paa Sygelejet (On the Sick Bed) reflected his defiant mood. He compared himslf to the dandelion — "the weed that grows the more you step on it,"[29] and adopted the slogans: Noli desperare[30]

---

26. Ibid., pp. 254–255.

27. Henrik Wergeland: Indlæg i Jødesagen til Understøttelse for Forslaget om Ophævelse af Norges Grundlovs Sidste Passus, Kristiania, 1841, pp. 14–16 (Plea for the Jewish Cause in Support of the Proposal to suspend Article 2, last paragraph, from Norway's constitution).

28. Joseph Fischer, "Rigsforsamlingen på Eidsvold i 1814 gav Nordmændene den frieste Forfatning, som da kendtes, men medens Danmark netop samme Aar, den 29. Martz, erklærede, at alle Jøder, som var født i Landet, eller havde faaet Tilladelse til at bosætte sig her, skulde 'nyde lige Adgang med vaare øvrige Undersaater til at ernære sig på enhver lovlig Maade,' vedtog Rigsforsamlingen 5 uger senere, den 4. Mai: 'Jøder ere fremdeles udelukkede fra Adgang til Riget.'", in Tidsskrift for Jødisk Historie og Literatur, Vol. 3, København, Levin og Munksgaard, 1925, p. 260.

29. In "Den Første Gang," Prolog til Campbellerne (1838): "Med eet af Løvetand den spredes, den Urt, der groer, jo mer den trædes" (In "For the First Time," a Prologue to Campbellerne).

30. In "Tidselskjærplukkeren" (The Thistledown Gatherer) from Jøden, 1842, Skrifter, Vol. 3, p. 334.

— do not despair — and *Vincere canendo*[31] — conquer by singing. And sing he did. Some of his best poetry stems from this period, notably in his collection of poems which he called *Jødinden, Elleve blomstrende tornekviste* (The Jewess, Eleven Blossoming Briar Shoots), 1844, where he continued to advocate the admission of Jews to Norway, as in his poem "Tornekviste" (Briar Shoots):[32]

> Noble women, such the bower
> Judah's stock has so richly borne;
> Gentle mothers, flower on flower,
> Heroines bold, when dangers lower;
> Judith's rose of the bleeding thorn.
>
> Why should Norway then feel dread of
> Welcoming these to every dale?
> why in the coldness we are bred of
> Should not our Northern vein be fed of
> Eastern ardour, and love instead of
> Law's harsh voice in our land prevail?

Wergeland was a deathly sick man when he wrote the prose and poetry contained in *The Jewess*.[33] He was at this late stage of his life particularly concerned about the forthcoming parliamentary session to start in the fall of 1845. A letter of May 3, 1845 to his friend Søren Sørensen, who again would sponsor a bill for admission of Jews, gives us an insight into Wergeland's courage on his deathbed:[34]

31. Aage Kabell, *Wergeland*, Vol. 1, *Barndom og Ungdom*, (Childhood and Youth). *Skrifter utgitt av Det Norske Videnskapsakademi i Oslo, Historisk-Filosofisk Klasse*, Oslo, 1957, p. 197 (Works published by the Norwegian Academy of Science in the Historical-Philosophical Category).

32. *Skrifter*, Vol. 3, pp. 341, 342. Translation by Charles Wharton Stork in *Anthology of Norwegian Lyrics*, New York, The American-Scandinavian Foundation, 1942, pp. 34–35, by permission of A.S.F.

33. *Skrifter*, Vol. 3, *Jødinden*, 1853, pp. 339–421: 1. *Tornekviste?* (Briar Shoots?), 2. *Blodet* (The Blood), 3. *Mødrene* (The Mothers), 4. *Den lykkelige Viv* (The Happy Wife), 5. *Sjelekamp og Seier* (Mental Agony and Victory), 6. *Kvinderne på Kirkegaarden* (The Women at the Cemetery), 7. *Drengen ved Blaaporten* (The Boy at the Blue Gate), 8. *Røst i Ørknen* (A Voice in the wilderness), 9. *Jeg er nu saaden, Jeg* (That's How I Am), 10. *Følg Kaldet* (Follow the Call), 11. *Kaadt Ukrud* (Wanton Weeds), 12. *Efterretningen* (The News). The latter poem was written in 1842 after the amendment to admit Jews to Norway had been defeated by Parliament. The original of this poem was first printed in *Jødesagen i det norske Storthing*, 1842. (The Jewish Cause in the Norwegian Parliament).

34. Jæger, op. cit., Vol. II, pp. 237–238: "*Naar Dagen kommer i Storthinget, da kjæmp, ras, græd, og naar intet hjælper, da demasker Egoismen og Raaheden med den Chirurgs Kulde, der flænger Huden af et Ansigt under en Obduction. —Det gælder Folkets Ære i Verden. Vær vred og tapper.*"

When the day comes in the Parliament, then fight, rage, cry, and when nothing helps, then unmask egoism and brutality with the detachment of a surgeon who slashes the skin off a face during dissection. The people's honor in the world is at stake. Be angry and courageous.

During his long illness, Wergeland received much encouragement from friends abroad. A special tribute was offered him by the Danish-Jewish author Meïr Aron Goldschmidt, who had written about Wergeland in glowing terms in his publication *Corsaren*. On July 7, 1845, Goldschmidt wrote him a personal letter:[35]

When I think of you, Wergeland, I am proud to be human. Here we have proof that immortality exists, that God has given the human being a divine soul. Let me greet you as the greatest of the contemporary Nordic poets.

It was, however, Bjørnstjerne Bjørnson who many years later expressed the nation's grief in Wergeland's untimely death by stating that there "had never been a more beautiful sight in the spiritual sphere of the Nordic countries than Henrik Wergeland on his death bed."[36]

Wergeland, who died on July 12, 1845, did not live to see the achievement of his objective: A constitutional amendment by the Norwegian *Storting* which opened the doors of Norway to the Jewish people in 1851. Before his own countrymen did so, Danish and Swedish Jews dedicated a monument to Wergeland in Stockholm on October 22, 1847.[37] The unveiling had to take place there because Jews were not permitted to enter Norway without permission. In 1849, however, a Jewish delegation consisting of Dr. Jakob Levertin, Dr. Axel Lamm, and Mr. Lipman Lipmanson received letters-of-safe-conduct, and the monument was again unveiled on "Our Savior's Cemetery" (Vor Frelsers Gravlund) in Kristiania on Wergeland's birthday, June 17.[38] The front of the monument contains this inscription:

35. Leiv Amunden, ed., op. cit., p. 331: *"Naar jeg tænker på Dem, Wergeland, er jeg stolt af at være Menneske. ... Her see vi Syn for Sagen, at der gives en Udødelighed, at der af Gud er givet Mennesket en guddommelig Sjæl."*

36. Harald Beyer, *Norsk Litteraturhistorie, Revidert og utvidet ved Edvard Beyer*, Oslo, 1963, p. 193 (The History of Norwegian Literature, revised and extended by Edvard Beyer).

37. Samuel Abrahamsen, "The Saga of Norway's Jews," *Congress Weekly*, Vol. 18, No. 25, October 8, 1951, p. 8.

38. Hugo Valentin, *Judarnas Historia i Sverige*, Stockholm, Albert Bonniers Forlag, 1924, p. 537.

"HENRIK WERGELAND, b. MDCCCVII - d. MDCCCXLV — The tireless Champion of Men's and Citizens' Freedom and Right."

On the back one reads:

"Grateful Jews outside Norway erected this in his Memory.[39]

On June 13, 1851, [40] the Norwegian Parliament finally passed a bill, with 93 in favor and only 10 against, lifting the constitutional restriction against the entering of Jews into Norway. A proclamation of September 24, 1851, signed by the Norwegian-Swedish Union King, Oscar I, formally opened the doors for Jews to enter Norway.

Far from flooding the country, as had been predicted, Jewish immigration into Norway was exceedingly slow. More than a year passed before the first Jew, Abraham Vollman from Copenhagen, arrived in Kristiania. By 1890 the Jewish population had grown to 214. By 1900 it had reached 642. By that time, a *Jødisk Samfund* (Jewish Society) had been formed in Oslo with Nathan Nachman Nathan as its first president. The following year the name of the community was changed to *Det Mosaiske Trossamfund* (The Mosaic Religious Community), which is still the official name of the congregation. [41] A synagogue at Bergstien 13 was inaugurated on May 21, 1920. In 1918, another congregation, *Den Israelitiske Menighet*, was formed with Isak Siman as the first chairman of the Board. A synagogue was built for the new congregation at Calmeyergaten 15, but in 1939, the two congregations were united, keeping the two synagogues, which served the Oslo community until

---

39. Alfred Werner, "Henrik Arnold Wergeland," *The Universal Jewish Encyclopedia*, New York, 1948, Vol. 10, p. 503. On the front of the monument: "Henrik Wergeland, f. MDCCVIII - d. MDCCCXLV den utrættelige kæmper for menneskets og borgerens frihed og ret." On the back one reads: "Taknemmelige jøder udenfor Norriges grændser reiste ham dette minde MDCCCXLVII."

40. Tønnes Andenæs, *Grunnloven vår. 1814 til idag*. Oslo-Bergen-Tromsø: Universitetsforlaget, 1966, p. 5. The Storting — Norway's Parliament was established in 1814, while the Parliament Building was built in 1860–1866. The Storting is elected every fourth year. It meets annually on the first weekday of October and remains assembled as long as necessary. It has a membership of 155. The Storting divides itself into two sections: The *Lagting* consisting of 39 members and the *Odelsting* consisting of 116 members. All legislative proposals which affect the citizen's rights and duties as well as relationship to the state are considered separately by both sections, while resolutions relating to treaties, budgetary and functional matters are dealt with in plenary sessions. The main work is done in 13 standing committees."Courtesy: Royal Norwegian Embassy Information Service, 825 Third Avenue, New York, NY 10022.

41. Harry M. Koritzinsky, *Jødernes historie i Norge* (The History of the Jews in Norway). Kristiania, 1922, pp. 65–66.

1942, when they were confiscated by the occupying power.[42]

The pogroms in Russia during the 1880s led to further immigration and to the establishment of a congregation in 1905 in Trondheim, Norway's third largest city. The congregation took the same name, *Det Mosaiske Trossamfund*, as the congregation in Oslo. The immigrants to Trondheim had come mainly from Russia, including Poland and Lithuania, but also from Germany and Denmark. Many had spent several years in Sweden before settling in Norway. On October 14, 1925, the world's northernmost synagogue was inaugurated in Trondheim with Salomon Abrahamsen as the Chairman of the Building Committee. At that time the Jewish population in that city was about 300. According to the census of 1920, the total Jewish population of Norway was 1457. The census of 1930 listed 1359 Jews, and that of 1990 listed 1,045 Jews as members of D. M. T.[43]

Despite the small number of Jews in the country, Jewish life was characteried by a number of religious, secular, and charitable organizations and publications. A youth organization was established in 1909 in Oslo; a Scandinavian Youth Society was founded in 1919 with nine chapters throughout Scandinavia; a WIZO (Women's International Zionist Organization) group and several other associations were founded, such as a home for the aged, a B'nai Akiva, and a children's home; a *Hevra Kadisha* (burial society) was founded in 1914 in Oslo.

A Zionist organization had been formed in 1912 in Oslo with a local chapter, "Herzliah," in Trondheim, the same year. A Zionist publication, *Jødisk Tidende (Jewish News)*, came out in 1918 and *News from Israel* after the establishment of the State of Israel. A building for social activities and classrooms for religious instruction were added to the synagogue in Oslo in 1960 with financial assistance from the American Joint Distribution Committee. Two publications, *Israeliten* (The Israelite) and *Hatikwoh*, were published up to the outbreak of World War II. Since 1975, *Jødisk Menighetsblad* has been issued three times annually. The Trondheim congregation, in 1927, had hired rabbi Abraham Israel

---

42. "Sammenslutning mellem de to jødiske menigheter i Oslo. Men begge synagoger bibeholdes," *Aftenposten*, Oslo, October 2, 1939 (Merger of the two Jewish Congregations. But both synagogues are being maintained.)

43. Alf B. Godager, *Islam seiler i medvind* (Islam sails with a fair Wind), *Aftenposten*, Olso, March 3, 1990, p. 23: "Det framgår ellers av statistikken at Det Mosaiske Trosamfunn har 1045 medlemmer." (Furthermore, it appears from the statistics that the Mosaic Religious Society has sl,045 Jews).

Jacobsohn (1891–1955) who had been born in Tiberias, Palestine. He had at first settled in Sundsvall, Sweden, before coming to Norway where he served the Trondheim congregation in many capacities with great distinction from 1927 to 1940.

Although the battle for admission of Jews had been won in 1851, the fight for complete emancipation still had a long way to go. While religious dissenting groups in 1845 had obtained legal right to organize outside the Lutheran State Church, this law did not in any way speed up the process of securing emancipation. The Law of Dissent of 1891 and Constitutional amendments from 1852 to 1971, led to gradual abandonment of various discriminatory laws, such as that of taking the citizen's oath, access to public offices, restricting cabinet positions to Lutherans only (1919), and requiring public school teachers to be members of the State Church. A liberal law of June 13, 1969 permitted dissenting religious communities to obtain public funds for religious education of children. [44] Article 2 of the 1814 constitution, which had rejected the central principle of the Age of Enlightenment — equality for all, [45], was remedied only on May 9, 1964, when the Norwegian Parliament unanimously passed an amendment to Article 2 guaranteeing "free religious exercise to all its inhabitants."[46] The Norwegian Constitution in Article 2 had given the official Lutheran religion a clear priority over the principles of freedom of religion. The protection of *Lutheranism*, furthermore, had been enforced by the denial of admission of Jews, and prohibition of Jesuits and Monastic Orders. [47]

---

44. *Lov av 13. juni 1969, nr. 25 om trudomssamfunn og ymist anna* (Law of June 13, 1969, No 25, regarding religious societies and other items). Article 19 stipulates regulations for appropriating public funds to support dissenting organized religious communities whose children were excused from religious instruction in the public schools.

45. Isaiah Berlin, *Dictionary of the History of Ideas*, New York: Charles Scribner's Sons, 1973, Vol. II, p. 109.

46. Article 2 of the Norwegian Constitution was amended on May 9, 1964 to read: "*Alle Invaanere af Riget have fri Religionsudøvelse*" (All inhabitants of the Kingdom have freedom of religion).

47. Tor Johan Sørensen, in *Kirke of Kultur* (Church and Culture), Oslo: Gyldendal, vol. 86, no. 2, 1981, p. 89: "*På Eidsvold ble den offentlige religion klart prioritert fremfor religionsfrihet. Vernet om den offentlige religion ble styrket ved direkte å forby virksomheten av jøder, jesuitter og andre minoriteter.*"

IV

The Roots of Anti-Semitism in Norway

The roots of European anti-Semitism were expressed in religious, economic, social, political, and racial terms. Religiously, Jews were commonly regarded as a people having committed deicide and ritual murder. Economically, Jews were regarded as usurers and exploiters. Anti-Semitism, in its various forms, was expressed most strongly in Norway during the period, when between the two world wars (1918-1939). The Jews were then accused of having caused the Bolshevik Revolution in Russia, of being leaders of a worldwide conspiracy to overthrow capitalist societies, and of destroying the "Aryan Race."

Anti-Semitism was virtually unknown in Norway until about the twelfth and thirteenth centuries, when it appeared in a number of literary works "imported together with the literature emanating from church and clergy."[1] During the Viking Age (780-1050), there had been no mention of words such as "Jew," "Judaism," or "Israel" either in runic inscriptions or in the Prose Edda or Poetic Edda. Snorri's *Kings' Sagas* contain no references to Jews, although Sigurd Jorsalfar (1103-1130) went on a pilgrimage to the Holy Land. There is mention of "Jorsal," (Jerusalem), "Jorsalaheim," "Jorsalaland" and "Jordan" in St. Olaf's Saga, the Saga of the Sons of Magnus, and in Harald the Hard's Saga. In the latter it is recorded that King Harald (1042-1066) went on a pilgrimage

---

1. Bjarne Berulfsen, *"Antisemitisme som litterær importvare"* (Anti-Semitism as a literary importation), in *Edda — Nordisk Tidsskrift for litteraturforskning*, Oslo, LVIII: 2 (1958): p. 125.

to the Holy Land, where he conquered all cities and castles. "Then he
went to Jordan and immersed himself there."[2]

The word for "Jew" in these later sagas (*Gythingr*) became known to
Nordic readers through missionary literature in which "Jews were
synonymous with pagans and blasphemers."[3] This particular prejudice
regarding Jews as pagans was incorporated into the Norwegian Church
prayers on Sundays.[4]

Most notorious among anti-Semitic literature was *Mariu Saga*, "a saga
about the Virgin Mary's miracles."[5] A Norwegian scholar, Dr. Bjarne
Berulfsen, has stated that when reading this saga it is impossible not to
recognize the "vicious character of the religious hatred of the Jews . . .
which will show that religious fanaticism could lead to bloodshed."[6] This
religious form of anti-Semitism, claiming that Jews killed the Son of
God, was also expressed in religious writings. As early as the fourteenth
century, books depicted Jews as usurers and sly swindlers. This showed
the contempt for Jews and their alleged economic exploitation of others.
By the sixteenth century, these prejudices had penetrated "even the
most isolated villages through the strangest literary channels."[7]

---

2. *Snorres Kongesagaer*, translated by Anne Holtsmark and Didrik Arup Seip, Oslo:
Gyldendal Norsk Forlag, 1942; *Harald Hårdrådes Saga*, p. 427: ("*Harald for med hæren
sin ut til Jorsalaland, og siden over til Jorsalaborg. Hvor han kom i Jorsalaland gav alle
byer og kasteller sign under hans makt. . . . Så gikk han ut til Jordan og lauget sig der.*"
(Harald went with his army to the Holy Land and later to the castle in Jerusalem. Wher-
ever he came in the Holy Land, all cities and castles subjected themselves to his power.
. . . Then he went to Jordan and immersed himself there.) Ibid., p. 503.

3. Bjarne Berulfsen, "*Jøder og Island*," (Jews and Iceland) in *Kulturhistorisk Leksikon
for nordisk Middelalder: fra vikingetid til reformasjonen*, Copenhagen: Rosenkilde and
Bagger, 1963, Vol. VIII, p. 77: "*. . . det har ført til at jøder blir sidestilt synonymt med
hedninger . . . gything er blitt folkeetymologisk omtydet til guthnithing (gudebespotter*,
i.e., to be blasphemous).

4. Carl Frederik Prytz, "*Jødene og kirkebønnen*," (The Jews and the Church Prayer),
Dagbladet, Oslo, No. 50, February 28, 1961, where two versions of this prayer are cited;
one which will "open up the door of faith for all pagan and for the people of Israel," another
to pray for the "ingathering of pagans and the remnant of Israel within the Christian
Church" (*Lukk opp troens dør for alle hedninger og for Israels folk.*)

5. Harald Beyer, *Norsk Litteraturhistorie* (History of Norwegian Literature), Oslo:
Aschehoug, 1952, p. 74: "*en saga om Jomfru Marias undergjerninger.*" (A saga about the
Virgin Mary's Miracles.)

6. Berulfsen, op. cit., p. 128: "*Når en leser en rekke av disse legendene om jomfru Marias mange jærtegn, kan en ikke unngå å bli slått av at det religiøse jødehatet kan få riktig
ondartet karakter . . . som nok vil vise at religiøs fanatisme kunne få blod til å flyte.*"

7. Bjarne Berulfsen, "*Jødehatet importert til Norge gjennom kirkelig og geistlig
literatur*" (Jew-hatred imported into Norway through ecclesiastical and clerical literature),
Dagbladet, Oslo, October 10, 1958: "*. . . på 15-hundretallet kan en merke hvordan*

Lutheranism was introduced into Norway through a Latin Church Ordinance to which King Christian III (1536-1559) affixed his signature on September 2, 1537.[8] Luther's anti-Semitic views were expressed in works such as "An Admonition Against the Jews" (1546) and "The Jews and Their Lies" (1543). The founder of the Protestant movement gave advice on how to deal with the Jews. Luther's anti-Semitic views were extensively reprinted in the controlled press at the time of the mass arrests and deportation of Norway's Jews. A directive of November 23, 1942, from Anders Beggerud's Press Directorate, stated:[9] "Citations from Luther regarding Jews should be mentioned in all newspapers in a prominent space." [10]

The Catholic paper, *St. Olav*, founded in 1889, was strongly influenced by both religious and political anti-Semitism right up to the outbreak of World War II. It was spread through articles translated from foreign clerical journals and printed notices about alleged Jewish ritual murders throughout the world.[11] Nonfictional anti-Semitic literature and publications during the pre- Nazi period were the work of many authors, newspapers, and periodicals such as Halldis Neegaard Østbye, A.C. Svarstad, Eivind Saxlund, and Ejlert Bjerke.[12] It is within this gen-

propagandaen mot jøder for økonomisk svindel trenger inn i den mest isolerte bygd gjennom de merkverdigste boklige kanaler."

8. Karen Larsen, *A History of Norway,* New York: Princeton University Press for The American-Scandinavian Foundation, 1948, p. 245.

9. Pressedirektoratet, November 23, 1943. Confidential to the editor: *"Citatet fra Luther om jødene bes inntatt i alle aviser på god plass."* Cf. *Aftenposten,* November 24, 1942.

10. *Luther's Works,* Vol. 47, "The Christian Society: On the Jews and Their Lies," Philadelphia: Fortress Press, 1972, pp. 268-274. See also Peter C. Clarkson, "Luther and Hitler, A Controversy Renewed;" *Journal of Ecumenical Studies,* XVII:3 (1980), pp. 445-453. It is to be noted that the World Congress of Lutheran Churches at Budapest in 1984 disassociated themselves from Luther's anti-Semitism.

11. Ibid., p. 18: *"Det katolske bladet St. Olav, som utkom med sitt første nummer i 1889, var sterkt preget av både religiøs og politisk antisemittisme helt til utbruddet av den annen verdenskrig. Det skjedde i form av artikler som ble gjengitt fra utenlandske kirkelige og andre blad og stadige notiser om angivelige jødiske ritualmord rundt om i verden."*

12. A partial listing of nonfictional anti-Semitic Norwegian books, newspapers, periodicals, and other publications includes: Irene Sverd, alias Halldis Neegaard Østbye, *Jødeproblemet og dets løsning* (The Jewish Problem and Its Solution), Oslo, 1938, and *Jødenes Krig* (The War of the Jews), Oslo, 1943; Eivind Saxlund, *Jøder og Gojim* (Jews and Non-Jews), Kristiania, 1910; A.C. Svarstad, "Jødenes Hevn" (The Revenge of the Jews), *Samtiden,* 1918; Ejlert Bjerke, *Judea drømmer* (Judea Dreams), Kristiania, 1913; Jon Alfred Mjøen, *Det norske program for rasehygiene* (The Norwegian Program for Race Hygiene), first edition, 1914, second edition, 1938; *Nationalt Tidsskrift Sandheten* (National Publication: The Truth), 1916-1945; *Den Nye Verdenskeiser* (The New World- Em-

eral cultural tradition of dislike for Jews and other dissenters that the reluctance to accept nonconforming groups in Norway must be seen.[13]

A leading Norwegian anthropologist, Hans Christian Sørhaug, offered a possible explanation why so many Jews in Norway were murdered during World War II. He stated that "Norwegian culture contains a special form for discrimination, which makes visibility of other ethnic groups difficult."[14] Sørhaug gave as examples the arrests of Jewish children while at school. "Norwegian police picked up Norwegian Jews without protest or resistance, as if it were an ordinary act of public office (*embetshandling*). Jewish schoolchildren were fetched at schools as if they were going to the school dentist and not to Auschwitz. The teachers did not lift a finger."[15]

From these episodes, Sørhaug proposed two hypotheses: (1) The Norwegian Jews are Norwegian. In that case they will not suffer anything worse than other Norwegians. The result of this interpretation would be that the Jewish children in fact went to the school dentist, or, at any rate, nothing more dangerous than that. (2) The Norwegian Jews are Jews. As strangers, they fall outside the Norwegian moral and practical horizon. It, therefore, does not concern us. The consequence of either of these interpretations means that the classroom instruction can continue as if nothing of importance had happened. The author added, "It is doubly tragic that many of the Norwegian Jews seem to have agreed with the first alternative."[16]

---

peror; i.e., the Protocols of the Elders of Zion), Kristiania, 1920, another edition, 1944; Nilus, *Jødefaren* (The Jewish Danger); *Fritt Folk* (Free Folk), the main publication of the National Union Party, March 1936 to May 1945, and its predecessor, *Nasjonal Samling*; Mikael P.O. Sylten, *Hvem er hvem i Jødeverden, samt fortegnelse over fremmedes forretninger i Norge*, first edition, 1925, last edition, 1941; *Fronten*, Oslo, 1932-1940; *Hirdspeilet* (The Mirror of the Hird), 1941-1945: *Huginn, Tidsskrift for norske studenter* (Publication for Norwegian Students); *Nasjonal-fascisten* (The National Fascist), published for the Norwegian Legion, 1925; *NS Ungdommen* (The National Socialist Youth), 1934-1941; *Nordisk Folkereisning i Norge* (Nordic Peoples' Uprising in Norway), Oslo, 1941; *Ragnarok*, 1935-1945.

13. Turid Larsen, "*Norge — Verdens største lokalsamfunn*" (Norway — The World's Largest Local Society), reviewing *Den norske væremåten* (The Norwegian Manner of Behavior), Arne Martin Klausen, ed., *Arbeiderbladet*, Oslo, March 29, 1984.

14. Hans Christian Sørhaug, "*Totemisme på norsk — betraktninger om den norske socialdemokratismes vesen*" (Totemism in Norway — Considerations of the manner of Being of the Norwegian Social Democracy), in Arne Martin Klausen, ed., *Den norske væremåten* (The Norwegian Manner of Behavior), Oslo: J.W. Cappelens Forlag, 1984, p. 72.

15. Sørhaug, op. cit., p. 72.

16. Ibid., p. 73.

A noted editor and author, Jahn Otto Johansen, stated that "the hatred of Jews in Norway is a kind of "refined prejudice." Among the youth in West Oslo, the word "Jew" is used as often as "pakkis" (for Pakistanis) as a defamatory expression."[17] The President of Norway's Parliament, Jo Benkow, wrote in his autobiography *Fra Synagogen til Løvebakken*, which became "the nation's best seller,"[18] that during his grammar school days he was often beaten up because he was a Jew.[19] When he ran for the first time for elective office for the City Council of Moss in 1951, he discovered that his name had been omitted from the election list. He commented that "the anti-Semites had shown their true face by eliminating my name from the list they had handed in."[20]

Continuing discrimination against Jews kept them out of civil service positions until 1891, and served to keep prejudice alive. This, in turn, led to only a limited degree of social and cultural integration of Jews within Norwegian society. A member of Parliament, Jakob Aano of the Christian People's Party, explained the singularity of Norway in terms of the attitude toward foreigners: "We are not used to living with strangers. Many of the causes stem from Norway having been and still being a society of a pure race."[21] Aano favored a long-range plan to change Norwegian attitudes toward their fellow-men of other colors and races.

In the twentieth century, Norwegian literary anti-Semitism was expressed by the leading author and Nobel Prize winner, Knut Hamsun, who had joined the Quisling party on December 22, 1940, and received membership number 26,000. He defended publicly his joining the Nazi party.[22] "His anti-Semitism consisted of the fact that he regularly,

17. Jahn Otto Johansen, *"Anti-semittismen idag,"* Kirke og Kultur, Særtrykk (Special Reprint), lecture at the Theological Faculty, University of Oslo, January 27, 1981, p. 132.

18. *The New York Times*, August 17, 1986.

19. Jo Benkow, *Fra Synagogen til Løvebakken* (From the Synagogue to the Parliament). Oslo: Gyldendal Norsk Forlag, 1985, p. 120: *"Jeg fikk mye juling fordi jeg var jøde."*

20. J. Benkow, op. cit., p. 231: *"I ly av valgets hemmelighet hadde antisemittene vist sitt sanne ansikt og strøket navnet mitt på den listen de leverte inn ... jeg ble vraket utelukkende på grunn av min herkomst."* p. 233: *"Tar man ikke kampen opp, vil man fortsette å få juling."* (If you don't fight back one will continue to be beaten up.")

21. Jakob Aano, *"Norge et ren-rase-samfunn,"* Nordisk Tidende, New York, February 19, 1981: *"Mye av årsaken ligger i at Norge har vært og fortsatt er et ren-rase-samfunn. Vi er ikke vant til å ha fremmede inn på livet. ... Vi burde forlengst ha igangsatt et langsiktig arbeid for å endre nordmenns holdninger til medmennesker av en annen hudfarve og rase."*

22. Arild Haaland, *"Nazisme, Litteratur og Knut Hamsun"* (Nazism, Literature and Knut Hamsun), in Bjarte Birkeland and Stein Ugelvik Larsen, eds., *Nazismen og norsk litteratur*, Bergen-Oslo-Tromsø: Universitetsforlaget, 1975, p. 59.

42 SAMUEL ABRAHAMSEN

throughout his fiction and nonfiction, created negative caricatures of Jews, showing them as destructive aliens on the soil of the host country."[23] Allen Simpson asserted that "there has been a distressing blindness on the part of Norwegian scholars to Hamsun's anti-Semitism." In a talk to journalists in Vienna in 1943, Hamsun had described Jews "exactly as Hitler, Rosenberg, Julius Streicher, and Himmler were describing them, as a disease bacillus infecting the German nation."[24]

A worsening of Christian-Jewish relations took place as Norway entered the crucial decades of the 1920s and 1930s. Especially detrimental to this relationship was the vociferous opposition to *shehitah*, the Jewish ritual slaughter of animals. A press debate regarding this ritual had started in the 1890s and increased in intensity during the 1920s, especially in *Nationen* (The Nation), the principal publication of the *Bondepartiet* (Farmer's Party) and in *Aftenposten*, Oslo, the main paper for the Conservative Party. The Storting debate started in 1926. The Agricultural Department had sought advice from Professor Halfdan Holth. His report of June 14, 1927, stated that *shehitah* was not painful for the animal.[25] The report by Professor Sophus Torup of June 7, 1927, was less favorable, claiming that he had never been present at a *shehitah* and therefore could not express any opinion as to procedure. He gave a scientific analysis and description of what happened to animals undergoing the ritual process.[26] The Jewish community in Oslo, through its president, J. Gittelsen, submitted a brief on May 16, 1927, to the Parliamentary Committee of Agriculture (*Stortingets Landbrukskomite*). The religious commandment of *kashrut* and Jewish ritual slaughter were stressed. The Jews regarded ritual slaughter as a Biblical law that could not be changed; it was part of the Jewish religion. Reference was made to Denmark, Finland, and Sweden where *shehitah* was permitted. G. Helsun stated that opposition in Norway was based on emotion and not facts. "A prohibition against *shehitah* will be felt as a strong breach of the old principle that all Norwegian citizens have a right to freedom of religion."[27] The document drew attention to a resolution passed by the

23. Allen Simpson, "Knut Hamsun's Anti-Semitism," *Edda — Scandinavian Journal of Literary Research*, No. 5, Oslo: Universitetsforlaget, 1977, p. 289.
24. Ibid., p. 287.
25. *Stortingsforhandlinger*, 1927, Vol. 5, Document No. 18, p. 2.
26. Ibid., pp. 1-2.
27. Ibid., p. 6: "*Et forbud mot schächtingen vilde av os føles som et sterkt brudd paa det gamle princip om at ille norske statsborgere har ret til fri utøvelse av sin religion.*"

League of Nations in Geneva at its third General Assembly in 1922 to the effect that "States, in regard to its minorities, will observe in the treatment of their own racial, religious, or linguistic minorities at least as high a standard of justice and toleration as is required by any of the Treaties and by the regular action of the Council." The petition ended with a plea that the Jewish congregation in Norway be permitted to continue ritual slaughtering of animals. In June 1929, however, the Storting passed a law — with 88 in favor and 21 opposed — prohibiting shehitah. This law became effective throughout Norway as of January 1, 1930,[28] and foreshadowed the prohibition of shehitah by Nazi-Germany in 1933.[29]

The Parliamentary debate over this issue had been acrimonious. A member of the Parliament and later prime minister, Jens Hundseid, stated that "we have no obligation to deliver our animals to the cruelties of the Jews; we have not invited the Jews to the country and we have no obligation to deliver our animals to the Jews for their religious orgies."[30] A leading Norwegian psychiatrist, Dr. David Abrahamsen, characterized the violent press agitation against shehitah as a comparatively mild example of mass psychosis.[31]

Examples of social anti-Semitism were expressed in Bærum municipality, a suburb of Oslo, on August 22, 1932, when the island of Gåsøya in the Oslo Fjord was deemed out-of-bounds for Jews. A resolution adopted unanimously by inhabitants at a general assembly, stated that sale or rental to people of Semitic descent (Jews) shall be denied by the governing body. Among those who signed were five lawyers. One owner, Mrs. Birgit Sorknes, who had been absent from the meeting, refused to sign the resolution. A noted Oslo lawyer, Leon Jarner, commented that the board's action was an example of the most vulgar form of anti-

---

28. Samuel Abrahamsen, "Norway," in the *Universal Jewish Encyclopedia*, New York, 1942, Vol. 8, p. 242.

29. It should be noted that one of the first acts of Nazi Germany in 1933 was the prohibition of *shehitah* in the various Landtage, i.e., through the legislative assembles. See H.J. Zimmels, *The Echo of the Nazi Holocaust in Rabbinical Literature*, New York, KTAV Publishing Company, 1977, p. xvi.

30. Oskar Mendelsohn, *Jødenes historie i Norge gjennom 300 år* (History of the Jews in Norway through 300 Years), Oslo: Universitetsforlaget, 1969, Vol. I, p. 578.

31. David Abrahamsen, *Jeg er jøde. En norsk jøde om jøder i Norge og om folket uten landegrenser* (I am a Jew. A Norwegian Jew about Jews in Norway and about the People without Frontiers), Oslo: Johan Grundt Tanum, 1935, p. 89: "... *et forholdsvis uskyldig tilfelle av antijødisk massepsykose.*"

Semitism.[32] Similar harassment of Jews took place when posters were put up in the county of Asker protesting summer rentals to Jews.

The tenacity of prejudice, authoritatively defined "as a set of attitudes which causes, supports or justifies discrimination,"[33] prevailed increasingly in Norway throughout the 1920s and 1930s which saw the rise of Vidkun Quisling's racist political movement.

---

32. Leon Jarner, "*Antisemittismen i norsk hverdagsliv*" (Anti-Semitism in Norwegian Daily Life), *Verdens Gang*, Oslo, November 29, 1947: "*Så sent som i 1932 opplevde vi et tilfelle som åpenbarte en antisemitisme i krasseste form og fra personer som man ikke uten grunn skulle tro bedre om. . . . Den 22. august holdtes generalforsamling i øyas Vel, og generalforsamlingen besluttet enstemmig at salg eller bortleie av eiendommene skal forelegges styret, som kun skal nekte godkjennelse hvis det gjelder salg eller bortleie til folk av semmittisk avstamning (jøder).*"

33. Arnold Rose, *The Roots of Prejudice*, Paris: UNESCO. 1958, p. 7.

V

Quisling's National Union Party and Its Ideology of Racism

Vidkun Quisling's name has become synonymous with treason and a symbol of European Nazi collaboration. During World War II, most European states had native traitors who sought positions of power. These self-styled national leaders, however, did not see themselves as traitors, but as patriots "who would save their countrymen from the corruption and inefficiency of democratic government."[1]

During the early 1920s unstable political conditions in Norway made non-socialist parties afraid of a Communist Party take-over following the Bolshevik revolution in Russia in 1917. The Norwegian Labor Party, of which the Norwegian Communist Party was an offshoot, had during several years maintained a friendly policy toward Moscow. There was fear of an armed revolution in Norway. In a speech in the *Storting* in April 1932, Quisling accused the Labor Party of treason.[2] As a countervailing force, several parliamentary organizations were formed by the bourgeois parties which had looked upon the growth of the Labor Party with great anxiety. Several right-wing organizations and parties were established to form a united front against Communism. Among them was *Fedrelandslaget* (the Patriotic League), established to fight against international revolutionary movements and to create a strong national government against Communism. At the height of its strength, the Patriotic

---

1. George N. Kren and Leon Rappaport, "Resistance to the Holocaust: The Idea and the Act," in Yehudah Bauer and Nathan Rotenstreich, eds., *The Holocaust as Historical Experience*, New York: Holmes and Meier, 1981, p. 212.
2. Per Ole Johansen, "*Kampen om Menstadslaget*" (The Fight over the Battle at Menstad)-, *Tidsskrift for arbeiderbevegelsens historie*, Vol. 1, 1982, p. 157.

League, headed by Fridjof Nansen and Christian Michelsen, had over 100,000 members. It was, however, Quisling's party, *Nasjonal Samling* (National Union Party) which became the only pro-Nazi party in Norway.[3]

Vidkun Abraham Lauritz Jonssøn Quisling (1887-1945) openly met the conquering Nazis as their closest collaborator. Born on July 18, 1887 in the valley of Fyresdal (in the southeastern province of Telemark), he graduated with distinction from the military academy of Norway and served as an officer on the General Staff (1911-1923). His special interest in Russia and his fluency in the Russian language brought about an appointment by the Norwegian government as military attaché to the Soviet Union in Moscow, where he also handled British interests after Great Britain broke off diplomatic relations in 1917. Quisling became an assistant to Fridtjof Nansen, who entrusted him with important tasks in helping the people of the famine-stricken Ukraine in 1922.[4] After fulfilling humanitarian tasks on behalf of the League of Nations, Quisling, who had changed from an avid Russophile to an ardent anti-Communist, returned to Norway after Nansen's death in 1930: "I had to return home and contribute what I could to save Norway."[5] This is Quisling's explanation, but the real reason was that there was no need to retain him at the Norwegian legation in Moscow after October 1, 1929, when Great Britain and the U.S.S.R. "agreed to renew their diplomatic relations."[6] Believing that the Viking Age represented the noblest epoch in Norway's history, Quisling adopted the flag of St. Olav, *Solkorset*, (The Sun Cross) as the symbol of his own party.

Although opposed to the democratic way of life and to the Norwegian democratic government, Quisling served as Minister of Defense from May 12, 1931 to March 3, 1933 in the governments of Peder Kolstad and

3. Andreas Norland, *Harde tider. Fedrelandslaget i norsk politikk* (Hard times. The Patriotic League in Norwegian politics), Oslo: Dreyers Forlag, 1973. See also, Bjørn Vidar Gabrielsen, *Menn og Politikk. Senterpartiet 1920-1970* (Men and Politics. The Center Party 1920-1970), Oslo: H. Aschehoug & Co. (W. Nygaard), 1977.

4. Gustav Hilger and Alfred G. Meyer, *The Incompatible Allies. A Memoir-History of German-Soviet Relatons 1918-1941*, New York: The Macmillan Company, 1953, p. 42.

5. *Straffesak mot Vidkun Abraham Lauritz Jonssøn Quisling, Utgitt på offentlig bekostning av Eidsivating lagstols landssvikavdeling* (Court proceedings against Vidkun Abraham Lauritz Jonssøn Quisling, hereafter referred to as *Quisling Trial*), Oslo, 1946, p. 572: "*Jeg måtte hjem og bidra det jeg kunne til å redde Norge.*"

6. Oddvar Høidal, "*Quislings stilling ved den norske legasjon i Moskva juni 1927–desember 1929,*" (Quisling's Position at the Norwegian Legation in Moscow, June 1927–December 1929), *Historisk Tidsskrift* (Oslo), Vol. 53, No. 2, (1974): 189.

Jens Hundseid of *Bondepartiet*, i.e., the Agrarian Party. During the parliamentary debate on April 7, 1932, Quisling charged the Communist and Labor Parties with treason, claiming they had secret contact with the Communist Party in the Soviet Union, which allegedly had supplied funds to prepare a revolution.[7] A special parliamentary committee investigated the charges, but found insufficient evidence for legal action.[8] The majority report agreed with the charges. Quisling felt vindicated.

On May 17, 1933, Quisling founded his own party, *Nasjonal Samling* (NS). Its vague and national-romantic program never gained popular support.[9] At the parliamentary election in 1936, the party polled only 26,576 votes, i.e., 1.84 percent of the electorate; this was rather less than the first election in 1933, where the NS Party received 2.2 percent of the vote.[10] NS was never able to elect a single delegate to the *Storting*. Furthermore, the 41 seats gained by the party in the 1934 municipal elections were reduced to 2 in the 1937 City Councils. The NS representations in rural councils were reduced from 28 to 5. The party, however, "did not put up lists in many communes and polled only 1,422 votes, i.e., 0.06 percent of the poll."[11]

At the time of the invasion, the party had barely 5,000 members. During the occupation, however, its membership reached a peak of 43,000 in 1943.[12] The legal accounting against the collaborators after the war recorded 54,651 registered members in the National Union Party from 1940 to 1945.

Quisling's habit of labeling opponents as "Jewish" or "agents of the world Jewry" was an attempt to manipulate public opinion and to gain

---

7. *Stortingstidende* (Parliamentary Gazette), April 7, 1932. See also *Documents from Special Committee: The Quisling Case (1932)* and the debates in the parliament (*Forhandlinger i Stortinget* Nos. 323 through 332 for the year 1932).

8. Sverre Hartmann, *Fører uten folk* (Leader without people), Oslo: Tiden Norsk Forlag, 1970, pp. 105 ff.

9. Paul M. Hayes, *Quisling: The Career and Political Ideas of Vidkun Quisling, 1887-1945*, London: David and Charles, 1971, p. 103.

10. *Norges Offisielle Statistikk*, Vol. IX, 26, p. 13: "Stortingsvalget 1933" (Parliamentary elections, 1933). Nasjonal Samling: 27,850 votes, i.e., 2.23 percent of the total vote. *Norges Offisielle Statistikk*, Vol. IX, 107, p. 38: Parliamentary Elections, 1936: Nasjonal Samling, 26,575.00 votes, i.e., 1.93 percent of the total vote.

11. Stein Ugelvik Larsen, "The Social Foundations of Norwegian Fascism, 1933-1945. An Analysis of Membership Data," in Stein Ugelvik Larsen, Bernt Hagtvet, Jan Petter Myklebust, eds., *Who Were the Fascists? Social Roots of European Fascism*, Bergen- Oslo- Tromsø: Universitetsforlaget, 1980, p. 599.

12. Tore Gjelsvik, *Norwegian Resistance*, London: C. Hurst and Co., 1979, footnote p. 14.

support among those who had come to regard Nazi-Germany as the wave of the future. After 1935, the attacks on Jews increased in the Quisling publications. According to them, World Communism was created and led by Jews, who controlled the world monetary systems and the world presses. National movements had to be anti-Semitic because Jews represented the evil aspects of internationalism. The Communists, led by Jews, were the foremost among the instigators of revolutions and wars. Paradoxically, Quisling's political philosophy was meant to be a synthesis of Communism, National Socialism, and Democracy. He called this organization of society "Soviets without Communism," declaring that this society was in accord with the nature of the Nordic race.[13]

From 1935, anti-Semitism, "the Jewish problem," and "pure racial theories" became central issues in the development of Quisling's party. After suffering defeats in parliamentary and municipal elections in 1936 and 1937, hatred of the Jews became a dominant theme in the Quisling press.[14] Benjamin Vogt, a leading Norwegian lawyer, stated that Quisling was a "Jew-baiter in a country where there were hardly any Jews and no Jewish problem."[15] Quisling's anti-Semitic policies alienated Christian party members. Some of them resigned, led by sogneprest (Parish Priest) Martin Tveto.[16]

Quisling opposed the awarding of the Nobel 1935 Peace Prize to Carl von Ossietzky (1898-1938), the leader of the peace movement in Germany after World War I. This award was a heavy, moral blow to the supporters of Nazism and led to Hitler's issuing an order that "henceforth no German citizen would ever be permitted to accept a Nobel Prize."[17]

---

13. Hans-Dietrich Loock, "Support for *Nasjonal Samling* in the Thirties," in Stein Ugelvik Larsen et al., eds., *op. cit.*, p. 667.

14. See especially *Vestlandets Avis* (The Western Coast Newspaper), *Hedmark Fylkesavis*, *NS Ungdommen* (The Youth of NS), and the main publication, *Nasjonal Samling* (National Union), and its successor after 1936, *Fritt Folk* (Free People).

15. Benjamin Vogt, "Quisling. The Man and the Criminal," *The American- Scandinavian Review* XXXVI, No. 1 (March 1948): 41.

16. Dag O. Bruknapp, "Idéene splitter partiet. Rasespørsmålets betydning i *NS's* utvikling," (The Ideas split the party. The significance of racial questions in the development of the National Union Party), in Roald Danielsen and Stein Ugelvik Larsen, eds., *Fra idé til dom. Noen trekk fra utviklingen av Nasjonal Samling* (From idea to sentencing. Some aspects of the development of the National Union Party), Oslo: Universitetsforlaget, 1978, pp. 44-47, "Letter of resignation of November 29, 1935 from Martin Tveto to Dr. Gudbrand Lunde."

17. Willy Brandt, *My Road to Berlin*, New York: Doubleday & Co., 1960, p. 72.

By this time Quisling had started to stress anti-Semitism and "Jewish Bolshevism" in his political campaigns. He stated that it was the goal of "secret international Bolshevism to drag the British Empire and the Nordic countries into a fratricidal war on the continent, which would lead to their mutual destruction."[18]

Quisling's efforts to attract members to the National Union Party led to recruitment from all strata of Norwegian society. The most famous member was the winner of the 1918 Nobel Prize for Literature, Knut Hamsun, whose membership gave legitimacy to the Norwegian Nazi Party.[19] Hamsun published a letter in *Fritt Folk* on May 4, 1940, in which he encouraged Norwegians to desert their King and country:[20]

"Norwegians:

When the English in their unspeakable savagery forced their way into Jøssing Fjord and violated our independence, you did nothing. When the English afterwards laid mines along our coast to bring the war into Norwegian territory, you did nothing then either.

But when the Germans occupied Norway and prevented our getting the war here in this country THEN you did something. You conspired with our runaway King and his private government and mobilized.

It is to no avail that each one of you has grabbed his gun and stands frothing at the Germans; tomorrow or the next day you will be bombed.

England is in no position to help you except with a few bands here and there who stroll about the valley and beg for food.

NORWEGIANS! Throw away your guns and go home again. Germany is fighting for all of us and is now going to break England's tyranny over us and over all neutrals.

Knut Hamsun."

Prior to this publication, Hamsun had not committed any treasonable act, but now he was subject to the strongest penalty of the law.[21]

---

18. Paul M. Hayes, op. cit., p. 123.

19. Hans Fredrik Dahl, Bernt Hagtvet and Guri Hjeltnes, *Den norske nasjonal-socialismen. Nasjonal Samling, 1933-1945, i tekst og bilder* (Norwegian National Socialism, the National Union Party, 1933-1945, in text and pictures), Oslo: Pax Forlag, 1982, p. 100.

20. *Fritt Folk*, Oslo, May 4, 1940. This letter was rejected by all Oslo newspapers except *Fritt Folk* (the Quisling organ) on the grounds that it attacked the person of the King and hence violated the Constitution.

21. Thorkild Hansen, *Prosessen mot Hamsun* (The Process against Hamsun), Oslo: Gyldental Norsk Forlag, 1978, p. 81. See also, Arild Haaland, "*Nazisme, litteratur og* Knut Hamsun" in *Nazismen og norsk litteratur*, Bergen-Oslo-Tromsø Universitetsforlaget, 1975. Hamsun was tried as a collaborator and fined $85.000 in 1947.

More than any other Norwegian, Dr. Jon Alfred Mjøen (1860-1939) contributed to the dissemination of racism in Norway by establishing the *Institutt for Rasehygiene* (Racial Hygiene Institute) in Oslo and publishing from 1919 to 1932 a periodical, *Den Nordiske Race* (The Nordic Race). In 1938 he published an extended edition of his *Racial Hygiene*, which became the main source for racial theories within the Quisling party program and in its publications. Dr. Mjøen maintained that the racially purest people lived in the Nordic countries and that it was possible in Norway and Sweden to find people of "one hundred percent Nordic race."[22]

The program of the National Union Party, adopted at its national convention in 1934, incorporated part of Dr. Mjøen's theories, especially Part III: "The Individual: The Race and the Health of the Nation," which stated in Article 2 that the race is to be protected, and that habitual criminals, the insane, and hereditary imbeciles, should be sterilized.[23] Furthermore, Norwegian foreign policy should seek worldwide connections with race- and culture-related people. The party program was never changed. According to the program, strict control of immigration was to be exercised. This was expressed in its main organ, *Nasjonal Samling* (National Union) in 1934, where articles objecting to the immigration of Jewish refugees were published.[24]

Dr. Mjøen had "proven" how important it was to prevent blood-mixing with inferior races. In 1934, the *Storting* passed a law to permit sterilization, which for some of the members of Quisling's party indicated a "clear acceptance of Mjøen's negative part of the race-hygienic program."[25] Racism and biology, which included elements of both anti-Semitism and the claim of race biology, were propagated throughout

---

22. Dag O. Bruknapp, op. cit., p. 26.
23. *Nasjonal Samlings Program, kap. III: Individet, slekten og folkehelsen, punkt 21:* ". . . *Vern om folkeætten, vaneforbrytere og arvelig sterkt belastede personer, som efter sakkyndiges mening ikke kan få sunne barn, berøves forplantningsevnen. Strengere kontroll med utlendingers oppholdstillatelse og innvandring.*" As reprinted in Ralph Hewins, *Quisling — profet uten ære* (Quisling — Prophet without Honor), Oslo: Store Bjørn Forlag, 1966, pp. 391-393. See also, Ralph Hewins, *Quisling — Prophet without Honor*, New York: John Day Company, 1966, p. 375: "The race to be protected. Habitual criminals, the insane, the hereditary imbeciles to be sterilized after examination by experts and certification that they cannot beget sound children."
24. *Nasjonal Samling*, Vol. 1, No. 8, May 9, 1934.
25. Bruknapp, op. cit., p. 42, footnote 116: "*Ved at Stortinget i 1934 vedtok en lov om adgang til sterilisering innebar dette vedtaket, for enkelte representanters vedkommende, en klar akseptering av Mjøens negative del av det rasehygieniske program.*"

Scandinavia. The claim of "superiority" of the Nordic race over other races was astonishingly readily accepted during the twenties. It was not just a matter of xenophobia and traditional anti-Semitism, but, teaching of racial categories, genetics, and cultural development.[26]

Quisling was convinced about the inequality of races as propagated by Nazi Germany. His concept of the superior Nordic race made it easy for him to accept the Nazi racial theories. The existence of the inferior Jews was regarded as an obstacle to the fulfillment of the ideal society,[27] which had a duty to keep the "Aryan race" pure.

Quisling had fully accepted vulgar anti-Semitism, quoting in his writings and speeches the untruths contained in the notorious forgery, *The Protocols of the Elders of Zion*. Quisling's publications and the press of his party which had accepted racism as an ideology led to dispute within the Quisling party over two different policies: whether to adhere to basic concepts of Christianity or to follow Nazi Germany's racial "*Weltanschauung.*" This debate led to a split in 1935-36, when Quisling's attitude became increasingly racist. His views were reflected in his establishing in 1937 of *Det Stornordiske Fredssamband* (The Greater Nordic Peace Union), which was clearly anti-Semitic. Quisling made no attempt to rescue the Jews in Norway.[28]

One of Quisling's most ardent and racist supporters was Mrs. Halldis Neegaard Østbye, a loyal party member and an editor of *Fritt Folk*. She based her anti-Semitism on biological and cultural differences.[29]

Immigration of Jews should be forbidden, she argued. It would only lead to racial mixing and to destruction of the superior Nordic race. In her book *Jødeproblemet og dets løsning* (The Jewish Problem and Its Solution), published in 1939 under the pseudonym of Irene Sverd, she stated that anti-Semitism was not racial hatred but self-defense. The aim of the book was "to open the eyes of her countrymen to the danger of the Jewish world conspiracy and to save us from the threatening destruction. The Jews stand behind World Communism, and they have under-

26. Ulf Lindström, *Fascism in Scandinavia 1920-1940*, Stockholm: Almqvist & Wiksell International, 1985, p. 56.

27. Hayes, op. cit., p. 312.

28. Berit Nøkleby. "Nyordning," (New Order) in *Norge i krig. Fremmedåk og frihetskamp 1940-1945* (Norway at War. Foreign Subjugation and War of Liberty). Oslo: Aschehoug, 1985, vol. 2, p. 211.

29. Irene Sverd (pseud. for Halldis Neegaard Østbye), *Jødeproblemet og dets løsning*, Oslo: Eget Forlag, Gjærder og Co., Boktrykkeri, 1939, pp. 1-11, 95.

stood how to collect most of the world's gold. The Jews are Asians, they signify a threat to this land when we permitted them to enter."

Throughout 1939, the papers of the National Union Party increased their attacks on the Jews. The intensity of these attacks may be gleaned from the headlines in *Fritt Folk* from that year: "Abolish the Jewish-Marxist Dictatorship in Norway,"[30] "The Voice of Jakob — Who Controls the British Press?"[31] "No More Room for Jews in Commerce!"[32]

In addition to this anti-Semitic propaganda, the National Union Party organized meetings protesting the admission of Jewish refugees. On February 7, 1939, Quisling spoke at a mass meeting on *Jødeinvasjonen* (The Jewish Invasion). Here a resolution was adopted, warning the authorities about granting foreign Jews admission and work permits while thousands upon thousands of Norwegians were unemployed; protested the use of public funds for support of refugees belonging to the world's richest nation, and asserting that actions favoring refugees "were mistaken humanitarianism serving certain international political aims which were against Norway's national interest and the desire of the country to be left at peace."[33]

On February 20, Mrs. Neegaard Østbye gave a lecture at the Oslo Klingenberg movie house, stating that the Jewish problem was the key to the world's problem.[34] The Jewish influence in Norway, 8-10,000 Jews, had determined its political, social, and cultural development. It was a secret Jewish conspiracy which had caused Europe's wars. "International Judaism is led by a small fanatic minority which built its power on the liberal and Marxist system. . . . Against these plans, against Communism and Marxism, against abolishing Christianity and family, National Socialism places preservation of property and a sound moral based

---

30. *Fritt Folk*, January 14, 1939: "*Vekk med det jødisk-marxistiske diktatur i Norge.*"
31. *Fritt Folk*, March 18, 1939: "*Jakobs røst. Hvem råder over den engelske presse?*" (Jakob's Voice. Who Rules the English Press?)
32. Ibid.: "*Ikke plass for flere jøder i handelen.*" (No Room for Additional Jews in Commerce)
33. *Fritt Folk*, February 11, 1939: "*Overfylt hus til Quislings foredrag tirsdag. Resolusjon mot jødeinvasjonen vedtatt med overveldende majoritet. . . . Vi protesterer mot aksjoner i flyktningespørsmålet som under en falsk humanitets maske tjener visse internasjonale politiske formål som er i strid med Norges nasjonale interesser og med folkenes fredsønske.*"
34. *Aftenposten*, (The Evening Post) Oslo, February 21, 1942: "*Jødeproblemet er nøkkelen til verdensproblemet. Også i Norge har den jødiske innflydelse været bestemmende politisk, sosialt og kulturelt. Norge huser 8-10,000 jøder. Fru Halldis Neegaard Østbye taler til fullt hus i Klingenberg Kino.*"

on family and the home. . . . But, luckily, the Jews have not succeeded in corrupting our people. This is proven by the constantly increasing membership in the National Union Party."

Under the impact of the rise of Nazism in Germany, Quisling's anti-Semitic and anti-democratic attitudes were strengthened. He favored a return to Article 2 of the Constitution of 1814, forbidding access of Jews to Norway, and advocated "a strong King and a government that did not have to resign because a majority in the Parliament voted against them."[35]

Quisling and his fellow-travelers had a policy of propagating anti-Semitic policies, even to the extent of participating "actively in the persecution of the Jews of Norway."[36] The aim was to build up a "new Norway" similar to Hitler's Nazi Germany. The Quisling regime had its own Storm troopers, the *Hird*, the party's paramilitary force, which was led until January 1937 by J.B. Hjort, the *Fylkesmann* (governor) of Akershus. Organized on the model of the Nazi S.A.[37] the *Hird* was the name properly given to "retainers in the service of Norway's medieval King."[38] The person in charge of the *Hird* in Oslo, Orvar Sæther, published in June 1941 a statement in *Fritt Folk* demanding that Norwegians avoid all contact with Jews. He urged Norwegians not to buy or sell to Jews, consult Jewish physicians and lawyers, work for Jews, admit Jews to theaters and movies.[39] Sæther made another statement about Jews on September 25, 1944, saying, "the Jews hate us because they are different from us, and they envy us. They envy our physical superiority and beauty, our courage and bravery."[40]

In order to prove himself a true follower of Hitler's racial theories, Vidkun Quisling felt the need to explain the "Jewish danger" in Norway. In March 1941 he traveled to Frankfurt-am-Main to address the inaugural meeting of the "Institute for the Investigation of the Jewish Ques-

---

35. Sverre Hartmann, op. cit., p. 167.

36. John. Andenæs, *Det vanskelige oppgjøret. Rettsoppgjøret etter okkupasjonen. De offentlige tjenestemenn* (The difficult settlement. The legal accounting after the Occupation. The Public Officials), Oslo: Tanum, 1979, pp. 47-48.

37. Oddvar Høidal, "Hjort, Quisling and *Nasjonal Samling's* disintegration," *Scandinavian Studies*, Vol. 47, No. 4 (1975): 467.

38. Gjelsvik, op. cit., p. 70.

39. *Jewish Telegraphic Agency News*, June 10, 1941.

40. Dahl, Hagtvet and Hjeltnes, op. cit., p. 120: "*Jødene hater oss fordi de er annerledes enn oss og de misunner oss. De misunner vår kroppslige overlegenhet og skjønnhet, vårt mot og vår tapperhet.*"

tion." Here he stated that the small number of Jews was not of main importance in Norway, but their destructive ideas, which had had a fatal influence on the inner development of Norway since the Jews had secured key positions and found eager and willing followers.[41]

To increase the number of Norway's Jews, Quisling invented the term *kunstige jøder,* i.e., "artificial" Jews, whose numbers he could inflate at will. Quisling estimated the number of Jews to be ten thousand, a number contradicted by a somber report by Terboven on November 6, 1942, addressed to *"Die Parteikanzler der NSDAP,"*: "There are about 1200 racial Jews who have led quiet and secluded lives. They have in Norway never succeeded in reaching a position in the economy. There are among them even capable farmers and craftsmen who are well-regarded (*"die in gutem Ansehen stehen"*) and who up to now have been considered as absolutely loyal citizens.[42] In December 1942 Quisling's Statistical Office prepared a graphic presentation of Norway's Jewish population according to occupations and trade, totalling 1140 persons.

The solution to the Jewish problem was offered by Mrs. Østbye in a letter to Quisling on October 7, 1942. Here she claimed that there was an urgent need for an Aryan law against racial mixing in Norway. The Jewish persecution, she said, should be undertaken "quietly and *through stages"* (underlined in text), for example, by bringing the Jews to concentration camps without official orders. The final arrangement "must, of course, be radical and not sentimental as it concerns the security of our own people and of Europe against a new Jewish advance. They have to be killed quickly and painlessly."[43]

---

41. Vidkun Quisling, *Kampen mellem arier og jødemakt. Tale i Frankfurt, 28. Mars 1941 om jødeproblemet* (The struggle between Aryan and Jewish power. Speech in Frankfurt about the Jewish problem, March 28, 1941), Oslo: *Nasjonal Samlings Rikstrykkeri 1941, p. 5.*

42. *Strafsache gegen Hellmuth Reinhard,* Baden-Baden, February 1, 1967: *"In Norwegian gibt es ungefähr 1200 Rassejuden, die still und zurückgezogen gelebt haben. Es ist ihnen in Norwegen nie gelungen, eine position im Wirtschaftsleben einzunehmen. Es gibt unter ihnen sogar tüchtige Bäuern und Handwerker, die in gutem Ansehen stehen, und die bisher als absolut loyale Staatsbürger gegelten haben."* Yad Vashem Doc./No. TR-10/608, p. 17.

43. *Fra Oslo Byrett. Dom 22.12 1948 over Halldis Neegaard Østbye,* "Tiltalens post 3" (From the Court Record of Oslo Municipality, December 22, 1948, Point #3 against the defendant), pp. 1-3: *"Det vil være en fordel om de tiltak som må gjøres, gjennomføres mest mulig i stillhet og etappevis. ... Det som det haster med er naturligvis arierloven så all videre raseblanding kan bli stanset ... alt det øvrige kan vel foregå mere i stillhet, anbringelse av jøder i konsentrasjonsleire o.s.v. uten offisielle forordninger. ... Det er en selvfølge at den endelige løsning av jødeproblemet må gjennomføres, uten*

The purity of the Nordic race had become a basic ideology of the Quisling party, i.e., prevention of pollution of the Norwegian race by means of "race control." This meant persecution of the Jewish people which, in Norway, started in earnest in October 1942. It had been preceded during the months of August and September by intense propaganda in the controlled press and in the official publications of the Quisling party. Writing in the monthly *Ideologisk månedshefte for Hirden*, the militant chief of the *Hird*, Oliver Møystad, stressed the racial, cultural, and moral superiority of the "Nordic man," which was the heritage of the Viking Age. He warned that blood mixing with Jews, Gypsies, and Blacks was sure to lead the Norwegian people into disaster.[44]

National Socialism was opposed to all race mixing. *Fritt Folk* summarized its ideology:[45]

> "Why should we let Norwegian culture be stamped by oriental characteristics? We do not hate the Jews, but we counteract any tendency on their part to dominate and interfere with our affairs."

According to *Aftenposten*, August 3, 1942, "the Jews are a racist people. Their laws have always provided for severe punishment of those who pollute the race with alien blood." The publication *Fronten*, in its program of 1938, stated that the Jews "confuse the mentality of our people and seriously threaten the purity of the race."[46]

During the war, the racial laws were enforced according to Nuremberg Laws of 1935. An office was established to certify Aryan descent and demanded documentation that grandparents of both sides were not "of Jewish descent." This declaration had to be verified by two persons who knew the family intimately, as was brought out in the case against Torleif Andreas Wulff, who had been arrested in November 1942, his properties confiscated and himself interned at Berg concentration camp. Baptismal certificates to prove Aryan descent for his grandparents were demanded and produced. According to the church registers, Torleif Wulff proved his "Aryan descent" as far back as April 1856, when his

---

*sentimentaliter når det gjelder å sikre vårt eget folk og Europa mot et nytt jødisk framstøt
... tiltalte har ment det hun har sagt, nemlig at jødene om nødvendig bør 'drepes raskt og smertefritt.'"*

44. Dag O. Bruknapp, op. cit., p. 24.

45. "Racial Questions and Persecution of the Jews in Norway," U.S. Legation, Stockholm, December 23, 1942, NND 730032, p. 6.

46. As cited in Bruknapp, op. cit., p. 17: *"Jødene forviller vårt folks mentalitet og alvorlig truer rasens renhet."*

grandmother was baptized.[47] But voices were heard opposing such bar-
barisms. One of the foremost Norwegian intellectuals, Ronald Fangen
(1895-1946), spoke and wrote against the Jewish persecutions, racism,
and Nazism as diminishing Christian spiritual values.[48] Many prominent Norwegian theologians were arrested for opposing Nazism, among
them Professor Kristian Schjelderup, a world renown theologian; Hans
Ording Professor of Theology, University of Oslo, and the lecturer Sten
Bugge, "well known for his missionary activities in China."[49]

47. *"Avstamningserklæring"* (Declaration of Descent), November 11, 1942;
Statsarkivet, Oslo, I.D. No. 00886 Il, February 2, 1943: *"Jeg forsikrer på ære og
samvittighet at nedennevnte personer — såvidt jeg vet eller har kunnet bringe i erfaring
— ikke er av jødisk avstamning."*
48. Carl Fr. Wisløff, *Norsk Kirkehistorie* (Norwegian Church History), Oslo:
Lutherstiftelsen, 1971, vol. III, page 415.
49. *Public Record Office*, FO 371/ 36877 London, pp. 11-12.

VI.

The German Invasion

Although Quisling had sought contact in the late 1930s with Nazi leaders, especially Alfred Rosenberg, *Reichsleiter* and head of the NSDAP Foreign Policy Bureau, German interest in Quisling and his movement did not become apparent until the summer of 1939.[1] Rosenberg and Quisling met in Berlin in June and again in December 1939, when a meeting with Gross-Admiral Räder and Adolf Hitler was arranged. At the meeting of December 11, Quisling explained that the Norwegian government, parliament, and foreign policy were "controlled by the well-known Jew, Hambro."[2] Furthermore, they discussed a proposal for a peaceful German occupation to forestall a British invasion of Norway. On December 18, before returning to Norway, Quisling had a last audience with "*der Führer.*" He left this meeting believing that he had been promised Germany's cooperation in a peaceful take-over in Norway by a pro-Nazi Norwegian government with himself as Prime Minister.[3]

Nazi Germany followed the domestic developments in Norway with great interest, as shown in the constant reports from the Oslo German legation to the Ministry of Foreign Affairs (*Auswärtiges Amt*) in Berlin, reporting the danger of Norway becoming judaized and flooded with

---

1. Magne Skodvin, *Kampen om Okkupasjonsstyret i Norge,* Oslo: Det Norske Samlaget, 1956, pp. 22 ff.

2. Harold Franklin Knudsen, *Jeg var Quisling's sekretær* (I was Quisling's Secretary), København: Eget Forlag, 1951, p. 90: "*Den nuværende norske regjering samt Storting og hele utenrikspolitikken ble behersket av den kjente jøde Hambro.*"

3. *International Military Tribunal,* Vol. 34, pp. 273–275, PS-#065, hereinafter referred to as IMT.

Jewish refugees who would dominate commercial and cultural life.[4] Intense commercial espionage was undertaken against Jews in Norwegian businesses in order to prevent them from continuing any representation of German commercial interests in Norway. The systematic discrimination was led by the Commercial Section of the Oslo legation, headed by its attaché, Dr. Memdeldorf, who reported to the *Reichsstelle für den Aussenhandel* in Berlin. Reports were also submitted by Norwegian credit offices, which gave information whether certain firms had "Aryan" or "non-Aryan" employees. In December 1938, *Tidens Tegn* (The Sign of the Times), a leading Oslo newspaper, reported that Norwegian firms were requested by German officials to "report whether Norwegian concerns were Aryan or otherwise."[5] The Norwegian Business Association advised its members in a circular letter of January 26, 1939 that the inquiries were an interference in domestic Norwegian affairs, and that businessmen should ignore the requests.[6] To conceal the real purpose of commercial espionage, an elaborate code had been developed in 1938 through a document entitled "*Stichwörte für dem schriftlichen und telegrafischen Verkehr der Auswärtigen Vertretung mit der Reichsstelle für den Aussenhandel bezîglich Rassenzugehörigkeit.*" In order to elicit racial information, the use of Greek or Roman female names (e.g., Ariadne, Cleopatra, or Xantippe) indicated questions, while the use of male names (Diogenes, Socrates) gave the answers. In Norway, the *Deutsche Handelskammer in Norwegen* (The German Chamber of Commerce in Norway) became a main center for racial intelligence.[7]

Quisling's National Union party willingly supplied the German Commercial Section of the Legation with details as to racial information through its many local agents throughout Norway. The *Deutsche Handelskammer* had become an effective organization in the spreading of anti-Semitic activities and in systematically collecting data on individual Jews and Jewish firms. During the occupation, the German Chamber of Commerce remained active. This machinery, often called "the

4. National Archives, Microfilm T-175, Roll 120. See also, Yad Vashem JM/2221 and JM/2261.
5. Helge Paulsen, "*Antisemittisk handelsspionasje i Norge*" (Anti-Semitic commercial espionage in Norway), *Dagbladet*, Oslo, May 18, 1965, p. 3.
6. Public Record Office, FO 371/23653 XC/A/5356; hereinafter referred to as PRO.
7. Paulsen, op. cit., p. 4, f. ex. Q: "*Ariadne Ole Olsen A/S*"? *Answer:* "*Herkules Ole Olsen A/S.*"

brown net," was involved with social and cultural associations, under the leadership of Günther Kern, the "Gauleiter" in Oslo. Nazi propaganda and espionage went hand in hand.[8]

After the outbreak of World War II in September, 1939, there was a growing concern by Norway for retention of her neutrality, which had been declared on September 1, 1939. The announcement made reference to the declaration of May 27, 1938, which Denmark, Finland, Iceland, Norway, and Sweden had issued for the purpose "of establishing common rules of neutrality."[9] Germany counted on Sweden's non-intervention during a planned invasion of Norway.[10] Having completed the conquest of Poland in the fall of 1939, a German spring offensive was to be expected. On April 5, 1940, Dr. Curt Bräuer, the German Minister to Norway, had invited members of the diplomatic corps and the Norwegian government to view a film of Germany's conquest of Poland, depicting especially the bombing of Warsaw. This film prompted Dr. Halvdan Koht, Norway's Foreign Minister, to state that it was intended to show neutral Norway what would happen if Germany attacked.[11]

Germany decided to strike hard and fast in order to obtain naval and airbases in Norway as well as to secure importation of iron ore from the Swedish mines in the Kiruna-Gällivare area through the Norwegian port of Narvik.[12] Hitler had stated that Germany could, under no circumstances, afford to do without the Swedish ore. "If we do, we will have to wage the war with wooden sticks," he said.[13] On February 21, 1940, Hitler put General Nikolaus von Falkenhorst in charge of preparing the invasion of Norway, under the code name of "Weserübung Nord."[14] On April 8, the British government laid mines in Norway's ter-

---

8. PRO, FO 371/32826 XC/A/5321, p. 2.
9. Nils Ørvik, *The Decline of Neutrality 1914–1941*, Oslo: Johan Grundt Tanum, 1953, p. 217.
10. Olaf Sundell, 9. April (The ninth of April), Stockholm, Sohlmans, p. 34.
11. Halvdan Koht, *Norway: Neutral and Invaded*, New York: The Macmillan Company, 1941, pp. 57–58.
12. Ivar Kraglund, *Narvik-Planen; tanker om en demarkasjonslinje i Nord-Norge, 1940* (The Narvik Plan; thoughts about a line of demarcation in Northern Norway, 1940). Hovedoppgave i historie, høsten 1981, Universitetet i Oslo (M.A. Thesis, Institute of History, University of Oslo, Fall 1981), Chapter 4: "The Battle for Narvik."
13. Nils Ørvik, op. cit., p. 237. *"Das Schwedenerz ist für uns absolut unentbehrlich. Fällt es aus, müssen wir bald den Krieg mit Holzknütteln führen."*
14. IMT, Vol. 28, p. 406, Doc. 1809-PS, as cited in Jodl, *Tagebuch*, February 19, 1940. See also, IMT, Vol. 34, Doc. 174-C, March 1, 1940: *"Weisung für 'Fall Weserübung,'"* pp. 729–32; p. 730: *"Mit der Vorbereitung und Führung des Unternehmens gegen Dänemark*

ritorial waters under the code name "Wilfred," named after St. Wilfred
because the operation was so "small and innocent."[15] Norway protested
the breach of her neutrality, which, according to the French General
Maxime Weygand, "is in a precarious position. It cannot be defended
by armed forces unless the two opponents are equally interested in pre-
serving it."[16] The concept of neutrality has been defined as "the legal
status arising from the abstention of a state from all participation in a
war between other states, the maintenance of it by an attitude of impartiality in its dealings with the belligerent states, and the recognition by
the latter of this abstention and impartiality. From this legal status arise
the rights and duties of neutral and belligerent states respectively. The
primary duty of a neutral state is strict impartiality in its relations with
both belligerents, whether such impartial conduct is obligatory or dis-
cretionary. There must not be any discrimination or preference. Even
a favor granted to one must be extended to another."[17]

Relying on speed, surprise, and camouflage, the German air and naval forces, with about 12,000 men, successfully occupied, during the
morning hours of April 9, Norwegian cities from the southern coast to
the Arctic Circle, including Oslo Stavanger, Kristiansand, Arendal,
Egersund, Bergen, Trondheim, and Narvik. The invaders suffered a serious loss in trying to secure the capital of Oslo. The German heavy
cruiser *Blücher* was sunk with important officers and Gestapo staff on
board. Lieutenant Jürgen Bieler survived the wreckage with top secret
documents from Hitler.[18] The Norwegian guns, dubbed "Moses" and
"Aron," and the torpedo batteries at Nordre Kaholmen caused the sinking of the *Blücher*.[19] One account from Berlin, dated April 18, 1940, stat-

---

*und Norwegen beauftrage ich den kommandierenden General des XXI. A.K. General N.
von Falkenhorst.*"

15. Magne Skodvin, *"Norge i stormaktsstrategien: Fra Finlandsfreden til 'Wilfred,'"* in
Norge og den 2. verdenskrig: 1940 fra nøytral til okkupert (Norway in the 2nd World War:
1940 from neutrality to occupation), Oslo, Universitetsforlaget, 1969, p. 19. Operation
"Wilfred" referred to the British laying of two minefields, one at Vestfjorden, north of
Bodø, another off stadtland, between Bergen and Ålesund.

16. Jacques Mordale, *La Campagne de Norvège*, Paris: Edition Self, 1949, p. 10: *"La
situation des neutres est delicate. . . . La neutralité est une situation precaire. Elle ne peut
être défendue que par la force des armes, à mine que les deux antagonistes n'aient un égal
interêt à voir subsister."*

17. Hugh Haile Leigh Bellot, "Neutrality" in *Encyclopedia Britannica*, University of
Chicago, 1945, 16: 2, pp. 264–65.

18. Sverre Hartmann, "Topphemmeligheter på svøm i Drøbaksundet" (Top Secrets
Afloat in the Drøbak Sound), *Aftenposten*, morning edition, June 16, 1983, pp. 2 and 49.

19. Othar Lislegaard and Torbjørn Børte, *Skuddene som reddet Norge: Senkningen av*

ed that "wounded sailors and soldiers who escaped with their lives from the *Blücher* are arriving with terrible burns on their faces and necks. It seems that when their cruiser went down, it set loose on the water a lot of burning oil. Many men swimming about were burned to death. I suppose half of them died from drowning, half from burning — a nice combination. Not a word about these things in the press."[20] The demise of the *Blücher* prevented the rest of *Angriffsgruppe* 5 from landing troops in Oslo and to capture King Haakon VII and the Norwegian government. The President of the *Storting*, Carl J. Hambro, organized an express train to Hamar and Elverum. The *Storting* voted late at night on April 9 to authorize the government to "safeguard Norway's interest, security and her future."[21] This declaration known as "*Elverumsfullmakten*" (The Elverum Authorization), provided the legal basis for continuing the war against Germany outside of Norway. On June 7, 1940, the King, government, and some members of the *Storting* left from Tromsø on the British cruiser *Devonshire* to establish the government-in-exile in London.

Warnings of possible German invasion had come from many sources and had reached Whitehall and the Norwegian government from various neutral sources in early April.[22] However, the British were not able

---

"*Blücher*," *April 9, 1940* (The shots that saved Norway: The Sinking of the *Blücher*, April 9, 1940), Oslo: Aschehoug, 1975, p. 78. For a fuller treatment of the invasion see Sverre Steen, ed., *Norges krig* (Norway's war), three volumes, Oslo: Gyldendal, 1948–1950; Chr. A.R. Christensen, *Vårt Folks Historie, Okkupasjonsår og Etterkrigstid*, Oslo: Aschehoug, 1961, Vol. 9; Kurt Assman, *Deutsche Schicksaljahre*, Wiesbaden, 1952; Frede Castberg, *Norge under okkupasjonen, 1940–43*, Oslo, 1945; T.K. Derry, *The Campaign in Norway*, London, 1952; Walter Hubatch, *Weserübung: Die Deutsche Besetzung von Dänemark und Norwegen*, Göttingen, 1960, 2nd edition; Koht, *Norway: Neutral and Invaded*, New York: MacMillan, 1941; Jacques Mordal, *La Campagne de Norvège*, Paris, 1949; A. Rosenberg, *Das Politische Tagebuch Alfred Rosenberg, 1934/35 und 1939*, München, 1964.

20. William L. Shirer, *Berlin Diary, The Journal of a Foreign Correspondent*, New York: Alfred A. Knopf, 1941, p. 319.

21. Johan Hambro, *C.J. Hambro, Liv og Drøm* (C.J. Hambro, Life and Dream), Oslo: Aschehoug, 1984, p. 221: "*Stortinget bemyndiger Regjeringen til inntil det tidspunkt kommer da regjeringen og Stortingets presidentskap etter konferanse innkaller Stortinget til neste møte, å ivareta rikets interesser og treffe de avgjørelser og beføyelser på Stortingets og regjeringens vegne som må anses for påkrevd av hensyn til landets sikkerhet og fremtid.*"

22. PRO, FO 371/24815/N3776/2/63 and N/3990/2/63, reports from British Naval Attaché, Oslo, and British Minister in Copenhagen, respectively. Warnings had also come from Norway's Minister in London, Erik Colban, on April 8, 1940.

to prevent the German military forces from successfully invading and occupying the country.

Prior to its departure from Oslo, the government had, at about 4:00 a.m., issued orders for a general mobilization.[23] In reality, this became only a partial mobilization. While the government and *Storting* fled the invading forces, the leader of the National Union Party, Vidkun Quisling, went into action. Since the capital was in chaos and the legal government had fled, Quisling saw his opportunity to undertake a *coup d'état*. *Reichsamtleiter* Hans Wilhelm Scheidt, who had visited Quisling in Norway during 1938–1939, soon became one of the most important persons surrounding Quisling.[24] At about 5:00 p.m. on April 9, Quisling was visited by Scheidt and Viljam Hagelin, a Norwegian businessman, who had spent many years in Germany and had established contact with Nazi leaders. Both reported that the Germans were shaken by the sinking of the *Blücher* with so much valuable material, including Bieler's *Geheime Kommandosache*.[25] Scheidt and Hagelin insisted that the National Union Party had to take over the power of governing, especially since they believed that Hitler would give his consent to a government in Norway headed by Quisling. Quisling believed that he would be Hitler's deputy in Norway. The German Minister to Norway, Dr. Curt Bräuer, had been kept in the dark about Germany's invasion plans until 11:00 p.m., April 8, when a special emissary, Colonel Hartwig Pohlman, from the Foreign Ministry in Berlin, opened in Dr. Bräuer's presence the sealed envelope outlining in detail the invasion plans.[26] Quisling's role as Prime Minister was not mentioned.

Nevertheless, at 7:30 p.m., April 9, 1940, Quisling spoke through the radio to the Norwegian people, announcing himself as Prime Minister in charge of a new government. He stated that England had broken Norway's neutrality and that the German government had offered the new

23. Trygve Lie, *Leve eller dø. Norge i krig* (To live or die. Norway at war), Oslo: Tiden Norsk Forlag, 1955, pp. 20–21.

24. Berit Nøkleby, "*Fra november til april — Sendemann Bräuers personlige politikk*" (From November to April — Minister Bräuer's personal policy). In *Norge og den 2. verdenskrig. Fra nøytral til okkupert. Studier i norsk samtidshistorie*, Oslo-Bergen-Tromsø: Universitetsforlaget, 1969, p. 20: "*Scheidt var Rosenbergs mann i Norge.*"

25. Sverre Hartmann, *Aftenposten*, June 16, 1983, p. 2, describes *Geheime Kommandosache*, such as "Top secret, mostly original documents — such as Hitler's directives, operational analyses in detail, plans for the conduct of war in Norway under different alternatives, including sketches and maps."

26. Arvid Brodersen, *Mellom frontene* (Between the Fronts), Oslo: J.W. Cappelen, 1979, p. 27.

Norwegian government its assistance against an occupation from England. Quisling maintained that, under such circumstances, his "National Union Party" had a duty and a right to take over the governing power to protect the best interests of the Norwegian people and to maintain Norway's security and independence. "We are the only ones who can do this and thereby save the country from a desperate situation into which our people have been led by party politicians." He announced that the government of Prime Minister Johan Nygaardsvold had resigned. A pro-Nazi government had taken power with Vidkun Quisling as chief of the government and as Minister of Foreign Affairs.[27]

Quisling's proclamation created great confusion, but also stimulated a will to resist among the Norwegian people. During the next few days, the Germans made several attempts to get King Haakon to accept the Quisling government, but the King refused. The German policy of forcing acceptance of a traitor as the new head of the national government was its first blunder in Norway, uniting the Norwegian government and hardening resistance.[28] Norway continued active warfare against Germany until June 7, 1940, when the Nygaardsvold government left from Tromsø to London to become the legitimate Norwegian government-in-exile (1940-1945).

Dr. Bräuer's main assignment had been to convince the King and the Norwegian government that resistance was hopeless and that Norway therefore had to submit to Germany's rule including Quisling as head of a new government. Furthermore, Dr. Bräuer's contention that an Administrative Council, subsequently created, was a genuine Norwegian government proved to be wrong. Dr. Bräuer was called back to Berlin, dismissed from the diplomatic corps, and sent to the Western front.[29]

On April 18, 1940, Hitler declared that the exploitation of Norway's economy could begin since Norway was henceforth to be regarded as an enemy country.[30] Norwegian workers completed the enormous con-

---

27. Hans Frederik Dahl, *Dette er London. NRK i krig, 1940–45*, Oslo: Cappelen, 1978, pp. 61–62: *"Proklamasjon til det norske folk"* (Proclamation to the Norwegian people).

28. Ronald G. Popperwell, *Norway,* London & Tonbridge: Ernst Benn Limited, 1972, pp. 154–155.

29. Chr. A.R. Christensen, *Vårt folks historie* (Our people's history), *"Okkupasjonsår og Etterkrigstid"* (Years of Occupation and Postwar Times), Oslo: H. Aschehoug & Company, 1961, Vol. IX, p. 218.

30. Finn Palmstrøm and Rolf Nordmann Torgersen, *Preliminary Reports on Germany's Crimes Against Norway,* Oslo, 1945, p. 64: *"Die Ausnüzung der Wirtschaft des Landes Norwegen kann beginnen. Norwegen ist hierbei als Feindesland zu betrachten."* A con-

struction and armament projects that benefited the German war machine. The three thousand people who were eventually sentenced for profiteering as laborers during the war, wrote Olav Riste and Berit Nøkleby, "hardly convey the lamentable willingness of many Norwegians to take the inflated wages offered for work which served the German interests."[31] One leading historian of the Norwegian occupation, Ragnar Ulstein, estimated that about two hundred thousand Norwegian workers volunteered to work on German fortifications, submarine bases, road building, airdromes, and military barracks.[32] Since Hitler was convinced that an Allied invasion of Norway was forthcoming, *Festung Norwegen* (Fortress Norway) was constantly being reinforced. During 1943 there were twelve infantry divisions, one armored division, and 250 coastal batteries in Norway. These forces helped to assure Swedish neutrality.[33]

Quisling's National Union Party claimed to have had a power base for establishing a Norwegian National Socialist government supported by Germany. After having been installed in February 1942 as "Minister President," Quisling made determined efforts to build up nazified unions. He planned to establish a *"Riksting"* (National Assembly) to which the unions would send representatives. The aim was to control schools, churches, and unions The Norwegian population answered this pressure by resigning from the unions *en masse* in 1942. The resignations had "the effects of a popular referendum with a vast majority against Quisling's plan for nazification of the Norwegian people."[34] During this national emergency, the Home Front had become the decisive force in thwarting the Quisling regime and the German occupiers in their common aim of nazifying the Norwegian population.

---

tention by the lawyer, Albert Wiesener, that Norway had not been at war with Germany since June 10, 1940, when Norway signed the capitulation documents, was rejected by the Norwegian Supreme Court in 1970. See *Annæus Schjødt, "Påstand om norsk kapitulasjon, 10 juni, 1940"* (Assertion regarding Norwegian surrender, June 10, 1940), *Aftenposten*, Oslo, June 30, 1981. See also, *Quisling*, p. 564. Letter from Finance Minister Prytz to Quisling, September 26, 1944.

31. Olav Riste and Berit Nøkleby, *Norway, 1940–45: The Resistance Movement*, Oslo: Johan Grundt Tanum Forlag, 1970, p. 58.

32. Erik Egeland, *"Ulstein's Saga," Aftenposten*, Oslo, January 24, 1978.

33. Aage Trommer, "Scandinavia and the Turn of the Tide," in Henrik S. Nissen, ed., *Scandinavia During the Second World War*, Minneapolis: University of Minnesota Press, 1983, p. 245.

34. Chr. A.R. Christensen, *"Hjemmefronten,"* (The Home Front) in *Våre Falne* (Our Fallen), Oslo: Published by the Norwegian State, 1950, Vol. III, p. 36.

Quisling and the Nazi leaders also suffered defeats in their attempted nazification of Norway's legal and sports organizations. The only striking success enjoyed by the NS was the ease with which the nazification of local governments was achieved. Since 1837, locally-elected councils had been in effect. Local elections, held throughout the country, were regarded as a cornerstone of Norwegian democracy. Despite their long tradition, however, local governments fell under NS control virtually without protest or efforts toward self-defense when the NS moved against them in December 1940.[35] From that point on, the chairmen of the councils were to be appointed, not elected, and the chairmen made all decisions on local affairs in accordance with Nazi principles of *"Gleichschaltung"* (coordination). The appointment of chairmen and local advisers were made by the Ministry of the Interior, which was made up of county governors (*Fylkesmenn*). Some collaborated in the nazification of local governments.

---

35. Ole Kristian Grimnes, "The Beginnings of the Resistance Movement," in Nissen, ed., op. cit., p. 190.

VII

The German Occupation and Domestic Policies

On April 15, 1940, Quisling's "government" was forced by the German authorities to resign in favor of a Norwegian Civilian Administrative Council.[1] The Germans agreed to the establishment of what they believed would be a cooperative body, namely the *Administrasjonrådet* (The Administrative Council), which had been organized by some Norwegian leaders who wanted to find an alternative to the Quisling government and secure a Norwegian administration in the occupied areas.

On April 15, 1940, Supreme Court Justice Paal Berg stated that the only governmental power left in Oslo was the Supreme Court and that, in order to prevent chaos, an administrative council of seven members had been appointed:[2]

> As German armed forces have taken over certain parts of Norway and thereby made it actually impossible for the Norwegian government to maintain its administrative authority in these parts of the country, and, as it is a compelling necessity that the civil administration be in operation, the Supreme Court has found it must provide for the maintenance during the occupation of these parts of the country by German troops, of a council to preside over the civil administration thereof.
>
> Confident that the King of Norway will approve the Supreme Court's

---

1. *Fritt Folk* (Free People). Quisling stated on April 16, 1940, that "because of the danger of continued loss of blood ... I therefore transfer my functions to this Administrative Council."

2. *"Proklamasjon fra Høysterett," Bestemmelser av Administrasjonsrådet*, No. 1, May 8, 1940, p. 1 (Announcement from the Supreme Court. Regulations by the Administrative Council.)

action under the existing extraordinary conditions in seizing this necessary solution, the Supreme Court appoints as members of this temporary administrative council:
Governor of Oslo Province I.E. Christensen, Chairman
Director J. Bache-Wiig
Chief Medical Officer Andreas Diesen
District Judge O.F. Harbeck
Director Gunnar Jahn
Lecturer R.J. Mork
President of the University of Oslo, Didrik Arup Seip.

In reply to the Supreme Court's announcement, the newly-created Administrative Council stated:[3]

There has been appointed today an Administrative Council for the occupied territory.

We who have taken over this commission make an earnest appeal to organizations and private individuals in these districts to give us assistance in our difficult work.

We ask that all show calmness and self-control and at the same time assist according to ability in continuing operations and work.

Everyone in thinking the matter over will realize that sabotage and rendering difficult civil operations merely bring disaster.

The Supreme Court's expectation that this action would receive the King's approval was not met. In a letter of April 17, 1940, the King and government replied:[4]

The Administrative Council which has in the last few days been set up in Oslo from those districts of the country which the Germans have occupied is an emergency institution which does not take the place of the Norwegian Government. The Council is forced to govern according to the direction of that Power which has forced its way into the country with brutal violence. It therefore does not represent the will of the Norwegian people, and has no legal basis in Norwegian law.

Hitler decided to rule Norway through a *Reichskommissariat* to be headed by *Gauleiter* Josef Terboven, a solid member of the German National Socialist Party and the Gestapo. Terboven was supported by the

---

3. Ibid., pp. 1, 2.
4. Monica Curtis, ed., *Norway and the War, September 1939–December 1940*, London: Oxford University Press, 1941, pp. 77-78. "Proclamation from the Norwegian Government, agreed to by the King in Council, April 17, 1940."

German Commander-in-Chief, General-Oberst von Falkenhorst, who, in his first proclamation on April 14, 1940, stated in part:[5]

> It is my task to protect Norway against an attack by the Western Powers. The Norwegian Government has declined several offers of cooperation. The Norwegian people must now themselves determine the fate of their fatherland.
>
> If my proclamation meets with the obedience which was very sensibly accorded by the Danish people when faced with similar circumstances, Norway will be spared the horrors of war.
>
> If opposition is offered and the hand of friendship is rejected, I shall be forced to employ the severest and most relentless means to crush such opposition.

The appointment of Terboven as *Reichkommissar* came through a *Führer-Erlass* of April 24, 1940, which stated that Terboven shall be in charge of the Norwegian occupied territories with headquarters in Oslo and that he shall exercise supreme governmental authority in the civilian sphere. For carrying out his functions he was given authority to use the Administrative Council as well as all other Norwegian authorities. In addition, the *Reichskommissar* was empowered to create laws by way of decrees.

It was also stated that:[6]

> The Reich Commissioner may use German police organs for the enforcement of his orders. The German police organs are at the disposal of the commander of the German troops in Norway, insofar as military necessities require and the duties of the Reich Commissioner permit.
>
> The Reich Commissioner is directly subordinate to me and receives directions and instructions from me.
>
> I appoint Oberpräsident Terboven as Reich Commissioner for Occupied Norwegian Territory.
>
> Regulations for carrying out and supplementing this proclamation are issued on my directions by the Reich Minister and Chief of the Reich Chancellery for the Civil sphere, and by the Chief of the High Command of the Armed Forces for the military sphere.
>
> Berlin, April 24, 1940
>
> (signed) Adolf Hitler
(Führer)

---

5. Ibid., pp. 73-74.
6. Ibid., pp. 78-79.

Who was this man, Josef Terboven, *Gauleiter* in Essen and *Ober-Präsident* of the Rhine Province where the Ruhr towns had been dominated by Terboven's SA?[7] Terboven had now been appointed Hitler's personal representative in Oslo, invested with absolute power, which he exercised ruthlessly and efficiently.

The British Consul General to Zürich, Mr. J. E. Bell, expressed his opinion of Terboven in dispatches to the Foreign Office in London dated April 23 and 30, 1940. From his communications the following composite picture emerges:[8]

> Terboven had gone into the trenches in 1916 at the age of seventeen or so and had become a ruthless killer. When I last saw him at an official dinner in 1939, Terboven had much deteriorated. He habitually drank too much. He would drink beer all night out of a silver mug and at 3 or 4 A.M. begin to top it off with cognac. Nothing has brought home to me more forcibly the fundamental transitoriness of the Nazi system than the appointment of a man like Terboven to be protector of a country with a history such as that of Norway. Terboven is nothing but a gangster and should be exposed as such. . . . Nothing destroys the self-confidence of the gangster more than the knowledge that his record is known. Terboven is not what I should call a demagogue. He was a true fanatic, a man who should not be underestimated. He can be both courageous and ruthless. I think he entirely believes the Nazi creed and that the Führer is to him something of a prophet.

Upon entering his new office on April 24, 1940, Terboven had two fundamental aims in mind: first to establish an administration subordinate to his wishes and, secondly, to utilize his power to let Germany win World War II by *all* means. Upon his arrival in Norway, Terboven found a political distribution of power which was not to his liking. His first declaration of April 26, 1940, outlined his functions and powers:[9]

7. Hermut Krausnik, Hans Buckheim, Martin Broszat and Hans Adolf Jacobsen, *Anatomy of the SS State*, New York: Walker and Company, 1968, p. 408.

8. PRO, FO 371/22263. Dispatch No. 57 (1170/A), April 23, 1940; No. 59, April 30, 1940: The British Consul General, Rotterdam, April 26, 1940, ibid., No. 883: "As to Terboven's efficiency, there could be no question. . . . Terboven is a particular protegé of Goering's. I must say it surprised me very much to hear that Terboven had been appointed to Norway. How different is the man appointed as Hitler's personal representative in Copenhagen, the German Minister Baron von Renthe-Fink. The lot of the Danes . . . will probably be paradise compared with that of the Norwegians at the tender mercies of Terboven."

9. Curtis, op. cit., p. 80.

By order of the Führer, I, as Reich Commissioner, have assumed full authority in the civil sphere for the duration of the occupation of Norwegian territory.

I regard my main task as the maintenance of peace, security and order, guarantee of orderly economic and cultural life of the population as well as the establishment of all conditions for military needs which prove necessary in the land in which, regrettably, there still is fighting counter to the will of the German Government.

To that end, the decisive condition is that the population loyally receives my measures and willingly follows them. Norwegian administrative authorities have offered their cooperation. They will remain in office and administer their duties as heretofore.

Terboven's organization, known as the *Reichskommissariat* for the occupied areas of Norway, was to function through the war.[10] Its offices worked closely with the willing collaborators, the quislings. Having failed to achieve a peaceful occupation of Norway, Terboven could with impunity exclude the German Foreign Office under Ribbentrop from any representation whatsoever in the *Reichkommissar's* rule of Norway.[11] The Administrative Council, which was supported by the Norwegian population, was abolished on September 25, 1940. Terboven instituted a new order which was to dominate the political power structure throughout the remainder of the Norwegian occupation: the appointment on September 25, 1940 of 13 *Kommissariske Statsråder*, ten of whom were members of NS.[12] On the same day, Terboven elevated all the State Councillors to the rank of "ministers."[13] In an order dated September 25, 1940, Terboven stated that the Royal House of Norway and

10. Helge Paulsen, "*Litt om forholdet mellom NS og Reichskommissariat i Norge 1940-45*" (Something about the Relationship between NS and the Reichskommissariat in Norway, 1940-45), in Rolf Danielsen and Stein Ugelvik Larsen, eds., *Fra idé til dom. Noen trekk fra utviklingen av Nasjonal Samling*, Bergen-Oslo-Tromsø: Universitetsforlaget, 1976, p. 205. Terboven's Reichkommissariat consisted of six main departments: *Hauptabteilung Verwaltung, Volkswirtschaft; Volksaufklärung und Propaganda*, and, somewhat later, *Hauptabteilung Technik; Der Höhere SS und Polizeiführer Nord*, and *Einstazstab Wegener* (called *Einsatzstab* from 1942 onward).

11. Christopher R. Browning, *The Final Solution and the German Foreign Office, A Study of Referat DIII of Abteilung Deutschland 1940-1943*, New York: Holmes and Meier Publishers, 1978, p. 87.

12. Odd Melsom, *På Nasjonal Uriaspost* (On National Post as Urias), Oslo: Institut for Norsk Okkupasjonhistorie, 1975, p. 108. The three non-members of Quisling's party were Johanessen (Commerce), Ø. Ravner (Industry), and Sandberg (Banking).

13. Ibid., p. 159.

its government had no further political importance and would not return to Norway.

> In accordance with the right conferred upon me by the decree of the Führer of April 24, I have appointed State Councillors who have taken over the conduct of government business as from today. . . . The activity of the Administrative Council is terminated.
>
> The old political parties are dissolved as from today. New formations for the purpose of political activity of any sort will not be allowed. The political developments of the last years have shown beyond doubt the correctness of the political views of *Nasjonal Samling* and its leader, Vidkun Quisling. . . . Henceforth there is only one road to a solution calculated to give the Norwegian people freedom and independence. It leads through *Nasjonal Samling*."[14]

With this proclamation, Terboven introduced the new official policy of Germany: nazification of the Norwegian people with the help of Quisling's party. The issues had been clarified from June to September during the *Riksrådsforhandlingene* (Negotiations for a National Council) with the Presidential Board and members of the *Storting* requesting a peaceful abdication of King Haakon on June 27, 1940. The King's dignified reply of July 3rd was a firm refusal.[15] The King agreed with Foreign Minister Halvdan Koht that a government could not be appointed that did not have the confidence of the Norwegian people. King Haakon stated that "if the government came to the conclusion that the interest of the country necessitated submission to the German demands he personally would not support the appointment of the Quisling government and would be forced to abdicate.[15a] The Quisling appointment was not made. The German policy went far beyond a military occupation of the territory which Hitler had characterized as *"das Schicksalgebiet in diesem Kriege"* (the fateful territory of this war).[16]

During the invasion of April 1940, the question had been raised with the Swedish government whether the King, Crown Prince, and the

---

14. Curtis, ibid., pp. 140-141. This is part of Terboven's order of September 25, 1940, which ended with: *"Til en løsning som er egnet til i vidtgående utstrekning å vinne tilbake frihet og selvstendighet for det norske folk, gis det nå bare en vei, og den går over Nasjonal Samling."*

15. Embassy of the United States, London, July 8, 1940, No. 5559. Subject: Position of Norwegian Government. Washington, D.C.: National Archives No. 730032.

15a. Herman Lehmkuhl, *Hitler Attacks Norway,* Montreal-London-Washington: Norwegian Information Services, 1943, p. 50.

16. Chr. R. Christensen, *Vårt Folks Historie*, Vol. IX, Oslo: Aschehoug, 1961, p. 239.

Government would be guaranteed safe conduct back to Norway if they were to enter Swedish territory. The Swedish Minister of Foreign Affairs Christian Günther stated that "no promise could be given that King Haakon would not be interned because the pressure from Germany could be too strong.[17]

After September 25, 1940, the constitutional powers had disappeared from political life in Norway. The King and his government were in exile in London; the *Storting* had been dismissed by Terboven; the Supreme Court had resigned over the principle of its constitutional right to review the *Reichskommissar*'s legislation.[18] Terboven's power over civilian life was now unlimited. He had the authority to create a new judicial system, to rule by edicts which made him in reality the life-or-death ruler over civilians.[19] Terboven insisted on complete control over personnel in public service in order to prevent members of the resistance from gaining access to the administration.[20] It has been ironically stated that Terboven was the real founder of the Resistance Movement and that Quisling, through *Nasjonal Samling*, created national unification against nazification.[21]

According to a German historian, Hans-Dietrich Loock, one of the purposes was now to establish a new Norwegian Nazi party built on *Nasjonal Samling* but without Vidkun Quisling as "führer."[22] In a memo of October 25, 1940, Quisling had demanded an independent Norwegian government and the abolition of Terboven's civilian administration. In this effort, Quisling failed.

This is the framework of the power struggle. Terboven regarded Quis-

17. Tim Greve, *Haakon VII. Menneske og Monark* (Haakon VII. Man and King), Oslo: Gyldendal Norsk Forlag, 1980, p. 289.

18. Th. Chr. Wyller, *Nyordning og motstand* (New Order and Resistance). *En framstilling og en analyse av organisasjonenes politiske funksjon under den tyske okkupasjon 25.9.-1940–25.9.-1942.* (A study and analysis of the political functions of the organizations under the German Occupation from September 25, 1940 to September 25, 1942), Oslo: Universitetsforlaget, 1958, p. 66.

19. Arvid Brodersen, *Fra et nomadeliv. Erindringer* (From the Life of a Nomad. Reminiscences). Oslo: Gyldendal Norsk Forlag, 1982, p. 96.

20. Magne Skodvin, *Som seilene fylles av stormen* (As the Storm Fills the Sails), Oslo: Gyldendal Norsk Forlag, 1982, p. 52.

21. Sverre Kjellstadli, *Hjemmestyrkene. Hovedtrekk av den militære motstand under okkupasjonen.* Vol. I, Oslo: Aschehoug, 1959 (The Home Forces. Main Accounts of the Military Resistance during the Occupation), p. 26.

22. Hans-Dietrich Loock, *Quisling, Rosenberg und Terboven. Zur Vorgeschichte und Geschichte der national-sozialistichen Revolution in Norwegen*, Stuttgart: Deutsche Verlags-Anstalt, 1970, pp. 558 ff.

ling as "an uncomfortable competitor"[23] and wanted to rule without him. Quisling had support from Berlin through Alfred Rosenberg. Eventually, Terboven, through the "Act of State" of February 1, 1942, signed at Akershus Castle, effectively blocked Quisling's quest for power by appointing him "Minister-President," basically an empty title.[24] Ultimate power remained where it had been since Terboven's arrival, in the hands of Terboven and the *Reichskommissariat*. The competitive interplay between the two protagonists was a crucial factor underlying the Norwegian Holocaust, for which Quisling worked assiduously.

Knut Hamsun supported Quisling against Terboven. During his visit to Hitler at Berchtesgaden in 1943, "Hamsun wanted nothing less than the removal through Hitler of the most hated man, Terboven, from his position as Norway's *Reichskommissar*."[25]

Soon after his installation as "Minister-President" on February 1, 1942, Quisling and his ministers reintroduced on March 12, Article 2 of the Norwegian Constitution of 1814. The March 1942 issue of *Norsk Lovtidend* (Norwegian Legal Gazette) published the following change in the Constitution: "Jews are prohibited from admission to the Kingdom," i.e., the wording of Article 2 except for the word "fremdeles" (furthermore) as originally adopted in 1814 by the Constituent Assembly.[26] This law received immediate coverage in the Nazi controlled press under the heading "Article Two of the Constitution Again in its Original Form." Minister Sverre Riisnæs praised Quisling for having resurrected

23. Sverre Steen, "*Riksrådsforhandlingene*" (Negotiations for a Riksråd — a National Council), in *Norge og den 2. verdenskrig, 1940. Fra nøytral til okkupert*, Oslo-Bergen-Tromsø: Universitetsforlaget, 1969, p. 137: "*Terboven så på Quisling som en ubehagelig konkurrent.*"

24. Magne Skodvin, "*Det store fremstøt*" (The great advance), in Sverre Steen, ed., *Norges Krig*, Oslo: Gyldendal, 1948, Vol. II, p. 582: "*Han hadde hindret at Quisling ble statssjef.*" (He had prevented Quisling from becoming chief of state.)

25. Harald Næss, review of Torkild Hansen, *Prosessen mot Hamsun*, *Scandinavian Studies*, Vol. 51, No. 3 (1979): 310.

26. *Norsk Lovtidend, 2nen Avdeling, Oslo: Grøndal og Søn, 1942:* "*Grunnlovsbestemmelse: I Grunnlovens paragraf 2 gjeninntas det ved grunnlovsbestemmelsen av 21de juli 1851 opphevede forbud i annet ledd, som skal lyde: Jøder ere udelukkede fra Adgang til Riget.*" Signed Quisling, Ministerpresident; Sverre Riisnes and R.J. Fuglesang." The word "*fremdeles*" (still) was omitted from Quisling's reintroduction of Article 2. The legal change in 1851 received this formulation as recorded in Tønnes Andenæs, *Grunnloven Vår 1814 til idag*, Oslo: Universitetsforlaget, 1966, p. 5, footnote: "*Grundlovens Paragraph 2 sidste Passus saalydende: 'Jøder ere fremdeles udelukkede fra Adgang til Riget' sættes herved ud af Kraft.*" (The last sentence of Article 2: "Jews are still excluded from admission to the Kingdom," is hereby suspended.)

the country's Constitution by prohibiting Jews from entering Norway and added:[27]

> Nasjonal Samling builds the new state with the Constitution as foundation. At the time of our ancestors at Eidsvold, we had still preserved our Nordic view of life. Our people acknowledged that one of the first duties of a people to gain its right to live is to take care of the people's blood. This sound race-conscious thought is closely connected with the ideological view of NS. That is why there is so much stronger reason for Vidkun Quisling to reestablish this constitutional prohibition, since Judaism today is a much more dangerous enemy for our race than it was at the time when the Constitution was adopted . . . blood and soil are the fundamental values which create a people's life. NS's first task is to protect these values.

The law did not, of course, have any practical effect, but it was a principal expression of a racist ideology and another example of the intensification of Jewish persecution.

Reichskommissar Josef Terboven had at his disposal the staff of the Reich Security Main Office (Reichsicherheitshauptamt, RSHA). One of these units, established in Norway, was headed by Oberregierungsrat und SS-Oberführer Franz Walther Stahlecker. He had been ordered on April 10, 1940 to be Himmler's personal representative for "Der höhere SS und Polizeiführer" (HSSP). He was in charge of the five Einsatzkommandos in Norway: Oslo, Stavanger, Bergen, Trondheim, and Tromsø, established in May and June of 1940. Other high Gestapo officials involved with Jewish persecutions in Norway were SS-Oberführer Heinrich Fehlis, in charge of Die Sicherheitspolizei und der Sicherheitsdienst (SIPO u. SD) from fall 1940 to spring 1945. Obtersturmbannführer Gerhard Friedrich Ernst Flesch had, in the fall of 1941, been transferred as Gestapo chief from Bergen to Trondheim, where the Jewish persecutions began the same fall.[28] Flesch was in

---

27. Aftenposten, March 14, 1942: "Nasjonal Samling bygger den nye stat med grunnloven som fundament. . . . På Eidsvoldsfedrenes tid hadde vi ennu bevart vårt nordiske livssyn. Vårt folk erkjente at en av de første pliktene for et folk som vil eie livets rett, er denne: å vareta folkets blod. Den sunde rasebevisste tanke er også i nøye samsvar med NS's ideologiske syn. Så meget sterkere grunn har det været for Vidkun Quisling til å gjenreise grunnslovbestemmelsen som jødedommen idag er en ganske annen farlig fiende for vår stamme enn den var på den tid da grunnloven ble gitt. . . . Nasjonal Samlings syn på de grunnverdier som skaper et folks liv (er) . . . folkets jord og blod. Det er Nasjonal Samlings første oppgave å verne disse verdiene."

28. Sverre Rødder, Bergen Politi under okkupasjonen (The Police in Bergen during the

charge of both the Gestapo and the *Sicherheitsdienst* (SD). *SS-Obergruppenführer* Walter Rediess was the Commander of *Allgemeine SS* in Norway. *Sturmbannführer* Leib in his office organized the *Germanske SS Norge*, which was a branch of the *Allgemeine SS* recruiting Norwegian members of Aryan descent as far back as "to their great-grandfathers."[29] The commander of *Waffen SS in Norway*, *SS-Obersturmbannführer* Pettersen, recruited Norwegians to fight on the Eastern front against the Soviet Union, where they suffered heavy losses. About one thousand were killed. Seven thousand Norwegians had been selected to join in this fight out of fifteen thousand who had volunteered.[29a] Many were graduate students or had completed their education as lawyers, teachers, civil engineers, medical doctors, theologians, or ministers. All had come from either *Nasjonal Samling*, *Fedrelandslaget*, or *Bygdefolkets Krisehjelp.* "They had grown up in a Nazi ghetto and had had no opportunities to adjust outside their milieu. They were fighting for a new Europe under the leadership of Germany."[30]

Adolf Eichmann's first representative in Norway, Criminal Commisar and *SS-Hauptsturmführer* (Captain) Wilhelm Esser, had arrived in Oslo on April 30, 1940, and he remained there until February 1941. On February 13, 1941, Eichmann's office in Norway, *Referat IVB4,* was taken over by *SS-Hauptsturmführer* Wilhelm Arthur Konstantin Wagner, as head of the Gestapo Office of Jewish Affairs. His immediate superior was *SS-Sturmbannführer* (Major) Herman Gustav Hellmuth Reinhard, born Patzschke on July 24, 1911.[31] He had joined the Nazi party on March 4, 1933, and had arrived in Norway on January 28, 1942, succeeding Norway's Gestapo Chief, Dr. Werner Knab. Reinhard, however, remained in charge of Norway's Gestapo office until February

Occupation) Bergen: Bergen Politikammer, 1, 1974, p. 115: "*Sikkerhetspolitiets avdeling i Bergen ble ledet av Sturmbannführer Gerhard Flesch. I oktober ble han flyttet til Trondheim som leder av sikkerhetspolitiets avdeling der."*

29. Records of the Office of Strategic Services, No. 32746, of April 23, 1943. A-4457, National Archives, Washington D.C.

29a. Svein Blindheim, *Nordmenn under Hitlers fane.* Oslo: Noregs Boklag, 1977, p. 7.

30. Svein Blindhem, *"Hvorfor sloss 7000 nordmenn under Hitlers fane på Østfronten?"* (Why did 7000 Norwegians fight under Hitler's banner on the Eastern Front?), *Nordisk Tidende,* Brooklyn, N.Y. June 9, 1977, p. 11.

31. *Strafsache Gegen Hellmuth Reinhard,* (Früher Patzschke) Baden-Baden, February 1, 1967, p. 1. TR/9/27-2; TR/10/608 and 10/765 Yad Vashem Archives, Jerusalem.

1, 1945.[32] The person in charge of *Abteilung 4N (Nachricten)* was *SS-Hauptsturmführer* Siegfried Wolfgang Fehmer, who cooperated closely with Hellmuth Reinhard.

The triumvirate of *Reichkommissar* Josef Terboven, *Obergruppenführer des Waffen SS*, Wilhelm Rediess, and Hellmuth Reinhard, aided by the close cooperation of the Norwegian State Police, Vidkun Quisling, and his party, *Nasjonal Samling*, were the protagonists in identification, roundup, arrest, confiscation of property, and deportation of Jews in Norway to Auschwitz. The Germans had many Norwegian collaborators outside and inside of the Norwegian State Police.[33] The German police in Norway had become consolidated under one central leadership.

The Norwegian police constituted the largest percentage of any civilian group to join the Norwegian Nazi party. During the fall and winter of 1940, more than 60 percent of the *politiembedsmenn* (police officers) and 30 percent of the *polititjenestemenn* (rank and file) had joined Quisling's National Union Party.[34] The NS Party had been particularly successful in recruiting policemen, so that the police became the most nazified of all the public servants during the occupation.[35] Nationally forty-two percent of all policemen had joined *Nasjonal Samling* without having been directly forced to do so. It was an alarmingly high percentage compared to the average of six percent among the other civil servants.[36] In March 1941 the Norwegian Police Department was reorganized. The State Police (STAPO), the Border Police (*Grensepolitiet* or GREPO) and Criminal Police (KRIPO) became an integral part of the Security Police. Throughout the occupation the police maintained secret contact with the Home Front.

Those among the police who had chosen to join the NS Party ignored the directive (*parole*) issued by Bishop Eivind Berggrav on October 23,

32. Odd Bergvald, *Hellmuth Reinhard. Soldat eller morder?* Oslo: Chr. Schibsteds Forlag, 1967, pp. 14, 15.

33. Berit Nøkleby, *Holdningskamp* (Steadfast Moral Struggle) in *Norge i Krig* (Norway at War), Oslo: Aschehoug, 1986, vol. 4, pp. 77-78.

34. Jon Arild Arnli, *Det norske politi: Perioden 1938–våren 1941* (The Norwegian Police; Period from 1938 to Spring 1941), Hovedoppgave #4918, M.A. Thesis, p. 1, University of Oslo: "*Over 60% av politiembetsmennene og over 30% av polititjenestemennene høsten og vinteren 1940 meldte seg inn i NS,*" Oslo: Universitetsbiblioteket.

35. Ole Kristian Grimnes, "The Beginnings of the Resistance Movement," *Scandinavia During the Second World War*, Minneapolis: The University of Minnesota Press, 1983, p. 190.

36. Nøkleby, op. cit., p. 65.

1940, to the effect that each individual was free to choose whether to join the NS Party or not. No civil servant should use as an excuse that there was no choice, but only forced membership. The organizations of lawyers and judges had instructed their memberships as to freedom of choice, each one had to follow his own conscience in the face of threats by the NS Party. The directive was explicit and also clearly raised the moral issue of choice. This policy indicated a way out of the dilemma, since everyone was free to refuse to join the Nazi Party. No civil servant had to feel trapped into thinking there was no way out. No one must feel forced to commit treason. If one joined, one would have to bear the brunt of responsibility.[37]

The Quisling organization had established a Police Department, headed by Jonas Lie, who had appointed Karl Alfred Nicolay Marthinsen (1896-1945) as chief of the Security Police and the State Police. Marthinsen was liquidated by the Resistance Movement on February 8, 1945 at Blindern, near Oslo.[38] An assessment of the crucial role played by the Norwegian police in the preparation, roundup, arrests, and deportation of Norwegian Jews has been documented by Dr. Knut Sveri, a noted criminologist and professor of Law at the University of Stockholm. He, as have many others, stated that arrest and deportation of Jews were against international law and punishable under Norwegian law:[39] "The occupying power has no right to arrest, deport, or murder human beings only because they belong to a certain religion or 'race.' This holds true also for the Quisling government which functioned on behalf of the occupying power. . . . The Norwegian criminal code in Article 223 penalizes those who 'illegally deprive anyone of liberty or participates in deprivation of such freedom.' The law is effective against all

37. Eivind Berggrav, "Paroler høsten 1940, *Morgenbladet*, Oslo, July 31, 1945: ". . . hver enkelt stod fritt til å nekte å melde seg inn i N.S. Ingen tjenestemann måtte få lov å falle tilbake på den betraktning at der ikke fantes noen vei forbi tvangssituasjonen. . . . Til landsforrederi må ingen la seg tvinge. Han får likevel sitt fulle ansvar."

38. Tore Dyrhaug, *Norge okkupert! Tysk etterretning om Norge og nordmenn 1942-1945*, Oslo-Bergen-Stavanger-Tromsø: Universitetsforlaget, 1985, p. 127.

39. Knut Sveri, *"Landssvikoppgjørets merkeligste rettssak,"* in Anders Bratholm, Helge Olav Bugge, Nils Christie and Terkel Opsahl, eds., *Lov og frihet. Festskrift til Johs. Andenæs, på 70-årsdagen 7. september 1982* (The Strangest Case in the Legal Accounting of Treason), Oslo: Universitetsforlaget, 1982, p. 346: "At arrestasjon og deportasjon av jøder var i strid med folkeretten er helt selvsagt. En okkupasjonsmakt har ikke rett til å arrestere, forflytte eller henrette mennesker bare fordi de tilhører en bestemt trosbekjennelse eller "rase". Det samme gjelder Quisling-regjeringen, som fungerte i kraft av sitt oppdrag for okkupasjonsmakten."

those participating in actions against Jews, regardless in which capacity
(as planner, participants, guards), and regardless of whether they knew
or did not know what later would happen to the Jews."

In his assessment of the Quisling contribution to the Holocaust, the
noted Norwegian criminologist Per Ole Johansen has stated that the
Quisling bureaucracy "did the job for the SS without lifting a finger in
defense of the Jews as a Norwegian minority.[40] . . . The noted scholar
on Norway's police during World War II, Nils Johan Ringdal characterized the attitude among the Norwegian police towards Jews as indifference and passivity. This might explain the "success" of the police actions
against Jews which constituted "the blackest chapter in the history of
the Norwegian police during the war. Forty per cent of Norway's Jews
died in German concentration camps and gas chambers. This was partly
the responsibility of the Norwegian police."[41]

---

40. As quoted by Ole Smith in *Politiken* (Copenhagen), December 23, 1984: *"Forum:
Det norske bidraget til Holocaust"* (Forum: The Norwegian Contribution to the Holocaust) in reviewing *Oss selv nærmest. Norge og jødene 1914-1943* (We are the nearest to
ourselves: Norway and the Jews 1914-1943) by Per Ole Johansen.

41. Ringdal op. cit., p. 229: *"Aksjonen mot jødene vil for alltid bli stående som det
svarteste kapitlet av det norske politis historie under krigen. 40% av Norges jøder døde
i tyske konsentrasjonsleirer og gasskamre. Dette var delvis det norske politis ansvar."*

VIII

Persecution of Norway's Jews

The destruction of Jews in Norway has been characterized as "the saddest chapter in the history of the Occupation."[1] From 1940–1942 Jews were exposed to various stages of discrimination: round-ups, arrests, torture, and finally deportation to death camps.

The first discriminatory measure was the confiscation of radios belonging to Jews, performed on May 10 and 11, 1940 by the Norwegian police upon the request of Criminal Commissar, Wilhelm Esser, Eichmann's representative in Norway.

A police report of May 10, 1940, stated that Commissar Esser had on that day asked for confiscation of radios "belonging to Jews who are members of Jewish communities or societies. . . . It is desired that the radios be stored in rooms to which both the Norwegian and German police will have access. Any mention of this prior notice in the press is desired to be prevented." A handwritten notification as to the latter request stated: "To be arranged through the Telegraph Office."[2] Confisction of radios belonging to Jews took place not only in Oslo but in other parts of the country as well. In a letter of September 5, 1941, to Oslo and Aker Police District, the request of May 10, 1940, was confirmed and "immediately

1. H. O. Christophersen, *Av nød til seir. Bilder fra okkupasjonstiden i Norge* (From Distress to Victory. Pictures from the period of occupation in Norway.) *Bind. I. Fra 9. april 1940 til kampåret 1942)* (Vol.I. From April 9, 1940 to the fighting year 1942. Oslo: Grøndahl & Søn Forlag A.S., 1977, p. 184.
2. Report from Oslo Police Precinct (J. Nr. 2089) of May 10, 1940: "*Kommissær Esser har idag kl. 14 bedt beslaglagt i løpet av idag og imorgen samtlige radioapparater hos jøder som tilhører jødiske trossamfund eller foreninger. . . . Apparatene ønskes oppbevart på rum hvortil både det norske og det tyske politi har adgang. Presseomtale av denne forholdsregel ønskes hindret.*"

complied with. Altogether (in Oslo) 107 radios were confiscated."[3] On May 28, 1941, a report was issued from Trondheim Police Precinct to the Chief of Security Policy in Oslo regarding confiscation of radios, and informing Jews that "it was forbidden to be in possession of radios."[4] All radio stores in Trondheim had been informed of the prohibition for Jews to possess radios.

The administrative Council had been well aware of the confiscation of radios on May 10 and 11. The minutes of the Council of May 16, 1940, reported that the Chief of Police in Oslo, Kristian Welhaven, had been called upon to explain the police action. Mr. Welhaven stated that the police had obeyed the German request without waiting for the issue to be dealt with by the superior authorities "because he thought that the police had no right to oppose such a decree, and furthermore, that protests would be of no avail."[5]

The German in charge of the Department of Administration of the *Reichskommissariat*, *Regierungspräsident* Hans Delbrügge, justified the actions by explaining to the Administrative Council that "the Jewish problem had to be handled internationally, and that the legal basis was to be found in one of Hitler's ordinances."[6]

---

3. Report to the criminal Police, Oslo-Department, September 5, 1941, by J. Trøgstad (førstebetjent) who confirmed the German request of May 10, 1940, and added: "*Henstillingen ble straks etterkommet og det ble beslaglagt i alt 107 radioapparater som kort tid efter blev overtatt av det tyske politi ved kommissær Esser.*" *Riksarkivet*, Oslo (National Archives, Oslo) hereinafter referred to as RAO), *Rapport fra Oslo Politi*, May 10, 1940, and September 5, 1941: "*Beslag av radioapparater hos jøder.*" (Confiscation of radios belonging to Jews).

4. Letter of May 28, 1941, from *Trondheim Politikammer* (Trondheim Police Precinct) to *Lederen av Sikkerhetspolitiet*, *Politidepartmentet* (Chief of Security Police), Oslo: "Besiddelse av radiomottagerapparat. Samtlige radioapparat hos jøder i Trondheim ble inndratt av det tyske sikkerhetspoliti i mai 1940. Man har i henhold til Politidepartementets rundskriv av 16. mai, 1941 foretatt kontroll hos samtlige jøder og funnet de apparat som vedlagte liste viser, samt gjort samtlige kjent med at det er forbudt å være i besiddelse av radiomottagerapparat. Samtlige radioforhandlere i Trondheim er tilskrevet i henhold til pålegget i ovennevnte rundskriv."

5. *Protokoll for møter i Det Administrasjonsråd som er oppnevnt av Høyesterett mandag den 15 April, 1940.* "*År 1940 den 16. mai*" (Protocol of the Administrative Council appointed by the Supreme Court, Monday, April 15, 1940. Minutes of May 16 regarding statements by the Oslo Chief of Police, K. Welhaven), p. 108: ". . . når politiet hadde fulgt tyskernes pålegg om å inndra jødenes radioapparater uten å vente til saka var behandlet i overordnede instanser, var det fordi han mente politiet ikke hadde adgang til å sette seg i mot et slikt pålegg og at protester ikke ville nytte."

6. Ibid., p. 115: "*Herr Delbrügge hadde framholdt at de tyske myndigheter måtte behandle jødespørsmålet internasjonalt . . . og at hjemmelen (for aksjonen) var å finne i der Führers forordning.*" *Regierungspräsident* Hans Delbrügge was in charge of

This incidence was characteristic of the defeatist attitude of the Norwegian civil administration during the first months of the occupation. There was, of course, no moral or judicial foundation for condoning confiscation of "Jewish" radios or for not protesting this discrimination at a time when arrests and interrogations by Gestapo seldom took place.[7] The motivation behind the confiscation might have been to identify Jewish families. In Norway, one had to obtain a state license in order to have a radio. By confiscating radios two aims might have been achieved at the same time: preventing the listening to foreign broadcasts and identification of Jewish families.

More systematic means of identifying Jews and Jewish enterprises had been undertaken by Commissar & *SS-Hauptsturmführer* Wilhelm Esser, who was born in Norway where he had lived until 1927, and returned to Oslo on April 30, 1940. He established a list of Jewish stores, based in part on the second edition of *Who's Who in the Jewish World, Including a Listing of Stores Belonging to Foreigners in Norway.*[8] The author Mikal P. O. Sylten stated that "Jews constitute a foreign and harmful element in every cultural society."[9] Demands for membership lists of the two organized Jewish societies in Trondheim and Oslo were made and complied with during the spring of 1940.[10]

Simultaneous with this harassment, the Norwegian Nazi party called for a crusade against the "Jewish international peril" in speeches and in the controlled press. In the fall of 1940, the quislings painted anti-Jewish slogans on store windows belonging to Jews. The slogans included, "Jewish store!" "Jews! Closed!" "Jewish Parasites!" "Palestine calling! Jews not tolerated in Norway!"[11]

"Hauptabteilung verwaltung/-Reichskommissariat"; as cited in Rolf Danielsen and Stein Ugelrik Larsen, eds. *Fra Idé til Dom,* Oslo: Universitetsforloget, 1976, p. 210.

7. Didrik Arup Seip, *Hjemme og i fiendeland* (At Home and in Enemy Country), Oslo: Gyldendal Norsk Forlag, 1946, p. 87.

8. Ole Kolsrud, *"For 40 år siden — Da nordmenn jaget jøder,"* (40 years ago — When Norwegians persecuted Jews), *Dagbladet,* Oslo, October 16, 1982, p. 19.

9. Mikal P. O. Sylten, *"Hvem er Hvem i Jødeverden samt fortegnelse over Fremmedes Forretninger i Norge,"* Oslo: *Nationalt Tidsskrift,* 1st Edition, 1925, 2nd Edition, 1932, 4th Edition 1941.

10. Oskar Mendelsohn: *"Jødeforfølgelsene i Norge — Norsk motstand — Hjelp til Flukt,"* (Jewish Persecutions in Norway — Norwegian Resistance — Help to Escape.) Oslo: *Jødisk Menighetsblad,* Vol. 2, No. 3, Kislev 5738/December, 1977, p. 14: *"Alt våren 1940 kom de første tyske tiltak: de jødiske menigheter ble tvunget til å levere inn medlemslister."* ("Already during the spring of 1940 came the first German actions: The Jewish organizations were forced to submit lists of membership.")

11. Magne Skodvin, *"Det store fremstøt," op. cit., p. 617: "Umiddelbart etter den 15.*

The campaign against individual Jews led to withdrawal of licenses issued to nine foreign Jewish medical doctors and to an announcement by Edward Sylow-Creutz, a quisling in charge of the Norwegian Broadcasting Corporation, that all Jewish music should be banned and that performers should be members of *Nasjonal Samling.* In the fall of 1940, Per Reidarson, a well-known musician, had submitted a proposal for an artists' and journalists' guild of Norway. In its program it was stated that only carefully selected persons, anti-Semites, and members of NS would be eligible for membership. This resulted in the harassment of a leading musician, Ernst Glaser, who was scheduled to appear as soloist in Sinding's Violin Concerto in A-major at a concert by Harmonien in Bergen on January 16, 1941, using Ole Bull's Guarneri del Gesù violin from 1742. While Mr. Glaser was entering the hall, anti-Semitic demonstrators held a rally organized by the local NS party, insisting that a Jewish artist should not be permitted to perform. The violinist was not permitted to play. Instead, demonstrations took place inside the concert hall, where leaflets were distributed stating that no Jew should be permitted to play on Ole Bull's violin, which was considered a national treasure.[12] The demonstrators shouted, "Down with Jews! Down with the Jew Moses Salomon."[13] Fistfights ensued, the police were called, and the demonstration continued until the orchestra played the national anthem. The demonstrators were not prosecuted, although the governing body of the *Harmonien* submitted the case to the police. None of the demonstrators were even interrogated.[14] In 1946, it was stated about this event: "The Norwegian authorities protected the mobs, of course. The

september begynte nazistisk pøbel å male inskripsjoner på vinduene. ..." Examples: "*Jødisk forretning!*", "*Jøde Lukket!*", "*Jødisk parasitt!*" or "*Palestina kaller! Jøder tåles ikke i Norge!*"

12. Hans Jørgen Hurum, "Musikk under okkupasjonen," *Kultur-Nytt, 1940–1942,* Oslo: 7:7 (1981): 22–23. See also Time Greve, *Bergen i Krig, 1940–1942, Bergen: J. W. Eide Forlag, 1979, pp. 172–173; Yad Vashem JM/1198; Adolph Berg and Olav Mosby, Musikselskabet Harmonien, 1765–1954,* Bergen: John Griegs Boktrykkeri, Vol. II, p. 186. The leaflets distributed at the Glaser concert stated: "*Ole Bulls violin er norsk nasjonaleiendom. Hans verker er grunnpillarene i norsk musikk. Norsk ungdom tillater ikke at vår germanske ære tilsvines av Jøden Moses Salomon* (alias Ernst Glaser). *Denne jødiske kramkar har tiltusket seg Ole Bulls fele, vår nasjonaleiendom, og reiser land og strand rundt og slår penger på dette. Vi krever at Moses Solomons kremmerturne stoppes her i Bergen.* ... *Nasjonal-Ungdom.*"

13. Kåre Fasting, *Musikselskabet "Harmonien" gjennom to hundre år,"* (The musical Society, "The Harmony," during two hundred years), Bergen, p. 16.

14. Kåre Fasting, op. cit., p. 17: "Harmoniens styre anmeldte saken til politiet uten at det kom noe ut av det."

German authorities seemed to greet the scandal with satisfacion. They declared that the 'national' Norwegian youth could really be moved to act."[15] It was a principle, as Müller Scheld, a member of the *Reichskommissariat*, said: "A Jew can have no official position in Norway."[16]

Further harassment took place in July 1941 with dismissals of Jews in public service. Jewish lawyers in private practice and other professionals were deprived of their licenses and could not continue in their professions. One of the lawyers, Willy Rubenstein of Oslo, received a letter dated September 6, 1941 from the Minister of Justice, Sverre Riisnæs. The letter stated:[17] "According to your declaration to the State Police of August 28, you are of full Jewish descent. As a Jew you are unworthy of having the confidence and respect necessary for your position. In conformity with the regulation issued on June 23 of this year, the Department has therefore canceled forever your license to practice law." A Supreme Court Justice, Einar Nathan, was arrested in December 1940, released in June 1941, but rearrested the following fall and deported in November 1942 to Auschwitz. He was shot to death by a prison guard for defending a co-prisoner who had been tortured.[18]

With the German invasion of the Soviet Union in June 1941, the racial war against the Jews took on a new dimension. In Harstad, Narvik, and Tromsø and also in other cities in Northern Norway, many Norwegian and stateless Jews were arrested, some even before the German invasion of U.S.S.R. Most of those arrested were incarcerated at the concentration camp "Sydspissen" (the Southern Point) on the island of Tromsø, located at the 70th degree northern latitude. One of the prisoners, Herman Smith from Tromsø, was arrested on June 12, 1941 and deported from Sydspissen to Birkenau-Auschwitz. He was one of the very few inmates who managed to send greetings that reached his family. A letter

15. Hans Jørgen Hurum, *Musikken under okkupasjonen*, Oslo: H. Aschehoug and Co., 1946, p. 61: "... de norske myndigheter holdt selvsagt sin hånd over pøbelen. Og på sin side syntes de tyske myndigheter å hilse skandalen med tilfredshet. ... De hadde fått utsagn for at den 'nasjonale' norske ungdom virkelig lot seg vekke til dåd."
16. Hurum, op. cit., pp. 61–62.
17. Letter from Department of Justice, Jrn. 511/41.S of September 6, 1941: "*Ifølge Deres forklaring for Statspolitiet den 28. f. m. er De av hel jødisk avstamning. Som jøde er De uverdig til den tillit og aktelse som er påkrevet for Deres stilling. Departmentet har derfor for alltid tilbakekalt Deres sakførertillatelse i medhold til forordningen av 23. juni d.å. 5. Oslo, den 6. september 1941. (Signed) Sverre Riisnæs. Reinhard Breien.*
18. Guro Nordahl-Olsen, *Krysning. En krønike fortalt av Guro Nordahl-Olsen* Oslo: C. Huitfeldt Forlag, p. 163. (Half-bred. A Chronicle as told by Guro Nordahl-Olsen.)

written in German from *"Arbeitslager Birkenau bei Neuberun"* was received by his daughter Mrs. Eva Fuksman.[19] The letter said:

> I write a few words to you to let you know that I am healthy, and I hope that you, Bergljot, and the children are also well. It is very cold here, but I hope that the winter will soon be over. I send special regards to all of you at home. Best regards!
>
>   Herman Smith

None of the Norwegian Jews deported from Northern Norway survived the war.

The Jews arrested in Trøndelag, Møre, and Romsdal were sent to Vollan prison in Trondheim and only later to Grini internment camp, which had opened on June 12, 1941, as *"Polizeihäftlingslager Grini."* By the end of the war, over 15,000 prisoners from all over Norway and eighteen foreign countries had been interned at Grini. On June 23, 1941, the day after the German invasion of the Soviet Union, sixty Jewish prisoners arrived at Grini. They were singled out for savage beatings. They had their hair torn off, skin and all. Afterwards the Jews had to clean up the "bloody mess." After about three weeks, however, the stateless Jews were inexplicably released.[20]

It is noted that the German contempt for foreigners gradually infected some of the Norwegian prisoners who, little by little, accepted the German view of East Europeans as belonging to an inferior race. The yellow Jewish star had been introduced at Grini.[21] When twelve Jews from Northern Norway arrived in Grini on April 3, 1942, Odd Nansen, a well-known architect and then a prisoner, was ordered by the camp com-

---

19. Letter to author of June 30, 1983 from Eva Fuksman, Oslo regarding her father Herman Smith and enclosing copy of the Birkenau letter. On back of the envelope is typed *"über die Reichsvereinigung der Juden in Deutschland Berlin-Charlottenburg 2, Kantstr. 158."*

20. August Lange and Johan Schreiner, eds., *Griniboken* (The Grini Book), Oslo: Gyldendal Norsk Forlag, 1946, Vol. I, pp. 33–34: *"Det var jonsokkveld, 1941, dagen etterat Hitlers arméer var gått til angrep på USSR. Ut på formiddagen rullet grå lastebiler inn, fangene hoppet ut og ble brutalt drevet inn gjennom porten. . . . Så ble de nye fangene jaget opp i hovedbygningen og stuet sammen på en sal i fjerde etasje. Det var 60 jøder av russisk avstamning. I to timer herjet vaktmansskapenes Zugführer med dem oppe på salen. Neste post var snauklipping. . . . 'Det går altfor langsomt' og røsket håret av dem i store dotter. Hodehuden fulgte med, og jødene ynket seg av smerte. Da behandlingen var over, lå det hauger med blodige hårtjafser på golvet. Jødene måtte feie opp, og såpevaske golvet til alle blodflekkene var borte. Jødene satt innesperret i fjerde etasje i to-tre uker. Så ble de til alles forundring løslatt."*

21. Holmboe, "De som ble tatt," op. cit., p. 450.

mander, *Unterscharführer* Walter Kunze, to make posters with the following text: "It is strictly forbidden to have contacts between Jew and Aryan." Nansen made the posters with large black frames expressing sorrow, and put the posters up on the doors of the Jewish rooms. This prohibition was not more effective at this time than it had been in the past.[22]

At Grini Jews were treated more cruelly than other prisoners. They could not be hospitalized or receive visitors and were forced to work at an accelerated speed. Their work consisted of heavy labor such as digging stones for the German guard barracks. Supervision was by SS-men. A prisoner who did this work wore two white stripes — a special designation — on his shoulder. On command, the Jews were required to sing songs with lyrics that said they were the cause of all misfortunes: *"Die Juden sind unser Unglück,"* or they had to stand with bent knees and upright arms to sing: *"Der Jude war einmal, der Jude ist nicht mehr"* (Once upon a time there was a Jew. The Jew does not exist any more).[23]

The Quisling government, through its State Councilor of Church and Education, Ragnar Sigvald Skancke, had, in September 1941, proposed changes in the marriage laws.[24] They would prohibit marriages between Norwegian citizens and persons of Lappish or Jewish descent up to the third generation. However, Bishop Eivind Berggrav, leader of the Church, expressed forcefully that the Church stood united against any attempt to introduce "aryan" marriage laws, whether against the Jewish or Lappish (Saamic) population.[25] Such racial laws were, of course, contrary the basic concepts of the Christian Church. The proposal was postponed, and, when put into effect in December 1942, was directed only against Jews.

On March 7, 1942, the first executions of Norwegian Jews took place when four Jews, who had been arrested in January 1942 on trumped-up charges of having spread hostile propaganda for a foreign power, were shot at *Kristiansten Festning* (Fortress) in Trondheim. They were Abel

---

22. Lange and Schreiner, op. cit., p. 118.
23. Ibid., p. 411. "The Jews are our misfortune."
24. Ludvig Schübeler, *Kirkekampen slik jeg så den* (The church struggles as I saw it), Oslo: Lutherstiftelsen, 1946, p. 70: *"Kirkedepartementat forsøkte også med en lov om forandring i ekteskapslovgivningen. Den skulle hindre jøder å inngå ekteskap med nordmenn."*
25. Torleiv Austad, *Kirkens Grunn, en analyse av en kirkelig bekjennelse fra okkupasjontiden 1940-1945* (The Foundation of the Church, an analysis of an ecclesiastical confession from the history of occupation, 1940-1945), Oslo: Luther Forlag, 1974, p. 128.

Bernstein, David Isaksen, Wulf Isaksen and David Wolfsohn.[26] A fifth person, Efraim Schilowsky, was released and returned to Sweden because he was a Swedish citizen. The announcement of the verdict in *Fritt Folk* on March 9, 1942, was forwarded to the Criminal Inspector Wiermyhr by Jonas Lie in an effort "to link Jews to criminal behavior against Germany."[27] The reaction to these murders were forcefully expressed in the Swedish press which, except for the Nazi papers, unanimously condemned the Trondheim murders. *Dagens Nyheter* commented that the murders represented "an attempt by the highest occupation authority to repeat his brutalities of last year, in order to force subjugation upon a people refusing to let itself be cowed in the usual Nazi fashion."[28]

In August, 1942, nine Oslo Jews were arrested at their summer homes at Nærsnes, near Oslo. Among them were Herman Bernstein and Paul Bernstein, Seleg Levenson and Gabriel Plesansky.[29] Rabbi Julius Isak Samuel, who had served the Oslo congregations since 1930, was arrested at the same time but was inexplicably released with orders to present himself daily at the Oslo Gestapo office. His wife, Henrietta, asked why he would not escape or go into hiding to which he answered: "As rabbi I cannot abandon my community in this perilous hour."[30] He was rearrested on September 2, 1942. At the Eichmann Trial in Jerusalem in 1961, Mrs. Henrietta Samuel testified that her husband had been murdered at Auschwitz on December 16, 1942.[31]

---

26. Fritt Folk, March 9, 1942: *"Dødsstraff for fiendtlig propaganda"* (Death penalty for hostile propaganda); *"De norske jøder, David Wolfsohn, Wulf Isaksen, David Isaksen og Abel Bernstein, alle fra Trondheim er dømt til døden for propaganda for en fiendtlig makt, ved dom av SS und Polizeigericht Nord. De dømte hadde spredt engelske nyheter på norsk som var avlyttet med et ulovlig radioapparat. Dommen er fullbyrdet ved skytning."* (The Norwegian Jews are condemned for having spread propaganda for a hostile power, by verdict of the SS and the Police Court of the North. . . . The verdict is fulfilled by shooting.)

27. Letter of March 9, 1942 from Jonas Lie to Criminal Inspector Jørgen Wiermyhr to prove alleged criminality by Jews;: Kripo, Jnr. 128/42B. National Archives, Oslo.

28. Office of Strategic Services, Washington, D.C., January 20, 1943, citing the illegal paper *Håndslag* (The Handshake), October 24, 1942, p. 2, "Sweden Reacts." National Archives, RG 226.

29. Marcus Levin, Letter, July 30, 1946, Stockholm, Department for American Joint Distribution Committee, *Wagner*, 17, pp. 2–3.

30. Ingebjørg Fosstvedt Sletten, "A Heroine of Norway," in Arieh L. Bambinger, *Roll of Honor*, Tel Aviv: Hamenorah Publishing House, Second Edition, 1971, p. 65.

31. Testimony by Henrietta Samuel, Eichmann Trial, November 5, 1961, p. N 1: "I have a document confirming that my husband was exterminated on the 16th of December 1942," Yad Vashem Archives, Jerusalem.

During the course of the proceedings against the Gestapo officer Wilhelm Wagner after the war, it was revealed that the nine Jews had been accused of anti-German propaganda, distribution of illegal newspapers, and having hidden couriers. Wagner testified that one of the arrested had admitted that the accusations were partly correct.[32] He failed to mention that the prisoner Nathan Fein was given no opportunity to read the "confession" prior to signing.

In the city of Trondheim, where about 150 Jews remained, the synagogue was confiscated by the Germans without warning in April 1941 and completely vandalized. The main sanctuary was used as a barracks, the women's gallery became a barbershop, the *Mogen David* (Shield of David) in the stained glass windows was replaced with swastikas, and all other Hebrew inscriptions were removed. Two of the four Torah scrolls were brought safely to the home of Aron Mendelsohn, a founder and leader of the Jewish congregation. His home at Kjøbmannsgaten 40 was used as a synagogue until his apartment was confiscated in the spring of 1942. After the confiscation of the synagogue in Trondheim, Arne Fjellbu, dean of the Nidaros Cathedral, warned the local Nazis and quislings in private conversations that if the synagogue action indicated a general persecution of Jews, "I can assure you that the Church will sound the alarm from one end of the country to the other. Here the Norwegian Church stands one hundred percent united. Such a thing we will not tolerate."[33]

At the same time, a generous offer of space for services was made by the Trondheim Methodist Church which, since 1937, had had cordial relations with the Jewish congregation through its president, Pastor Einar Anker Nilsen. A room in the attic of the church was made available

32. The Wagner Case, Doc. 2, pp. 17–18: "*Avhørt pånytt i Akesrhus Fengsel den 12.4.46, siktede Wilhelm, Ad Nærsnes saken: "Tiltalte opplyser at det kom en anmeldelse fra et NS tjenestested om illegal virksomhet blandt jødene på Nærsnes som drev antitysk propaganda, illegal avisvirksomhet og at de skjulte kurerer." For å undersøke om anm. var riktig ble det foretatt anholdelse av de navngitte personer i anm. Forhørene varte i flere dager og ble ledet av Böhm. Tiltalte var bare tilstede engang iblandt under avhørene. Det er godt mulig at han da kunne komme med spørsmål som de avhørte slettes ikke likte og at han av den grunn ble betraktet som den farligste av de tyskerne som deltok i avhørene. Under avhørene tilstod de avhørte at det som, stod i amneldelsen var delvis riktig, og dokumentene ble sendt til Reinhardt [sic!] som ga ordre til fengsling." R.A.O.*
33. Arne Fjellbu, *Minner fra Krigsårene*. Oslo: Land og kirke, 1945, pp. 105–106: "*. . . det er spørsmål om jødene skal komme i en klasse for seg selv. Hvis det skjer, kan jeg forsikre Dem at kirken skal alarmeres fra landsende til landsende. Her står den norske kirken 100% samlet; noe slikt finner vi oss ikke i.*"

for synagoge services. The two remaining Torah scrolls were transferred there together with ceremonial objects for synagogue services. Nobody had to see that Jews congregated in the Methodist church. Members of the congregation were "instructed to arrive and leave the church one by one, or not more than two together in order not to attract undue attention. This functioned very well, although it was dangerous."[34] A plaque commemorating these events was unveiled in November 1981.

After the final arrests and deporation of the Trondheim Jews in October and November, 1942, the Methodist Church continued to defy the Nazi authorities by hiding the two Torah scrolls and other objects in the vault of the church until the end of the war. In 1945 they were returned to the survivors of the Jewish congregation and used at the rededication services of the synagogue on October 14, 1947.[35] The church's generosity was not the only example of sympathy and practical help extended to Norway's Jews. Notable were the personnel within customs control who had strict orders to confiscate all packages to Jews, especially food packages from Denmark or Sweden. The personnel, however, would contact the recipients immediately without informing the Nazi authorities at great risk to their own personal safety.

In contrast to the Trondheim synagogue, the synagogue in Oslo at Bjergstien 13 remained almost intact. The superintendent, Anton Sleipnes, took good care of all the possessions, including the Torah scrolls which were used at the rededication ceremonies of the synagogue on August 31, 1945. The synagogue at Calmeyer Street 15, belonging to Den Israelitiske Menighet (The Israelitic Congregation) was vandalized, but not to the extent of the one in Trondheim.[36]

Confiscation of stores belonging to Norwegian Jews had started in the fall of 1941 in the city of Trondheim. On October 21, 1941, three stores belonging to the family Abrahamsen were confiscated by the State

34. *Kirken i sentrum. Trondheim Methodistmenighet 100 år, 1881–6. november, 1981,* Oslo: Norsk Forlagsselskap, 1981. (The Church in the Center. The Trondheim Methodist Church Society through 100 years, 1881–November 6, 1981), p. 120: "... *Ingen måtte se at jødene samlet seg i Methodistkirken. De ble bedt om å komme helst en og en eller maksimalt to i følge, og forlate kirken på samme måte for ikke å vekke oppsikt. Dette fungerte fint, selv om det var farlig."*

35. *Adresseavisen,* Trondheim, November 6, 1981: *"Hemmelig jødisk synagoge på loftet"* (Secret Jewish synagogue in the attic.)

36. Interview, July 4, 1981, with Mendel Bernstein, President from 1939 to 1945 of the Mosaic Religious Society in Oslo.

Police.[37] "Aryan" managers were appointed by the Norwegian Gestapo agent, Reidar Johan Duner Landgraff, who had served the Nazi interests since Fall 1940. The three Abrahamsen stores were opened on November 3 under "new management." The family members were not arrested but left for Sweden at 5 a.m. on October 28. After crossing the border south of Magnor with the help of members of the Home Front, the two brothers, Heiman and Abel Abrahamsen and their mother, Mirjam, were detained overnight by the Swedish District Sheriff. The next morning, in spite of pleading asylum, they were told in no uncertain terms to return to Norway, which they did. They crossed the Swedish border at a different point the next day and were subsequently admitted to Sweden.[38] A protest was lodged by the Norwegian legation in Stockholm through the minister *(sendemann)* Jens Bull, who opined that "we must insist that political refugees not be returned to Norway."[39] This indicated that Sweden had been unwilling to admit Norwegian Jews without their having been at first cleared as political refugees. The Norwegian bureaucracy in Stockholm would seldom give such clearance.[39a]

37. *Riksarkivet*, Oslo: Bishop Eivind Berggrav, Private Archive 320, Map No. 78, p. 1. folder marked 1. Israel Mission 2. The Jewish Question. In the margin of the report is the hand-written notation, *"Mottatt anonymt i posten 12.11.41"* (Received anonymously through the mail November 12, '41): *"Straks etter 20/10 ble tre firmaer tilhørende Fam. Abrahamsen lukket av statspolitiet. Familiens gårder og øvrige eiendommer, bankbokser beslaglagt."* (Right after October 20th the three stores belonging to the family Abrahamsen were closed by the State Police. The family homes and other properties, safe deposit boxes were confiscated.)

38. Interview with Heiman Abrahamsen, Trondheim, Norway, June 5, 1983. Cf., interview with Abel Abrahamsen, Norwegian Broadcasting, Oslo, September 7, 1975: "Escape to Sweden during the Occupation," Tape No. 54159/2.

39. *Norges Forhold til Sverige 1940–45. Aktstykker utgitt av Det Kgl. Utenriksdepartement* (Norway's Relation to Sweden During the War 1940–45. Documents published by the Department of Foreign Affairs), Vol. III, Oslo: Glydendal Norsk Forlag, 1950, No. 446, p. 212: *"Notat av chargé d'affairs Bull dat. Stockholm 22. novbr. 1941 om samtale med utrikesråd Engzell 21 s.m.: '... det hadde vært mange klager over at folk var blitt vist tilbake til Norge. Jeg hadde nettopp igår fått meg forelagt en ny sak (jeg tenkte her på beretningen om de to brødrene Abrahamsen) og vi måtte fastholde at politiske flyktninger ikke måtte bli sendt tilbake til Norge."* (There had been many complaints that people had been returned to Norway. I had just yesterday been presented with a new case (I thought of the account by the two brothers Abrahamsen) and we had to insist that political refugees must not be returned to Norway.

39a. Nils Johan Ringdal, *Mellom Barken og Veden. Poltiet under okkupasjonen* (Between the Bark and the Wood: Police during the Occupation). Oslo: Aschehoug, 1987, p. 242: *"På svensk side var man lenge ikke villig til å ta imot norske jøder uten at de var klarert som politiske flyktninger. Det norske buråkratiet i Stockholm ville sjelden gi slik klarering."* See also Steven Koblik, *the Stones Cry Out. Sweden's Response to the Persecution of the Jews 1933-1945.* New York: Holocaust Library, 1988, pp. 53-54.

On Monday, November 3, 1941, the store belonging to the Trondheim firm, H. Klein, was confiscated, again by Landgraff and his cohorts. This time the owner and his oldest son were arrested, imprisoned at Vollan Prison, and accused on trumped-up charges of breaking the various rationing regulations.[40] It appeared as though a major anti- Jewish action was about to take place in 1941 with the arrests of male Jews in Northern Norway and submission of lists by the *Fylkesmenn* (County Governors) to the Department of Justice for Jewish-owned properties throughout Norway. However, nationwide confiscation of Jewish properties did not take place until the fall of 1942, when mass arrests of Jews took place.

On October 26, 1942, a law was issued, signed by Quisling, regarding "Confiscation of Properties Belonging to Jews." The law was to take effect immediately, regardless of constitutional provisions to the contrary. It stated that assets of any kind belonging to Jews with Norwegian citizenship or stateless Jews would be confiscated for the benefit of the State.[41] This law of October 26 specifically concerning Jews was followed by a proclamation by the Norwegian State Police of October 28, 1942, which stated that "pursuant to the law of October 26, 1942," Jews were notified that:[42]

> (1) the total possessions of your own and those of the rest of the family have been confiscated;
> (2) the oldest member of the remaining family is obliged to present himself at the police precinct where the family resides. Attempts or participation in avoiding confiscation of possessions or avoidance of complying with the duty to present oneself will lead to the strongest punishment which this law permits.

Part of the confiscation procedure was to dispose of movable Jewish

40. The Trondheim newspaper *Dagposten*, November 3, 1941, and *Adresseavisen*, November 4, 1941. See Steven Koblik, *The Stones Cry Out. Sweden's Response to the Persecution of the Jews 1933–1945.* New York: Holocaust Library, 1988, pp. 53–54.

41. "*Lov av 26 oktober 1942 om inndraging av formue som tilhører jøder,*" *Norges Handels — ogs Sjøfartstidende,* October 27, 1942 (Law of October 26, 1942 regarding confiscation of Jewish properties. ... This law is effective immediately). Signed by Quisling, Hagelin, Sverre Risnæs and R. J. Fuglesang. "*I samsvar med paragraf 3, annet ledd, i Ministerpresidentens kunngjøring av 5. februar fastsettes følgende som gjelder uten hensyn til Grunnlovens bestemmelser: Paragraf 1. Formue av enhver art som tilhører jøde som er norsk statsborger, eller jøde uten statsborgerrett som oppholder seg her i landet, inndras til fordel for statskassen. Det samme gjelder formue tilhørende jødens ektefelle og barn.*"

42. *Kunngjøring, Statspolitet, Oslo og Aker Avdeling, Riksarkivet,* Oslo, STAPO-O.A.Arv. 5000/42.

property by auction, the proceeds to be turned over to the Quisling State Treasury. Office furniture, however, was to be transferred to government offices while real estate was not to be sold but put under government administration. According to Quisling's order, all confiscated gold, silver, and jewelry should be remitted to the occupation power as a voluntary contribution to the German war effort. Furthermore, various instructions stated that it was of the utmost importance that confiscated property be handled carefully and honestly, and that all persons involved with confiscation and liquidation behave in a dignified and professional way. It was reported at that time, both in information bulletins of the Norwegian legation in Stockholm and in Swedish newspapers, that a number of policemen and officials connected with the liquidation of confiscated Jewish properties had been discovered by the German security police to have made undue profits on the confiscations. [43]

On November 20, 1942, managers of confiscated properties in Oslo and the surrounding area received notice that houses located at Bygdøøy should be confiscated for Quisling's personal guards as soon as possible. The houses should be located as close as possible to Quisling's residence, Gimle. [44] The Ministry of the Interior published, on December 10, 1942, a list of Jews whose properties had been confiscated.

Detailed instructions for implementing the principles of confiscation were signed by the Minister of Finance, F. Prytz, on November 20, 1942. [45] The machinery of confiscation was set up in great detail through the establishment of a Board of Liquidation, with a judge of the Quisling Supreme Court, Reichborn-Kjennerud, as Chief of the Board. He was appointed to implement the detailed regulations, including Article 3 of the basic law of October 26, 1942, where provisions were made for the disposal of Jewish apartments, to be taken over by members of the Quisling party. [46] Already on November 13, 1942, an application had been

---

43. "Instruction No. 1: Confiscation of Jewish Properties: *Information Bulletin of the Norwegian Legation at Stockholm, No. 230, February 25, 1943.*

44. *Letter from "The Board of Liquidation of Confiscated Jewish Properties," Oslo, November 20, 1942: "Til bobestyrerne i Oslo og Omegn: Huset må ligge på Bygdøy, og så nær Førerens bolig, Gimle, som mulig."*

45. *Forskrifter i medhold av lov av 26 oktober 1942 vedrørende inndragning av formue som har tilhørt jøder.* (Regulations in reference to the Law of October 26, 1942 concerning confiscation of properties which have belonged to Jews), *Norwegian Law Gazette, January 8, 1943.*

46. *Ibid. Article 8, last paragraph: "Ledige leiligheter som jøde kun har hatt eiendomsrett til, disponeres av likvidasjonsstyret. Til disse skal NS-medlemmer i stats —*

92   SAMUEL ABRAHAMSEN

submitted by a Nazi member, Stian Bech, to the lawyer Håkon Høst, a manager of confiscated apartments. The applicant stated he wanted to take over an apartment which had "belonged to the Jew Bernstein in Fagerborggt. 27, second floor: I have today seen the apartment and it suits me. I am a member of NS and K.O. and I have served in the Waffen SS for months; I have participated in the winter campaigns of 1941–42 in Russia, came back to Norway in July this year, and have since then served in the State Police." At the bottom of the letter is noted: "Recommended,. November 20, 1942."[47] Members of the Quisling party had priority of occupying confiscated apartments.[48]

Norway's three synagogues, one in Trondheim and two in Oslo, had been confiscated without any compensation in 1941 and 1942, respectively. In January 1943, the two Jewish communities were dissolved and their bank accounts and properties transferred in favor of "N.S. hjelpefond." (Relief Organization).[49] In a letter of January 23, 1942, the attorney general wrote to the Minister of Interior Dahl, that it was unfortunate that the Department of Church and Education had appeared as "a decisive authority in connection with the persecution of the Jews." This indicated that the department had played a significant role in the persecution and deportation of Norway's Jews.[50]

A letter of March 7, 1942 from Trondheim Police Precinct to the Security Police in Oslo signed by the Police President Christopher Lange and Police Major Egil Lindheim stated that all Jewish stores in Trondheim had been closed. "The last action took place on February 26.

og partistillinger være fortrinnsberettiget. Deretter kommer andre NS-medlemmer i betraktning."

47. Letter dated November 13, 1942, from Stian Bech to Håkon Høst, a lawyer and manager of confiscated apartments, with office at Tordenskjoldsgt. 77, Oslo. National Archives, J. Nr. 2190/1942.

48. Wisløff, op. cit., v. III, p. 460.

49. "Kjennelse 27 mars 1947 Lnr. 133: Høyesterettsadvokat Annæus Schjødt, aktor imot Ragnar Sigvald Skancke," point 25, (Supreme Court Attorney A. Schjødt, Counsel for the Prosecution, against Ragnar Sigvald Skancke), p. 169: "Den 19. desember 1942 skrev Kirkedepartementet til Innenriksdepartementet at det intet hadde å innvende mot at det mosaiske trossamfund og den israelitiske menighet ble oppløst og deres eiendommer og formuer inndratt og erklærte samtidig sin tilslutning til at de verdier som ble inndratt skulle gå til N.S. hjelpefond."

50. Ingvald B. Carlsen, Kirkens kamp i Norge under Besættelsen, 1940–1945 (The Struggle of the Church of Norway during the Occupation), København: P. Haase Forlag, 1946, p. 129: "... det var uheldig at K.D. (i.e., Kirkedepartementet) traadte frem som en bestemmende myndighet i Forbindelse med Jødeforfølgelsene."

As managers of these stores, the security police has engaged Norwegians."

It has been estimated that properties valued at close to nine million Norwegian crowns (about one-and-a-half million dollars) were taken from Jews during the occupation, and properties valued at about "sixteen million Norwegian crowns from Norwegians."[51]

51. *Nordisk Tidende*, Brooklyn, New York, March 3, 1967: *"Verdier for nærmere 9 millioner kroner tatt fra jøder i Norge da landet var okkupert av tyskerne."* P. 1: *"I alt regner man med at tyskerne tok verdigjenstander for over 9 millioner kroner fra jødene i Norge, og for omkring 16 millioner fra nordmenn."* (All in all, one estimates that the Germans took valuables worth 9 million crowns from Jews in Norway, and about 16 millions from Norwegians.

IX

Mass Arrests of Norway's Jews

During the years 1941-42, regulations were being prepared by the Quisling government to clarify various issues in defining the concept of "who is a Jew." Decisions were based on the First Ordinance of the Reich Citizenship Law, published in Berlin in 1935, which defined who is a Jew, an Aryan, or so-called "*Mischlinge*" (mixed-blood) of First or Second Degrees. However, Quisling's interpretation of "*Mischlinge*" was stricter than the original formulation of the infamous "Nüremberg Laws" of 1935 insofar as he ordered the arrest of Jewish women married to "Aryans."[1]

An office was established in Oslo in the fall of 1942 to certify Aryan descent and to demand documentation that grandparents on both sides were not "of Jewish descent." This declaration had to be verified by two persons who knew the family intimately, as was brought out in the case against Torleif Andreas Wulff. He had been arrested in November, 1942, his properties confiscated, and then interned at Berg concentration camp. Baptismal certificates to prove Aryan descent for his grandparents were demanded and produced. According to the church registers. Torleif Wulff proved his "Aryan descent" as far back as April, 1856, when his grandmother was baptized.[2]

While preparing the rules governing "who is a Jew" and thus defining who would be subject to registration, arrest, and deportation, *Nasjonal Samling* cooperated very closely with the German authorities, especially through *Einsatzstab Wegener*, named after Paul Wegener who had

---

1. Sveri, op. cit., p. 348: "*Den 14. januar 1943 innskjerpet han* (i.e., Rød) *i en generell ordre at alle heljøder skal etterspores og anholdes, også kvinner gift meed 'arier.'*"

2. "Avstamningserklæring" (Declaration of Descent), November 11, 1942, Statsarkivet, Oslo, I.D. No. 00866 Il, February 2, 1943.

arrived in Norway on April 21, 1940, together with Joseph Terboven.[3] This *Einsatzstab* had the unusual assignment of counseling Quisling on political matters, to increase party membership, and to develop propaganda to that effect.[4] This did not prevent the Norwegian collaborators from exercising great zeal and initiative in the persecution of Norway's Jews.

On October 10, 1941, the Norwegian State Police was requested in a letter from the chief of the German Security Police, Wilhelm Rediess, to prepare a law requiring the stamping of all identity cards belonging to Jews with a "J." The law stated that the stamping is *gratis*, and that as far as possible it should be done in *red* ink. On January 10, 1942, Jonas Lie, the Minister of Police, issued the order to have a large "J" stamped onto the identification cards of Jews.[5] The problem of "who is a Jew" was clarified in an announcement from the Police Department issued on January 20, 1942, on the same day that the infamous "Wannsee Conference" implemented the "Final Solution."[5A]

The announcement was published in the daily press on January 22, 1942.[6] It stated that persons are Jews when they are:

---

3. Helge Paulsen, "*Litt om forholdet mellom NS og Reichskommissariat i Norge, 1940-45,*" (Something about the relationship between NS and RK in Norway, 1940-45), in Rolf Danielsen and Stein Ugelvik Larsen, eds., *Fra Idé til Dom*, Oslo: Universitetsforlaget, 1976, pp. 205-206.

4. Magne Skodvin, "*Det store fremstøt,*" in Sverre Steen, ed., *Norges Krig*, Vol. II, Oslo: Gyldendal Norsk Forlag, 1948, p. 606.

5. *Stempling av jøders legitimasjonsbevis* from the Chief of Security Police, January 10, 1942. National Archives, Oslo, Ref. No. 5289/41A. *Bergens Tidende* of May 3, 1973 stated that "J" for "Jew" was instituted by Berlin after strong pressure from Sweden. ("J for Jøde" — et svensk initiativ.)

5a. Robert Wolfe, "Introduction," *The Holocaust. The Wannsee Protocol and a 1944 Report on Auschwitz by the Office of Strategic Services*, New York-London: Garland Publishing, Inc., 1982, p. 1

6. *Aftenposten*, Oslo, January 22, 1942: "*Kunngjøring fra Politidepartementet. Stempling av jøders legitimasjonskort, grenseboerbevis, passersedler og tjenestebevis. Som jøde etter denne bestemmelse ansees: (1) Den som nedstammer fra minst 3 av rase fulljødiske besteforeldre, uansett hvilket statsborgerskap han måtte ha. Som fulljøde blir i ethvert tilfelle den av besteforeldrene å regne som har tilhørt det jødiske trossamfund. (2) Som jøde regnes også jødisk bastard som nedstammer fra 2 fulljødiske besteforeldre: (a) Når han ved utferdigelsen av denne kunngjøring tilhører det jødiske trossamfund eller senere blir opptatt i dette. (b) Når han ved utferdigelsen av denne kunngjøring er gift med jøde eller senere gifter seg med jøde. (3) Samtlige medlemmer av det mosaiske trossamfund· er å anse som jøder. Personer som i henhold til foranstående bestemmelser skal være i besiddelse av J-stemplet legitimasjonsbevis må innen 1. mars d. å. melde seg til den politimester eller lensmann som har utstedt hans legitimasjonsbevis, for å få stemplingen foretatt. Unnlatelse herav straffes med bøter opptil et tusen kroner eller med fengsel inntil 3 måneder. Oslo, 20. januar 1942.*"

1. Descendants from at least three full racially Jewish grandparents, regardless of citizenship he might possess. In any case a full Jew is to be
regarded as those of grandparents who have belonged to the Jewish congregation.

2. As a Jew is also included a Jewish bastard (*Mischlinge*) who is descended from two Jewish grandparents:
    (a) Who at the time of the date of the announcement belongs to the Jewish community or at a later date becomes a member.
    (b) Who at the time of the date of this announcement is married to a
Jew or later on marries a Jew.

3. All members of the Mosaic religious community are to be regarded as
Jews.
    Persons who are covered by these regulations must be in possession of
identity cards stamped with "J" and must report before March 1 to the
police precinct or country sheriff who issued the identity card in order
to obtain the stamp. Violations will be penalized with fines of up to 1,000
crowns or imprisonment of up to 3 months.

On February 6, 1942, Oliver Møystad, head of Norway's Security Police, forwarded to all police precincts a "Questionnaire for the Jews in
Norway," to be filled out by everyone with a "J" on their identity cards.
It consisted four pages which, in addition to vital data, also asked whether one belonged to a religious society and asked for detailed information
about one's economic situation. The last page was to be filled out by the
local police as to whether the person had previously been in conflict with
the law. The questionnaire had to be completed in triplicate by everyone
who possessed an identity card stamped with a "J."[7]

The Norwegian police were governed by laws established in 1920
known as *Instruks for rikets polititjenestemenn* (Police Instructions). It
was clearly stated that "the police has as its task to protect persons, property, and all legal activities, and to prevent punishable actions which
may expose the safety of society to criminal action."[8]

In defiance of these laws, the police arrested the Jews without a war

---

7. *Rundskriv fra Lederen av Sikkerhetspolitiet, Oliver Møystad, til politimestrene i
Norge* (Circular Letter from the Chief of Security Police to Chiefs of Police Precincts) regarding "Spørreskjema for Jøder i Norge" (Questionnaire for Jews in Norway), Oslo, February 6, 1942, Jnr. 00746/42.

8. Thorleif Karlsen, *Lang dag i politiet* (Long Day in the Police). Oslo: Gyldendal Norsk
Forlag, 1979, pp. 25-26.

rant and disregarded other legal procedures. Arrests and deportations were clearly a breach of domestic and international law. These severe suspensions of civil rights prompted one recognized authority on police justice to state later that "it was difficult to believe that Norwegian police participating in these actions later dared to say: 'We did not know what was going to happen to the Jews.'"[9]

The 12,000 questionnaires were printed by Nelson Trykk, Kongensgt. 16, Oslo, and ordered on February 2, 1942, the day after the installation of Quisling as minister-president. They were delivered to Quisling's Statistical Office on February 21, 1942. Seven hundred stamps with a large "J" were mailed on March 1, 1942, from Johs. Krogstie, Storgt. 19, to the Police Department of Oslo. The stamps and the questionnaires were distributed to the police and sheriff precincts throughout the country as part of the destruction machinery through roundup and arrest of Norway's Jews. [10] The stamping of "J" in the identification papers of Norway's Jews was undertaken independently of the nazified State Police and without the Home Front protesting this action. [11]

During the fall of 1942, the tempo of Jewish persecutions in Trondheim increased under the command of one of the most cruel Nazis in Norway, the Gestapo chief in that district, Gerhard Ernest Flesch. On October 6, the Nazi authorities declared a state of emergency in the Trøndelag province following serious sabotage committed against German installations at Majavatn and Glomfjord. [12] Proclamations of a civil state of emergency in Trondheim and in the districts of North and South Trøndelag were issued by Reichskommissar Terboven during the early morning of October. [13] The communiqué stated that several acts of sabotage had been committed which, if they had succeeded, would have endangered Norway's supply situation. Therefore, a civil state of emer-

9. Odd Bergfald, *Gestapo i Norge*, Oslo: Hjemmenes Forlag, 1978, pp. 83-84: ". . . *det er vanskelig å fatte at norske politifolk som var med på disse aksjoner senere våget å si 'Vi visste ikke hva som ville skje med jødene.'!*"

10. *Dagbladet*, Oslo, October 16, 1982, p. 19.

11. Per Ole Johansen, *Oss selv nærmest. Norge og Jødene 1914-1943*, Oslo: Gyldendal Norsk Forlag, 1984, p. 144.

12. Sverre Kjellstadli, *Hjemmestyrkene. Hovedtrekk av den militære motstand under okkupasjonen* (The Home Forces. Main Features of the Military Resistance During the Occupation). Vol. I. Oslo: H. Aschehoug & Co., 1959, pp. 165-167; 404, footnote 84.

13. As quoted in *Bulletin #1096*, U.S. Legation, Stockholm, October 28, 1942: "Norway's Civil State of Emergency in Trondheim from October 6-11, 1942." Enclosure No. 1, pp. 2, 3. National Archives, Washington, D.C. See *Morgenbladet*, Oslo, October 7, 1942.

gency had been declared, followed by an order by General Wilhelm
Rediess stating that unlimited power had been given to the Quisling
Fylkesfører (County Leader) Henrik Rogstad. A curfew was imposed
from 8 p.m. to 5 a.m. and, in addition, all public institutions and res-
taurants were to be closed at 7 p.m. Indoor and outdoor meetings were
forbidden, movie houses and theaters were closed indefinitely. Rediess
warned that resistance would be suppressed by armed force. This was
no empty threat.

A reign of terror followed with the arrest and subsequent execution
of 34 hostages. The following 10 persons were executed on October 7,
1942, in Trondheim:

Otto Skirstad, attorney in Trondheim
Henry Gleditsch, chief of the Trondheim theater
Harald Langhelle, newspaper editor in Trondheim
Hirsch Komissar, engineer in Trondheim
Hans Konrad Ekornes, Bærum
G.S. Birch, bank director in Trondheim
Per T. Lykke, shipbroker in Strinda
Gunnar Bull Aakran, attorney in Røros
Peder Eggen, master builder in Klæbu
Captain Finn Berg, from Trondheim.

Another twenty-four hostages were shot on October 6 and 8, 1942.
Willy Brandt wrote that the hostages had been shot after having heard
on the radio about their own execution.[14] Among the ten hostages who
were shot on October 7 was Hirsch Komissar, an active member of the
Jewish community in Trondheim.[15] He had been arrested in January
1942, sent to prison camp at Kjøllefjord in northernmost Norway, and
brought back to be executed. That a Jew was included in this massacre

---

14. Willy Brandt, *Krigen i Norge* (The War in Norway), Oslo: Aschehoug, Vol. II, p.
119, 1945: *"Gislene ble ikke skutt på den tid som var nevnt i Gestapos bulletin. De ti gisler
ble skutt ... ved Falstad Konsentrasjonsleir om morgenen den 7. oktober etterat de om
kvelden før gjennom radio hadde fått høre om sin egen henrettelse."* (The hostages were
not shot at the time which was mentioned in the Gestapo Bulletin. The ten hostages were
shot ... at the Falstad Concentration Camp in the morning of October 7 after they had
heard the previous evening on the radio about their own execution.)

15. The Jewish cemetery in Trondheim has a special memorial erected for "Hirsch
Komissar, b. June 9, 1887, shot as a hostage by the Germans in the Falstad Forest, October
7, 1942."

along with thirty-three other patriots reinforced the impression that no particular attack on Jews *as Jews* was forthcoming.

On October 7, 1942, the property and apartments of the murdered individuals were confiscated by the Gestapo office headed by Commissar Landgraff, a member of the Norwegian Nazi Party. He was dubbed "Landgraff the grave plunderer." The Jewish women and children were removed from their own apartments and assembled under Norwegian guards at the Museumsplass No. 3 or at Innherredsveien No. 27 and 31. The oldest prisoner at the Museumsplass was Dora Steinfeld, 83 years old; the youngest was Mina Mahler, 15 years old.[15a]

The execution of the hostages had been unparalleled, but members of *Nasjonal Samling* applauded the announcement of the first ten executions.[16] The hostages had not been tried by a court, and they were given no opportunity to defend themselves. They were allegedly executed for a series of acts of sabotage. As reported in *Deutsche Zeitung in Norwegen* on October 8, 1942: ". . . they had been transporting weapons for ridiculously small cash compensations. These weapons were to serve for sniper warfare in the event of a British invasion."

The reactions of the Swedish press to the execution of Norwegian hostages were strong. The Stockholm paper, *Dagens Nyheter* (Daily News) of October 8, 1942, announced the executions on the front page. The newspaper declared that the horrors of war and massacre of innocent people were foreign to Nordic mentality and the Nordic concept of justice:[17]

> Nothing can soften the blow which this sort of news means to the Swedish people. It is still almost incomprehensible to the concept of justice, which we like to regard not only as Swedish, but as European, that a person should atone with his life for a crime which he has not committed.

The anti-Nazi weekly newspaper, *Trots Allt*, published a special issue on Norway on October 13, 1942, and announced that a collection of poems by 34 Swedish poets had been published by Bonnier to commemorate the tragic events in Norway.[18]

15a. Jahn Otto Johansen, *Det hendte også her*, op. cit., p. 69.

16. "Concerning Events in Trondheim During Civil State of Emergency, October 6-11, 1942," National Archives, Washington, D.C., RG 226, Records of the Office of Strategic Services, #29116, pp. 3, 6.

17. Public Record Office (London), FO 371/33063 xc/A/5356, from British Legation, Stockholm, October 15, 1942, p. 1.

18. Ibid., p. 2.

During this civil state of emergency, all male Jews in Trondheim over
the age of fourteen were arrested by Norwegian police under the command of Chief of Criminal Police Landerud. One of the Trondheim Jews
arrested on October 7, 1942, was Julius Paltiel, 17 years old. He had received a warning by a former policeman who had seen his name on a
list of Jews to be arrested that night. Julius Paltiel related that he walked
down to a neighbor, Ole Tiller, on the first floor in his building,
Brattørgaten No. 6, where he remained until about 5 a.m., when he felt
sure the danger was over. Returning to his flat, he went to sleep for an
hour, only to be awakened by the door bell at 6 a.m. "I opened the door
and there was the police: 'You are arrested. Come with us.' I asked permission to take along toilet articles, which was granted. The police came
in and met my mother who was very upset. I was transported to the District prison at Kongens Gate."[19] Paltiel, along with about thirty other
arrested Jewish males, was sent by train to Rognlan station, where German guards took over. The Jews were forced to run the seven kilometers
from Rognlan to Falstad Concentration Camp at Ekne near Levanger,
where they were treated brutally.

The person in charge of Falstad Concentration Camp was SS-
Obersturmführer Denk, who was under the command of
Obersturmbannführer Gerhard Flesch in Trondheim.[20] During an inspection of the concentration camp in November, 1942, accompanied by
Acting Commander Gneist, Gerhard Flesch noted three sick Jews in
bed in the attic. At the trial against Flesch, Dr. Leo Eitinger, a native
of Czechoslovakia and fluent in German, testified on April 26, 1946, that
he was present at the Falstad inspection by Flesch in November, 1943,
and heard him say loudly to be heard by all prisoners: "But Mr. Gneist,
you don't let sick Jews lie down! Dig a grave outside and everything will
be all right."[21] On November 13, 1942, the three inmates, Moritz

19. Norwegian Broadcasting, Trøndelag, "Jewish Persecution in Trondheim,
1940-1942," First program, September 2, 1982. Transcript, p. 4.

20. Odd Bergfald, *Gestapo i Norge*, op. cit., p. 255. Dr. Eitinger mentions the name
of Scharsmitz as commander at Falstad.

21. Testimony by Dr. Leo Eitinger, April 26, 1946, in the case against Gerhard
Friedrich Ernest Flesch. Dr. Eitinger had come to Falstad on May 14, 1942. He was present at the inspection in November 1942 and heard Flesch state: "*Aber Gneist, Sie lassen
doch keine kranken Juden liegen? Draussen ein Grab graben, und alles ist in Ordnung.*"
This encouragement to murder was not lost on the court. For these murders and other
major crimes against humanity, Flesch was condemned to death on February 28, 1948.
The verdict was carried out the same day at Kristansten Fortress, Trondheim. "*Rapport*

Nevezetsky Abrahamsen, Kalman Glick, and Herman Schidorsky were removed, ostensibly to receive medical treatment in Trondheim.[22] Asriel B. Hirsch testified during Quisling's trial that they were shot that same night. They had become sick at Falstad because of the torture and mistreatment there.[23] After an intensive search between 1945 and 1947, their bodies were found and buried at the Lademoen Jewish Cemetery on June 16, 1947.[24]

A noted Norwegian historian, Ragnar Ulstein, has related that at Falstad one of the prisoners was ". . . a mature artist, but he was otherwise impractical and helpless. But when he sang he was transformed. The Jew was commanded to sing every evening, but during the day they treated him worse than dirt. . . . The officer commanded the Jew to start singing. He stepped forward. He had jacket and pants that were too short for him, he looked more like a scarecrow, a fool and nothing else. . . . Then he started singing from the operetta *Zarewitsch* by Franz Lehar. Immediately, everyone was transformed. The world around them listened and mourned; the prisoners stood as if in church, and the hundreds of prisoners lifted their faces towards the darkening clouds and hummed with him quietly:

"Hast du dort oben vergessen auch mich?
Es sehnt doch mein Herz auch nach Liebe sich,
Du hast im Himmel viel Engel bei dir
Schick dock einen davon auch zu mir."[25]

---

til Politimesteren i Oslo, 'Landssvikssak mot Gerhard Friedrich Ernst Flesch.'" 26. april 1946, *Riksarkivet* (National Archives), Oslo, pp. 2, 3, 17-18.

22. Egil Ulateig, *"Verre enn Auschwitz. De jødiske fangenes skjebne. Historien om Falstad — en konsentrasjonsleir i Norge,"* in *Vi Menn,* Oslo, No. 24, June 14, 1983, p. 13. (Worse than Auschwitz. The Fate of the Jewish Prisoners. The History of Falstad — a Concentration Camp in Norway).

23. Asriel B. Hirsch's testimony, see *Quisling,* p. 159. "Three Jews were shot while we were there. The reason was that they were weak, they had become ill during the stay at Falstad because of mistreatment." (". . . *jeg ble ført av det norske politi til Falstad. . . . På Falstad ble det skutt tre jøder mens vi var der. . . . Grunnen var at de var svake; de var blitt syke under oppholdet på Falstad på grunn av mishandlingen der.)" Quisling,* p. 159.

24. The newspaper *Nidaros* reported on June 17, 1947: *"De tre drepte jøder ble gravlagt i går." (The three Jews were buried yesterday).* The Jewish cemetery in Trondheim has this memorial: *"Skutt i Falstadskogen 13. november 1942 under det tyske voldsherredømme:* Herman Shidorsky, f. 1887; Kalman Glick, f. 1877; Moritz Abrahamsen, f. 1884. Stedt til hvile her 16. juni 1947. (Shot in the Falstad Forest November 13, 1942, during the German reign of terror. . . . Buried here June 16, 1947).

25. Ragnar Ulstein, *Englandsfarten,* Vol. I. *Alarm i Ålesund,* (Transport to England,

Over 6,500 prisoners were incarcerated at Falstad, out of which 200 were shot. The concentration camp was closed on December 8, 1943.[26]

The questionnaires for Jews, completed during spring 1942, became a basis for identifying Jews for roundup and arrest on October 25-26, 1942. The arrests were allegedly based on Terboven's decree of September 25, 1940, ordering arrests of persons who were suspected of being hostile to the state.[27] The Germans were not fully prepared for the mass arrests and deportations of Norwegian Jews at that time. The Wannsee Conference of January 20, 1942, called together by Heinrich Heydrich, was attended by Martin Luther, Under Secretary of State of the German Foreign Office, a party man and a driving force in the Jewish deportations. Luther warned that the Germans would meet obstacles in deportations of the small Jewish populations of Scandinavia and argued for a postponement.[28]

The arrests of Norwegian Jews reportedly came as a surprise to Berlin. The Quisling authorities had great difficulty in obtaining the ships necessary for deportation. Only one month after the October arrests did the German navy allegedly provide the S.S. *Donau* for deportation purposes. Until November 1942, Adolf Eichmann and his staff had not been concerned with the deportation of Norway's Jews, realizing that without a ship, deportation could not take place.[29]

The pretext for the start of mass arrests of Jews had been an event on October 22, 1942, when nine young Jews tried to escape to Sweden by

Vol. I. Alarm in Ålesund). Oslo: *Det Norske Samlaget*, 1967. Chapter 17: "The Song," pp. 266-267.

26. Ulateig, op. cit., *Vi Menn*, No. 22, May 31, 1983: "*Et glimt av helvete — Historien om Falstad — en konsentrasjonsleir i Norge,*" p. 8 (A Glimpse of Hell — The History of Falstad — A Concentration Camp in Norway).

27. Tim Greve, *Bergen i krig, 1940-42*, Bergen: J.W. Eide Forlag, 1979, p. 256 (Bergen at War, 1940-42). "*Ved en meget generelt utformet lov av 24. oktober 1942 skaffet NS-regjeringen seg en slags hjemmel for å gå til arrestasjon av personer 'som med skjellig grunn' kunne mistenkes for folke- eller statsfiendtlige holdninger.*" Cf. *Deutsche Monatshefte in Norwegen* (The German Monthly Journal in Norway), September, 1940.

28. Raul Hilberg, *The Destruction of the European Jews*. Chicago: Quadrangle Books, 1961, p. 355.

29. Towiah Friedmann, *Dokumentensammlung über "Die Deportierung der Juden aus Norwegen nach Auschwitz,"* Ramat Gan: Stadt-Verwaltung, 1963, p. I: "*Bis November 1942 hatte sich der Eichmann-Stab der Gestapo-Berlin um die norwegischen Juden nicht gekümmert und es auch für aussichtslos gehalten, Juden von dort deportieren zu können.*" (Until November 1942, Eichmann and his staff did not bother with the Norwegian Jews and thought it meaningless to be able to deport Jews from there).

train under the leadership of Karsten Løvestad, a resistance member who served as a border pilot. On the train, between Skjeberg and Berg, a border policeman in civilian clothing, Arne Hvam, asked for identification. The Jews had a "J" stamped on their cards. The leader, Karsten Løvestad, shot the policeman. The trip had been arranged so hurriedly that the train conductor, Thomas Hansson, had not been told about the rescue mission.[30] Now, with the policeman shot, the Norwegian and German police searched the whole district and arrested the nine Jews. The next day, the families of the arrested men were rounded up. In the controlled press, the Jews were accused of murder.[31] Among those arrested was Hermann Feldmann. His foster parents, Rakel and Jakob Feldmann, decided to leave Oslo in order to reach the Løvestad family, with whom they had had business contacts. They sought help trying to escape to Sweden.

The rescue party set out early on October 27 for the Swedish border. The two border pilots, Peder Pederson and Haakon Løvestad, upon reaching *Skrikerudtjernet* (the Skrikerud Pond) decided to murder the Feldmanns.[32] They stole money and jewelry and left the bodies in the pond. The bodies were found in May 1943 with stones securely fastened with telephone wires.[33] Pederson and Løvestad were tried in 1947 by a court in Sarpsborg and accused of murder. However, they were acquitted of murder and given only minor sentences for theft. They defended themselves by claiming that the Feldmanns would not have been able to reach Sweden on foot because of their weakened condition. Moreover, the pilots were afraid that if captured, the Feldmanns might reveal to the Gestapo the transportation routes to Sweden. The acquittal of

---

30. Ulstein, op. cit., p. 206.

31. *Fritt Folk* (Free People), Oslo, October 24, 1942, front page: "Atter en skjendig udåd — norsk politimann skutt ned av jøder." (Again a cowardly act — Norwegian policeman killed by Jews).

32. Yad Vashem Archives, Doc. B/28-1, p. 10: "*Ekteparret Jakob og Rakel Feldmann ble myrdet ved Skrikerudstjernet, 27/10-1942*" (The couple Jacob and Rakel Feldmann was murdered at the Skrikerud Pond, October 27, 1942). The Feldmanns were buried on January 10, 1947, at Helsfyr Gravlund. The tombstone has this inscription: "*De falt som ofre under flukten fra Norge 27.10.1942*" (They fell as victims during escape from Norway, October 27, 1942).

33. Sigurd Senje, *Ekko fra Skriktjenn. En dokumentarroman basert på 'Feldmann-saken, 1942-47'*" (Echo from Skrik Pond. A documentary novel based on the Feldmann Case). Oslo: Pax Forlag, 1982, pp. 15-17. See also, Even Stengelknoll, "Også vi tok livet av jøder," (We also killed Jews), *Dagbladet*, August 4, 1979 and Ingebjørg Sletten Fosstvedt, *Dagbladet*, September 4, 1947; "Noen spørsmål til mine landsmenn om Feldmann-saken," (Some Questions to my countrymen as to the Feldmann Case).

Pederson and Løvestad caused the greatest debate in history of Norway's *rettsoppgjør* (legal accounting) after the Second World War.[34]

An order to arrest male Jews according to criteria set forth previously on January 20, 1942, was issued by K.A. Marthinsen, chief of the State Police. At ten-thirty in the morning of Sunday, October 25, 1942, express telegrams were sent to all police precincts throughout Norway.[35] The telegrams stated that all male persons over the age of 15 whose identity cards contained "J" should be arrested and transported to Kirkeveien No. 23 in Oslo. The arrrests must take place on Monday, October 26 at 6 a.m. Those arrested could take along tableware, ration cards, and all identity documents. Their property would be confiscated. Special attention should be paid to valuables, jewelry, and cash. A search had to be made for these items. Bank accounts were to be closed and safe deposit boxes emptied. The instructions stated that confiscated items should remain at the precinct until further notice, but the registration documents were to be forwarded to the chief of the State Police. Furthermore, a manager had to be appointed for the confiscated stores. A report as to the arrested person's citizenship, especially if formerly German, was to be forwarded immediately to Police Headquarters. The instructions ended with an order that all adult Jewish women had to report daily to the Police of the Criminal Department.

The mass arrest of Norway's Jews was organized in close cooperation between German and Norwegian authorities. This is shown by Wilhelm Wagner's testimony at the trial of Hellmuth Reinhard at Baden-Baden in June 1967. Wagner testified that he had gone by car to the home of Marthinsen on October 24, 1942 to inform him about the impending arrests of Jews to be made by Norwegian police. The German police

---

34. Ted Olson, "Death at Skrikerud Pond," *Harper's Magazine*, Vol. 206, No. 1236, May 1953, p. 71.

35. *Iltelegram fra Statspolitisjefen den 25. oktober 1942 kl. 10:30* (Urgent telegram from Chief of State Police, October 25, 1942, at 10:30 a.m.), National Archives, Oslo: "*Alle mannlige personer over 15 år hvis legitimasjonskort er stemplet med "J" skal arresteres uansett alder oppover, og transporteres til Kirkeveien 23, Oslo. Arrestasjonen skal skje mandag den 26. oktober kl. 0600. Arrestantene må medta skaftetøy, rasjoneringskort og alle legitimasjonsdokumenter. Formuen beslaglegges. Oppmerksomheten hendledes på verdipapirer, smykker og kontanter, og heretter må det ransakes. Bank-konti sperres og bankbokser tømmes. Det beslaglagte beror hos Dem inntil mærmere ordre. Registreringsdokumenter innsendes hertil snarest. Der må innsettes bestyrer av de arrestertes forretninger. Oppgave over de arresterte med angivelse av stasborger-forhold, specielt om tidligere tysk borgerskap, innsendes omgående hertil. Alle voksne jødinner pålegges daglig meldeplikt ved ordenspolitiets kriminalavdeling.*"

should only give technical help. Marthinsen issued the order to all Norwegian city and rural police precincts. The arrests of the Jews then took place at the local precincts all over Norway. They were to be sent to Germany, their citizenships revoked, and they were never again to return to Norway.[36]

During the weekend of October 24-26, the Norwegian police worked at full speed compiling as complete identification lists as possible. According to Criminal Police Inspector J. Wiehrmyhr's report of October 27, 1942, the registration of Jews was undertaken by *Nasjonal Samling*'s Office of Statistics and exclusively by that office without pressure by the Germans.[37] All the preliminary work, such as questionnaires, lists of names and addresses, roundups, and arrests had been made by Norwegian authorities. The arrests of male Jews on October 26 were carried out by the Norwegian police.[38] There were very few examples of police officers refusing to comply with the arrests of Norway's Jews.[39]

Herman Sachnowitz recounted his arrest and that of his father and four brothers at their farm, Gjein, at Stokke in Vestfold county, on October 26, 1942:

> I was awakened about 5:30 a.m. by a persistent knocking on the main gate. I heard shouting and loud voices. It was the local sheriff at Stokke, Gran, who had arrived with his assistants to arrest all male members of the Sachnowitz family. . . . We were taken by car to the newly-established prison camp at Berg, at Tønsberg; some cold barracks, a place for roll-call and a main building for the guards. We were the first Jewish family to

36. Odd Bergfald, *Hellmuth Reinhard, Soldat eller Morder?* (Hellmuth Reinhard, Soldier or Murderer?). Oslo: Chr. Schibsteds Forlag, 1967, pp. 58-59. Testimony by Wilhelm Wagner: "*Jeg sørget selv for muntlig å gi ordre til det norske politi, via den norske politisjef Marthinsen. Han brakte ordren videre til samtlige norske politikamre og lensmannsdistrikter. Arrestasjonene av jødene foregikk så ved de lokale stasjoner rundt omkring i Norge.*" ("I, myself, made sure to give an oral order to the Norwegian police through the Norwegian Chief of Police, Marthinsen).

37. J. Wiehrmyhr, *Registrering av jøder i Norge*, letter of October 27, 1942. Ref. No. 1205/42B, p. 1. National Archives, Oslo, stating, "The aim, as far as it is possible to ascertain is to collect material for statistical preparation of the Jewish problem in Norway."

38. Oskar Mendelsohn, "Jøder i Norge" (Jews in Norway) in Hallvard Rieber-Mohn and Leo Eitinger, eds., *Retten til å overleve. En bok om Israel, Norge og antisemittismen* (The Right to Survive. A Book about Israel, Norway and anti-Semitism). Oslo: J.W. Cappelens Forlag, 1976, p. 80: "*Samme morgen ble razziaene mot jødiske menn satt i gang av norsk politi.*"

39. Greve, op. cit., p. 257: "*Man kjenner dessverre bare meget få tilfeller der lensmennene og politifolk unnlot å utføre oppdraget.*"

arrive there. The guards were Norwegian members of the *Hird*."[40]

Many were arrested at their places of work or, if students, while in school. There are examples of Norwegian police entering classrooms to arrest Jewish children. Knut Nygaard, principal of Sydneshaugen School in Bergen, related that one of his most painful memories of the war was the day when the Norwegian police came to fetch the Jewish schoolchildren. "We never saw them again. On the staircase I met one of the policemen who was completing the action. He stated that he was not a member of *Nasjonal Samling.* 'We are forced to do this,' was his answer to my question whether he understood what he was doing while others were dying for freedom and humanity. Today the name of grade school student Oscar Müller is on the memorial tablet in the main hall of Sydneshaugen school. He ended his life in the gas chambers."[41]

Dr. Robert Savosnick, a medical student, was arrested on October 28, 1942 at Orkdal Hospital and taken to Oslo by train, "guarded by two Norwegian patriotic policemen."[42] According to the police records at the Trondheim precinct, Dr. Savosnick was arrested together with Leopold Levin, a Jewish merchant at Orkdal. They were transported by car from Orkanger to Trondheim by a Norwegian policeman, Arne Grut, of the Orkdal Police Precinct. They were sent by train from Trondheim to Oslo, escorted by two patriotic policemen, Ivar Grong and Bjarne

---

40. Sachnowitz, op. cit., p. 9: "*Ved halv-femtiden om morgenen våknet jeg ved hissig dundring på hoveddøren. Det var Gran, lensmannen i Stokke som kom med sine hjelpere for å arrestere alle mannlige medlemmer av familien Sachnowitz. . . . Så ble vi fraktet med bil til den nyoppretted Berg fangeleir ved Tønsberg, noen kalde brakker, en appelplass og en hovedbygning for vaktmannskapet. Vi var den første norske jødiske familien som kom dit. . . . Vaktene var norske hirdmenn.*"

41. Knut Nygaard, "*Hva visste vi?*" *Bergens Tidende,* "*Kronikk,*" June 29, 1983: "*En av mine såreste minner fra krigstiden er den dagen da norske politifolk kom og hentet de jødiske elevene på skolene. Vi så dem aldri mer igjen. I trappeoppgangen (på Sydneshaugen skole) møtte jeg en av politifolkene som gjennomførte rassiaen. Han var ikke medlem av NS, sa han. "Vi er nødt og tvunget," svarte han på mitt spørsmål om han forstod hva han var med på, mens andre døde for friheten og mennskeverdet. Idag står vesle Oscar Müllers navn på minnetavlen over de falne i vestibylen på Sydneshaugen skole. Han endte sett liv i gasskammeret. Hva tenkte og følte disse nordmennene i politiuniform da de utførte sin 'plikt' og da de senere fikk greie på jødebarnas endelige skjebne? . . . særlig store illusjoner om tyskernes behandling av jøder kan ingen ha hatt.*"

42. *Rettslige forklaringer fra hjemvendte norske fanger* (Legal depositions by returning Norwegian Jews), Testimony, February 26, 1946, Oslo Tinghus: "*Vitnet ble arrestert på Orkdahl Sykehus ... og ble sendt til Oslo under bevoktning av to norske jøssingpolitimenn.*" (The witness was arrested at Orkdal Hospital ... and was sent to Oslo by two patriotic policemen (that is, loyal to the Home Front). *Yad Vashem Archives* JM/1198.

Glasø. The two prisoners arrived at Bredtvedt concentration camp on November 3, 1942. They were held there until deported on November 26 on board the S.S. *Donau* to Stettin and hence to Auschwitz, where Dr. Savosnick received #79224 on his left lower arm. He survived. Leopold Levin did not.[43]

The Mahler family of Tempevegen 4, Trondheim, consisted of eight members: parents, five children, and a grandmother on the mother's side, Lea Leiman from Lund, Sweden, and a Swedish citizen. In 1938 the Mahler family had opted for Norwegian citizenship, but the grandmother decided to retain her Swedish citizenship. That saved her life.[44] The parents, Malke and Simon, the latter born in Frauenburg, Latvia, were murdered at Auschwitz together with three of their children, Abraham (b. 1920), Selik (b. 1923), and Mina (b. 1927). On the day the father, Simon Mahler, was arrested, October 27, 1942, by two Norwegian policemen, Bjørnebo and Reidar Dahl, from Ut-Trøndelag Police precinct, they also arrested Selik in the classroom at the *Katedralskolen* (The Cathedral High School). "Selik went at the front of the class, said goodbye to his classmates and teacher, and read some lines from a German poem dealing with liberty: One may take the body, but the thoughts are free."[45] His brother Salomon escaped on bicycle and took the main road to Sweden via Hommelvik, from where he got a lift to Stjørdal, and hence to Selbu, where he was taken in late at night by a farmer whom he had known from previous visits. The next morning two of the farmer's sons lent him skis and accompanied him to the Swedish border. He arrived in Sweden on November 1, 1942, and settled in Gothenburg. His mother and sister Mina were arrested on November 25, 1942 and sent to the Bredtvedt concentration camp. They were murdered at Auschwitz.

The oldest daughter, Sara, had married Asbjørn Dagfinn Uthaug, a non-Jew, on April 7, 1942, but this did not prevent her from being arrested on March 15, 1943, in her home, Holtermannsvei 35, Trondheim.[46] The arrest was made by members of the *Hird*, the Nor-

---

43. Interview with Dr. Robert Savosnick, Trondheim, June 2, 1983. See also his book, *Jeg ville ikke dø! Fortalt til Hans Melien*; Oslo: J.W. Cappelen, 1986, (I did not want to die! As told to Hans Melien.)

44. Interview with Mrs. Uthaug, Trondheim, June 6, 1983.

45. Laila Holm, *"Familien Mahlers tragiske skjebne" (The tragic fate of the Mahler family), Arbeider-Avisa*, Trondheim, March 30, 1983, p. 18.

46. *Rapport til Statspolitisjefen den 15.3.1942 avgitt av politibetjent Leif Carlsen, Trondheim Politikammer. "Angår pågripelse av jøde Sara Bella Uthaug, f. Mahler,*

wegian Storm Troopers. Sara was taken to *Kretsfengslet* (District Prison), Munkegaten 16, and sent by train the next day to Bredtvedt Concentration Camp near Oslo. In December 1943 Sara had obtained permission to leave for Sweden but was stopped by German border police and returned to the Gestapo H.Q. in Oslo, Viktoria Terasse, and then transported to Grini concentration camp. Here she remained until May 2, 1945 when she was released together with approximately 50 other Jews married to non- Jews and sent to Sweden.[47]

The release of these Norwegian prisoners had come about through negotiations by *Reichsführer-SS* Heinrich Himmler and his chief of staff, SS-General Walter Schellenberg on one side. On the other side were Arvid Richert the Swedish Minister to Berlin; Norbert Masur, Swedish Section, World Jewish Congress; and Dr. Felix Kersten, Himmler's Finnish physician and masseur. The negotiations took place at Himmler's headquarters near Orianenburg between 2:30 and 5:00 a.m. on the morning of April 21, 1945.[48] Mr. Masur related that he had met alone with Himmler for a half hour, "a free Jew, face to face with the frightening and cruel chief of the Gestapo, who had five million Jewish lives on his conscience."[49] By May 1945 over 20,000 "German-held internees from over twenty countries had been transported to Sweden."[49a]

There were petitions from Jews in Norway to be exempted from deportations. On December 27, 1942, Esther Hirsch of Bremsnes wrote to the Chief of Police in Kristiansund precinct. Esther explained that her father, Jakob Hirsch, age 76, and her mother, Frida, age 75, were so weak that they could not take care of themselves without assistance. "My

---

Trondheim. Den 15.3.43 kl. 15.45 ble Sara Bella Uthaug . . . pågrepet og transportert til Stapos kontor i Trondheim, Søndre gate 6."

47. *1945 Års Svenska Hjälpexpedition till Tyskland. Förspel och förhandlingar.* Stockholm: Kungl. Utrikesdepartementet, 1956, p. 36: "*50 norske judar enligt UD's lista frigives och föras av de tyska myndigheterna i Norge till den svenska gränsen.*" (According to the list from the Swedish Ministry of Foreign Affairs fifty Norwegian Jews are to be released and escorted by German authorities in Norway to the Swedish border."

48. Norbert Masur, *En jude talar med Himmler* (A Jew Speaks with Himmler). Stockholm: Albert Bonniers Förlag, 1945, pp. 25, 34.

49. Masur, op. cit., p. 28: "En halv timma var jag ensam med honom, en fri jude ansikte mot ansikte med den fruktade och ubarmhärtiga Gestapochefen, som hade fem millioner judiska liv på sitt samvete."

49a. Steven Koblik, "No Truck with Himmler. The Politics and Rescue and the Swedish Red Cross Mission, March-May 1945," *Scandia, Tidsskrift för Historisk Forskning,* vol. 5, Nos. 1-2, 1985, p. 173. See also Prof. Koblik's article "Sweden's Attempts to aid Jews, 1939-1945," *Scandinavian Studies,* vol. 56, no. 2, Spring 1984, pp. 89-113.

mother is ill as shown by the medical report, and it would, of course, be best that I, who know her illness and how to treat her, would be permitted to continue to take care of her. . . . I look forward to a consenting reply to my petition since I cannot imagine that my old, weak parents shall be left to struggle by themselves."[50] This petition was sent with a recommendation to the chief of police in Kristiansund who, on December 29, 1942, forwarded the petition to the Oslo State Police. It was stated that disapproval of the petition would lead to the daughter being transported to Oslo. "The parents, however, are regarded as being too weak and too old to endure a transportation."[51] A letter from the Oslo State Police of January 6, 1943, gave the order that "the Jew Jakob Hirsch, b. May 20, 1866, the Jewesses Frida Hirsch, b. December 12, 1868, and Esther Hirsch, b. May 26, 1905, should be transported to Oslo as soon as possible. The transportation should be undertaken discreetly so as *not* to afford an opportunity for people to congregate on the pier." All three members of the Hirsch family were transported on board the S.S. *Gotenland* on February 24, 1943, destined to Auschwitz. The Hirsch family did not survive.[52]

In Southern Norway, especially in Oslo, which had a Jewish population of about 800, there had been only a few indications of the Nazi intent. In a 1942 report, Harry Koritzinsky, the long-time secretary of the Oslo Jewish community, stated that until the fall of 1942, the Jews in Oslo had undergone a relatively calm period. "Terboven's declaration of September 25, 1940, had by and large had a quieting effect on the Norwegian Jews."[53]

Some of the Jews arrested in 1942 had actually fled to Sweden in 1940, only to return to Norway believing in the promise of amnesty by Terboven for those who had fled during the invasion, or in Terboven's speech on September 25, 1940, promising protection to all religious denominations. The Jews were sure their faith was included in this an-

50. Holm, op. cit., p. 19.

51. Letter of December 27, 1942, from Esther Hirsch, Bremsnes, to Roald Theisen, Chief of Police, Kristiansund. K.P. Jno. 3194, 1942, RAO, Oslo.

52. Letter of 7 December 29, 1942, from Roald Theisen to the State Police, Oslo, K.P. Jno. 3195, 1942, RAO: *"Fortegnelse over personer som med bestemthet vites à være deportert fra Norge den 24. februar 1943"* (Listing of persons who with certainty are known to have been deported from Norway on February 24, 1943), Yad Vashem, B/28-10.

53. Harry Koritzinsky, *"Jødene i Norge 1940-1942,"* Redegjørelse avgitt i Stockholm, 30. November 1942 (The Jews in Norway, 1940-1942. A report given in Stockholm, November 30, 1942), p. 14..

nouncement. The return to Norway turned out for many to be a fatal mistake. There were, of course, requisitions of Jewish apartments and houses for the benefit of the Germans, but that happened to all Norwegians and the Jews felt fairly safe that there would be no specific actions taken against them as Jews. They had gone through the same problems of Nazi occupation as anyone else. Just like the rest of the population, the Jews had adjusted themselves to the hardship of German occupation, except for anti-Semitic attacks in the controlled press.

Norwegian Jews wanted to share the same difficulties as the rest of the nation. Little did they know that they were singled out for destruction. The state of siege and the arrests of all male Jews over the age of fifteen in Trondheim and other parts of Norway in the beginning of October 1942 had affected the tranquility of the Oslo Jewish community. Nevertheless, the mass arrests at the end of October 1942 came unexpected to Jews and non-Jews alike. The element of surprise, thorough planning, and relentless persecution were some of the major reasons for "success" in doing away with about half of Norway's Jewish population.

The procedure for the arrest can be followed in detail in a police report of October 4, 1946, by the two criminal investigators, Thorbjørn Frøberg and Knut Ebeling. They stated that altogether 260 male Jews were arrested between October 26 and 27, 1942.[54] Three police inspectors, Sverre Dürbeck, Jørgen Wiermyhr, and Thorvald Undhjem, brought along the *Spørreskjema* (inquiry forms) which the Jews had filled out in the spring of 1942 and filed with local police precincts throughout the country. In charge of preparing the lists of names and addresses was Police Officer Homb and eight other civil servants. Police Inspectors Knut Røed, Ragnvald Kranz, and others arrived on Sunday, October 25. The mimeographed lists of Jews to be arrested were distributed to arresting squads consisting of all available personnel from the State Police, thirty members of the Criminal Police, and twenty from the "Germanske SS-Norge," and others totaling 124 persons.[55] The action was led by Deputy Chief of the Oslo State Police, Knut Røed.

On Monday, October 26, everyone involved met at 5:30 a.m. at Kirkevien 23. The 124 policemen were divided into 62 task forces. Each

---

54. *Rapport til Oslo Politikammer*, Landssvikavdelingen, avgitt av Kriminalassistene Thorbjørne Frøberg og Knut Ebeling, *Aksjonene mot jødene* (The Actions against Jews), Oslo, October 4, 1946, pp. 1, 2.

55. Per Ole Johansen, op. cit., p. 149.

received an envelope with ten names.[56] Knut Røed gave instructions as to the arrests, which cars were to be requisitioned, and how to proceed in hunting for individual Jews. The zeal of the Norwegian police is illustrated by the repeated attempts to arrest Jews who were not at home at the first call; in those cases, second and third calls were made.

The arrested Jews were transported first to Bredtvedt, and the next day to Berg concentration camp near Tønsberg. Ernest Aberle, a refugee from Czechoslovakia, arrested in his home at Lillehammer (about 150 miles north of Oslo), has given a detailed description of those events. He recounts arriving at the Berg camp October 18, 1942, which was under Norwegian administration, with Major Eivind Wallestad and Lieutenant Leif Lindseth in command. The camp was totally unfit for human habitation, lacking water and toilet facilities.[57] Of the 292 Jews deported from Berg Internment camp, only 7 survived.[58]

A group of about 350 Jews arrived at Bredtvedt, a concentration camp near Oslo on October 28 and were greeted by Lindseth's statement that they would receive the harsh treatment they deserved; any attempt to escape would result in being shot. Suffering from hunger, lack of medicine, clothing and bedding, they received some help from the Norwegian Red Cross and a local doctor, Anton Jervell, who sought to bring in additional supplies. He was prevented from doing so by Wallestad's statement that they were not needed. The prisoners' stay came to an abrupt end at 4:00 a.m. on November 26, when about 280 Jews were transported by special train from Berg concentration camp to Oslo harbor Pier I, with police officer Ragnvold Kranz in charge. He had received orders during the night not to deport Jews married to "Aryans." Lindseth stated that those who claimed to be married to an "Aryan" but were not would be shot.

The German assessment of the Norwegian reaction to mass arrests of Jews may be gleaned from a report of November 14, 1942, in *Meldungen aus Norwegen*.[59] Under the heading *Allgemeine Lage* (the General

---

56. Dag Tangen, "*Norges Krystallnatt, 1942: 10 jøder i hver konvolutt*" (*Norway's Crystal Night: 10 Jews in Every Envelope*), Dagbladet, Oslo, April 4 and May 28, 1979.

57. Ernest Aberle, *Vi må ikke glemme* (We must not forget), Oslo: J.W. Cappelens Forlag, 1980, p. 50.

58. Carl Haave and Sverre J. Herstad, *Quislings Hønsegård. Berg Interneringsleir.* Oslo: Alb. Cammermeyers Forlag, 1948, pp. 290-293, "*De som ble sendt til gasskamrene.*" (Those who we sent to the gas chambers).

59. Tore Dyrhaug, op. cit., p. 64: "*Folk flest reagerte ikke større på arrestasjonene. Bortsett fra enkelte ytringer av det vanlige slaget, at her kunne man bare se hvor*

112   SAMUEL ABRAHAMSEN

Situaion), it was stated that the population had not reacted to any large
extent to the arrests. "Setting aside the few comments of the usual kind,
that here one could see how inhuman Germans are, demonstrations of
sympathy to any large extent have not been registered."

The reaction of Norway's Minister of Foreign Affairs, Trygve Lie, in
London, was that "the arrests of Norwegian Jews and the transport to
Germany did not come unexpectedly. Nevertheless, we had difficulties
understanding such expression of systematic inhumanity, which could
have no other motivation than deranged malice."[60] Trygve Lie did his
best to mitigate this madness. During 1942-1943, he made several attempts to rescue the deported Norwegian Jews. The Norwegian government in London made inquiries about the deportations of November
1942 to the International Red Cross at its Headquarters in Switzerland.
The proposal was to exchange the Jewish deportees for wounded German prisoners-of-war held by the Allies. The Norwegian legation in
Bern informed the Red Cross officials that the Norwegian government
was deeply shaken over the serious breach of human rights which the
German authorities had committed against innocent Jews in Norway, including women and children. It asked the International Red Cross to use
its good offices to stop the deportation of Jews from Germany to Poland,
so that the unfortunate victims might avoid the bitter fate that was sure
to await them there.[61] The International Red Cross replied that all attempts to contact the deported Jews had been in vain, but that the efforts would be continued, and asked for financial assistance to send supplies to the Jews. But the Norwegian Red Cross, through its director,
Irgens, stated that the one thousand British pounds which the Norwegian government had granted as a contribution to the I.R.C. could not
be used for this purpose, since the monies were intended for the agency's administrative expenses.[62]

*umenneskelige tyskerne er, er det hittil ikke registrert sympatidemonstrasjoner for jødene
i større omfang."*

60. Trygve Lie, *Hjemover* (Homeward), Oslo: Tiden Norsk Forlag, 1958, p. 16:
"*Arrestasjonen av norske jøder og transporten til Tyskland kom ikke uventet. Det samme
hadde tidligere hendt i det ene okkuperte land efter det andre. Ikke destomindre hadde
vi vondt for å fatte slike utslag av systematisk umenneskelighet, som ikke kunne ha annet
motiv enn en sinnsyk ondskap."*

61. Tim Greve, *"Norsk forsøk på å redde jødene i 1942-43. Britene sa nei"* (Norwegian
attempts to rescue Jews during 1942-43. The British said no) *Verdens Gang*, Oslo, October
4, 1983, pp. 4-5.

62. *"Jødeforfølgelsene i Norge. Melding fra legasjonen i Bern"* (The Jewish Persecutions in Norway. Report from the Legation in Bern). Det Kgl. Utenriksdepartementet

Support for the exchange of prisoners came also from Norwegian Jews residing temporarily in Stockholm. On January 8, 1943, a letter was sent through the Norwegian legation to the Norwegian government in London. It stated that every attempt had to be made to rescue the deported Jews, "since a quick and terrible destruction awaits them if we can not promptly obtain positive results. The deported are shouting to us for help. They plead that their lives must be saved as far as it is humanly possible."[63] The letter was signed by the former president of the Oslo Jewish Community, Mendel Bernstein, and by its long-time secretary, Harry Koritzinsky, as well as by Marcus Levin and Charles Koklin, former chairmen respectively of the Oslo Rescue Committee and the Jewish Youth Organization in Oslo.

Other prominent Norwegians residing in Sweden also signed the petition on January 20, 1943. They were Annæus Schjødt, Supreme Court attorney; Martin Tranmæl, editor; and City Judge Harald Gram. Furthermore, Gunnar Josephson, president of the Stockholm Jewish Community, as well as its treasurer, Theodor Levy, supported this appeal, which was forwarded on February 2, 1943, to the Royal Ministry of Foreign Affairs in London.[64] Here, the Minister of Foreign Affairs, Trygve Lie, took action immediately. In his letter of February 16, 1943, to Erik Colban, the Norwegian Minister in London, Lie asked that the possibilities for such an exchange should be investigated.

The reply of February 25, 1943, signed by A.W. Randall, stated that His Majesty's Government was sympathetic to the fate of Norway's Jews. However, the proposal could not be submitted to the German government, since it would not conform to the Geneva convention as to prisoners-of-war and that first priority would be to liberate the British troops in German captivity.[65] In a letter of July 7, 1943, from Jens Bull to the Foreign Ministry in London, he stated that the experience in Swe-

(London), Jnr. 266605/42. "Dir. Irgens i Røde Kors opplyser at de £1000 som regjeringen har bevilget som bidrag fra Norges R.K. ikke kan tenkes anvendt for ovennevte formål, da pengene er bestemt for I.R.K.s administrasjonsutgifter." (Dated April 1, 1943, initialed by C.P.R.), U.D. Archives, Oslo, Dossier 342, 39F "Jødeforfølgelsene i Norge."

63. Letter, Stockholm, January 8, 1943, Jnr. 00862, "Til Den kgl. Norske Regjering p.t. London: En snarlig og fryktelig undergang venter dem om man ikke hurtig kan oppnå positive resultater. De deporterte roper gjennom oss på hjelp. De bønnfaller om at deres liv må reddes, så sant det står i menneskelig makt." U.D. Archives, Oslo, Dossier 3/42, 39F.

64. Jens Bull, Norwegian Minister to Stockholm, to Royal Ministry of Foreign Affairs, p.t. London: "Deportasjoner av jøder fra Norge" (Deportations of Jews from Norway), 26 U. 8.1.43 J.nr. 26605/42, U.D. Archives, Oslo.

65. Time Greve, "Norsk forsøk etc." op. cit., p. 5.

den had been that it was useless "at the present time to send packages or letters to Jews in Germany. The legation, however, would like to learn whether the Red Cross in London or other institutions have opportunities to contact the prisoners . . . or if any action will be taken to obtain permission for relatives to at least correspond with the prisoners."[66] Herman Florence of Oslo sent a letter on December 31, 1942, from the Norwegian training camp at Öreryd in Småland, Sweden, to Annæus Schjødt. Mr. Florence stated that the number of Norwegian Jews deported to Germany was "between 400 to 600" and suggested that at least the women and children among them should be given the opportunity to be exchanged. "I for my part think I have not fully done my duty until every opportunity has been tried to assist the unfortunate."[67]

66. Letter, July 9, 1943, from Norwegian Legation, Stockholm, to Ministry of Foreign Affairs, London, No. 3615: "Jøder fra Norge i tysk fangenskap" (Jews from Norway in German Imprisonment), U.D. Archives, Oslo: "Etter de erfaringer man har her i Sverige nytter det for tiden ikke hverken å sende pakker eller brev til jøder i Tyskland. Legasjonen vil imidlertid gjerne høre om Røde kors i London eller andre institusjoner har anledning til å komme i forbindelse med slike fanger. Legasjonen tør ennvidere forhøre om der er eller vil bli foretatt noen aksjon for om mulig åpne adgang for de pårørende til iallefall å korrespondere med fangene."

67. Letter from Herman Florence, Reg. Nr. 9519, Öreryd, December 21, 1942, to Attorney-at-Law Annæus Schjødt, Stockholm. For further reading about Öreryd, see Ole Kristian Grimnes, "Et Flyktningssamfunn vokser fram" (The Growth of a Community of Refugees), in Nordmenn i Sverige (Norwegians in Sweden), Oslo: H. Aschehoug & Co., 1969, pp. 50 ff.

X.

Deportations of Norwegian Jews to Auschwitz

Willy Brandt reported in his book *The War in Norway* that by 1942 the horrors of the German concentration camps were known, but "few envisaged that before the end of the year, regular pogroms and deportation of hundreds of men, women and children would take place in Norway."[1]

For the Norwegian Jews, the bitter end was now at hand. The night of October 25–26 had been one of terror. The night of November 25–26, 1942 has been recorded as the most fateful night in the history of Norway's Jews. On November 25, the Jewish prisoners at the Falstad concentration camp at Levanger in Central Norway started on their journey to Auschwitz, first by rail to Oslo via Trondheim. There the arrested men were joined at the railway station by their wives and children, arrested in Trondheim. It was the last time they saw each other.

Since transportation of Norway's Jews to the German destruction camps by rail through Sweden and Denmark had been ruled impossible, a ship had to be made available. Shipping was in short supply, but on November 25, 1942, *Untersturmführer* (Second Lieutenant) Heinrich Grossmann of the RSHA informed *Oberführer* Heinrich Fehlis in Oslo that "a sudden opportunity of transportation (*plötzlich*

---

1. Willy Brandt, *Krigen i Norge*, Oslo: *Aschehoug*, 1945, Vol. II, p. 133: ". . . *Det var få som i januar 1942 ante at Norge innen året var gått, skulle bli skueplass for regelrette jødepogromer med deportasjon av hundrevis av menn, kvinner og barn.*"

angebotene Möglichkeit) had appeared.[2] The German Navy had put S.S. *Donau* at the disposal of the Gestapo. The prisoners from Trondheim arrived too late to be loaded on board the *Donau*, which had left Oslo on November 26 at 3 p.m. for Stettin.

On the train from Falstad to Oslo, the Jewish prisoners were accompanied by Norwegian police in civilian dress who told them they were being sent to Poland. Upon arriving in Oslo on November 26 at 9 p.m., they were met at the Oslo railway station by a delegation of women from *Nasjonalhjelpen* (The National Help), including "Mrs. Helliesen Lund and Ingebjørg Sletten."[3] They had, during the night of November 25–26, received a message from the city of Lillehammer alerting them to the transportation of Jewish prisoners from Falstad.[4] There were 36 men, women, and children in this group.[5] Five persons who should have been deported were not present at the roll call at 8 p.m. at the Trondheim railroad station.[6]

As chairperson of *Nasjonalhjelpen*, Mrs. Helliesen Lund had access to the Quisling chief of police, Marthinsen, whom she had met on previous occasions. Now she asked permission to visit and to bring warm clothing, blankets, and medicines to the Jewish prisoners who had been interned at Bredtvedt.[7] Here they were to stay for another three months, awaiting the S.S. *Gotenland* to transport them to Stettin. With great courage and resourcefulness, Mrs. Helliesen Lund obtained per-

2. Raul Hilberg, *The Destruction of the European Jews*. Revised and Definitive Edition, New York and London: Holmes and Meier, 1985, Vol. II, p. 556.
3. Fritz Lustig, testimony in the case against Wagner, *Rapport til Oslo Politikammer (Landssvikavdelingen), 28.1.1948. Ad sak 3064/45 Wilhelm Wagner, p. 1: "På toget fra Falstad til Oslo ble de ledsaget av norske politifolk i sivile klær, og de fortalte at de skulle til Polen. Ved ankomsten til Oslo Ø. ble de møtt av flere norske damer. Vitnet kjente bare fru Helliesen Lund og Ingebjørg Sletten fra Nasjonalhjelpen."*
4. Celine Wormdal, *Kvinner i Krig* (Women at War), *Gløtt inn i en forsømst samtidshistorie* (Glimpses into a neglected contemporary history), Oslo: Aschehoug, 1979, p. 13.
5. *Report of November 26, 1942: "Til Politipresidenten i Trondheim. Angår: Arrestasjon, transport av jødekvinner og barn til Oslo."* Signed by police officer, Kr. Vik. Oslo (Report regarding arrest and transportation of Jewish women and children to Oslo).
6. "Erkjennes mottatt 27/11-42 kl. 1:15. Bredtveit Fengsel 27/11-42" (Receipt of 36 is hereby acknowledged. Bredtveit Prison, November 27, 1942 at 1:15 a.m.). Signed by *N. Daae Tvedt*, a member of N.S. in charge of the prison camp at Bredtveit. The five persons who had escaped arrest were Liebe Klein, Sara Jacobsen, Leopold Paltiel, Rosa Philipson, and Sara Mahler.
7. Sigrid Helliesen Lund (*i samarbeid med Celine Wormdal*) *Alltid Underveis*. (Always on the Road. (In cooperation with Celine Wormdal)), Oslo: Tiden Norsk Forlag, 1981, p. 101.

mission and eventually made a total of six visits.[8] The visits were abruptly curtailed when a Norwegian, married to a Jewish person, had been caught trying to escape to Sweden. When arrested, he had given Mrs. Helliesen-Lund's name to the Gestapo as the person who had advised him to escape.

In Oslo, a large and well-organized police force of about 300 men was available for the action on November 24–26: 60 from the State Police, 60 from the Criminal Police, 60 from the *Hird*, 30 from the *"Germanske SS-Norge"*,[9] and about 100 from the Emergency State Police.[10] This was a very large police action "demanding exact and careful preparation."[11] On November 25, detailed instructions had been issued by K.A. Marthinsen, chief of the Norwegian State Police, for the arrest of *all* remaining Jews, including women, those over the age of 65, children under 14, the sick, the mentally ill, and the retarded. "Exceptions are made for women and men married to persons not having 'J' on their passports. Exempted are, furthermore, persons with British, U.S., Mexican, Central or South American citizenships, of the neutral countries, and those countries allied to Germany."[12] Instructions for deportation by ship on November 26 at 3 p.m. were issued by Marthinsen. His report of the events was as follows:[13]

---

8. Sverre M. Nyrønning, *"Reddet jøder fra nazistenes Helvede"* (Saved Jews from the hell of the Nazis), *Forsvarets Forum* (The Forum of the Defense), No. 5, March 31, 1980, p. 20.

9. Tore Dyrhaug, *Norge okkupert. Tysk etterretning om Norge og nordmenn 1942–1945*, Oslo-Bergen-Stavanger-Tromsø: Universitetsforlaget A/S, 1985, p. 43: *"Skjema for innmelding til "Germanske SS-Norge"* (Application for admission to "Germanic SS-Norway").

10. *Riksadvokatens Meddelsesblad*, Supreme Court Decision L.nr. 187 S.nr. 669/1946, Case against Wilhelm A.K. Wagner, p. 26: "... *ca. 300 mannskaper ... sto til disposisjon for gjennomførelsen av denne aksjon"* (About 300 men were made available for the execution of this action [i.e., on November 24-26, 1942]).

11. Knut Sveri, *"Landssvikoppgjørets merkeligste rettsak. Aksjonen mot jødene i Norge"* (The strangest judicial proceeding of the legal accounting against collaborators. The action against the Jews in Norway), in Anders Bratholm, Nils Christie, Torkel Opsahl, eds., *Lov og Frihet.* (Law and Freedom), *Festkrift til Johs. Andenæs på 70-årsdagen* (Festschrift to J. Andenæs on his 70th birthday), September 7, 1982, p. 345: *"Dette var en etter norske forhold meget stor politiaksjon, som fordret en nøyaktig og omhyggelig planlegging."*

12. Instructions from State Police, Department of Oslo and Aker, November 25, 1942: *"Alle kvinnelige jøder med J. i passet samt deres barn skal anholdes. Eventuelle mannlige jøder med J. i passet som påtreffes, anholdes også. De anholdte må være norske, statsløse, tyske, slovakiske, kroatiske eller statsborgere av et av de Tysklands besatte land. Unntatt er de kvinner og menn som er gift med personer som ikke har J. i passet. Unntatt er videre de personer som av statsborgerskap tilhører det britiske rike, U.S.A., Mexico, De Midt- og Syd-amerikanske stater, de nøitrale land og de med Tysklands forbundne stater."*

Evacuation of Jews: On the 24th of November, 1942, at 20.00 hr., I received orders from the German Security Police, *Hauptsturmführer* Wagner, that Jews with a 'J' stamped on their identification cards, as well as their families, should be evacuated from Norway. Ship transport was available with the date of departure set from Oslo, November 26, 1942, at 15.00 hrs.

The order for the deportation of Norway's Jews had allegedly come from Berlin to SS *Oberführer* (Brigadier General) Heinrich Fehlis of *Der Höhere SS* and *Polizeiführer* of the *Reichkommisariat*. Furthermore, there were instructions about confiscation of Jewish properties and revocation of Norwegian citizenship as soon as the deportees left Norway. None should expect to be returned to Norway.[14] A telegram of November 25, 1942, sent by Hellmuth Reinhard to the Gestapo in Stettin, stated that on November 26, a "ship transport of about 700 to 900 Jewish men and women of all ages will leave Oslo for Stettin." It was clearly stated that the Jews were to be brought to Auschwitz.[15] The RSHA had already been informed, and further instructions would come from them. The telegram, stamped *Geheim* (secret), also stated that the voyage would take three days. The ship, which had been made available by the *Kriegsmarine* (German navy), had to be returned forthwith; the telegram asked for the immediate disembarkation of the Jews to be shipped to Auschwitz.

The next day, November 26, additional detailed information was sent by Reinhard to Stettin, giving the name of the troop transport ship, the S.S. *Donau*, and that it had left Oslo at 2:55 p.m. with 532 Jewish prisoners. The transport leader was *Untersturmführer* Grossmann, who was held responsible for return of a typewriter that had been used for listing the names of the Jews. The telegram stated that the arrival in Stettin would be during the early morning of November 29.[16] Stormy weather,

13. Report from Norwegian State Police of November 27, 1942, K.A. Marthinsen. Document R. I. 06644 *Eidsivating Lagstol, Landssvikavdelingen*, pp. 1–6: *Evakuering av jøder* (*Eidsivating* Court, Department for Dealing with Treason: Evacuation of Jews).

14. Odd Bergfald, *Hellmuth Reinhard*, op. cit., pp. 58–59.

15. Telex from Norway's Gestapo Chief, Hellmuth Reinhard, of November 25, 1942, regarding deportation of 700 to 900 Norwegian Jews to Stettin. "*Die Juden sollen nach Auschwitz verbracht werden.*" Signed Reinhard.

16. Telex from Hellmuth Reinhard regarding the departure of S.S. *Donau* at 2:55 p.m. from Oslo, November 26, 1942, and arriving in Stettin on November 29. There were 532 Norwegian Jews on board, with SS *Untersturmführer* Grossmann as transport leader. Signed Reinhard.

however, delayed the arrival until November 30, as witnessed by the transfer of documents signed in Stettin confirming arrival of 302 Jewish men and 230 women and children.[17] Another ship, the S.S. *Monte Rosa*, had left Oslo on November 19, and again on November 26, 1942, with respectively 21 and 26 Jewish prisoners on board destined for Auschwitz. Some of those deported on the *Monte Rosa* had been arrested at their summer homes in Nærsnes in the Bundefjord. Many were members of the board of *Jødisk Hjelpeforening* (Jewish Rescue Association) in Oslo.[18] According to testimony by Marcus Levin, the families had been interrogated by Gestapo, arrested, and sent to Grini where they were severely mistreated. The interrogations prior to arrest had been led by Wagner and *Untersturmführer* Erhard Böhm. A prisoner, Nathan Fein, had been forced to sign a confession which he had had "no opportunity to read through."[19] The majority of the men arrested at the end of October were kept at Berg concentration camp until November 26, when they were transported to Pier I in Oslo.

The round-up and arrest of Norwegian Jews still at liberty took place in the early morning hours of November 26. The action was carried out in the following manner: On November 24, Marthinsen received a communication from *Hauptsturmführer* Wagner that all Jews with 'J' on their identity cards should be arrested together with their families and evacuated from Norway by ship. Wagner's order of deportation included children, women, and all male Jews over the age of 65, as well as Jews in hospitals, at the Jewish home for the aged, the Jewish children's home, and other institutions. Marthinsen called together all police officers to clarify special assignments. Inspector Sverre Dürbeck was to arrange for the arrest and transportation of Jews from Eastern Norway, Southern Norway, and, if possible, from Trondheim and Bergen. At his disposal he had the civil servants at police headquarters, the local chiefs

---

17. Transfer protocol (*Übergabeprotokoll*), signed by *Untersturmführer* Grossmann verifying the handing over at Stettin on November 30, 1942, of 532 Norwegian Jews: 302 men and 230 women and children. Raul Hilberg, *The Destruction of European Jews*, 1985, op. cit., p. 557, note 10.

18. Marcus Levin, *Rapport til Oslo Politikammer (Landsvikavdelingen)* (Report to Oslo Police Precinct, Department for Dealing with Treason), August 31, 1946. *Case Against Wagner*, op. cit., pp. 1, 2.

19. Ibid., p. 3: "Nathan Fein . . . *hadde blitt tvunget til under forhørene å underskrive en erklæring som han ikke fikk anledning til å lese. . . . Samtlige er avgått ved døden i Auschwitz unntatt Nathan Fein som levet helt til våren 1945 da han ble skutt i Bergen-Belsen.*"

of police, and the out-of-city precincts of the State Police. Inspector
Knut Røed was in charge of the arrests of Jewish families brought to Pier
I, where the S.S. *Donau* would be waiting. Røed was also in charge of
embarking the prisoners. *Politifullmektig* (Police- Lieutenant) Ragnvald
Krantz was assigned to arrest Jews in hospitals, the mentally ill and retarded at other institutions, as well as male Jews over the age of 65 within
the Oslo and Aker precincts. Krantz organized the transportation of the
Jews from Berg concentration camp to Oslo. *Politifullmektig* Lindvig
was in charge of ordering about 100 taxis and buses for local transportation in Oslo on November 26, and also for obtaining the necessary provisions for the duration of the voyage.[20]

The instructions with which the Norwegian police implemented the
arrests of Jews were given to the policemen by the State Police on November 25, 1942. It outlined procedures and policies for arrests of Jewish women and children; what the arrested Jews were allowed to bring
along for four days; the delivery of keys, ration cards, and valuables; and
the transportation to Pier I.[21]

During the late evening of November 25, air raid sirens in Oslo went
off repeatedly between 9 p.m. and midnight to keep people off the
streets. At 5 a.m., November 26, the well-planned and carefully- executed round-up of the Jews took place. The Norwegian police went from
house to house according to lists carefully compiled from the
spørreskjema (questionnaire) which the Jews themselves had filled out
during the spring and summer of 1942. Some addresses were inaccurate
because of changes, but the zeal of the police, already manifested the
previous month, had not waned. By utilizing the National Register, most
of the new addresses were traced. Some of the Jews now arrested had
escaped from pogroms in their previous homelands. One of the deportees, Mrs. Olga Scheer from Oslo, age 81, had avoided a Jewish massacre
37 years earlier in Lithuania. She was arrested together with two daugh-
ters, three sons-in-law, and seven grandchildren. All were transported
aboard the S.S. *Donau* and died at Auschwitz.[22]

Some persons were known to have been removed from *Donau* prior
to its departure from Oslo. A prominent Norwegian scientist, Victor

    20. Frøberg and Eberling, "Regarding action on November 26, 1942. Evacuation of
Jews," op. cit., October 4, 1946, pp. 2, 3.
    21. Haakon Holmboe, *"De som ble tatt,"* op. cit., p. 475.
    22. Robert Levin, *Med Livet i hendene* (With my life at stake), Oslo: J.W. Cappelens
Forlag, 1983, p. 21.

Morris Goldschmidt (1888–1947), who was born in Zürich and had settled in Norway, was in 1936 appointed by the University of Oslo to teach
mineralogy and geology. He was arrested on October 22, 1942, released,
re-arrested, and put on board the *Donau* on November 26 for transportation to Auschwitz. Professor Goldschmidt has given his own account
of his dramatic release:[23]

> At 10:50 came a state policeman, seemingly the same who had arrested
> me the previous day, and called out to see whether Victor Moritz
> Goldschmidt was present. When I answered yes, he told me to walk for-
> ward toward the ship and said I was free and could return home. He added
> that he was glad to give me this message. I drove home in a taxi, which
> was paid by the state police, as I had had to hand in all my money at
> Bredtvedt the day before.... As I learned my release had been engineer-
> ed by Professor Hans Solberg, the dean of our faculty and protector [of
> the university] Rector Adolf Hoel, who ... had gone to the chief of the
> state police Marthinsen, and impressed on him that I had to be set free
> for work vital to the state.

Professor Arvid Brodersen stated that the release of Professor
Goldschmidt was caused by "colleagues at the university who had convinced the Gestapo agent Wagner to issue an order to that effect."[24] The
Donau left without Goldschmidt, who three weeks later was transported by the Resistance movement to safety in Sweden.[25]

Those who had avoided arrest during previous round-ups were now
brought to Pier I for embarkation aboard the S.S. *Donau*; special trains
and buses from the various detention camps arrived at the pier where
those previously arrested "were united with their families."[26]

Hauptsturmführer Wagner was in charge of the embarkation of Jews
at the pier. The court proceedings against him after the war brought out
the fact that he had left the pier at about 11:00 a.m. to pay a personal
visit to Mr. Schei, director of the Norwegian Department of Supply. According to orders from Berlin, there was food on board for tour days
only. Wagner asked Schei for additional supplies for 14 days, claiming

23. Arnold Kramisch, *The Griffin. The greatest untold Espionage Story of World War II*. Boston: Houghton Mifflin Company, 1986, p. 134.

24. Arvid Brodersen, *Fra et Nomadeliv. Erindringer.* (From a Nomadic Life. Reminiscenses), Oslo: Gyldendal Norsk Forlag, 1982, p. 139.

25. Kramisch, op. cit., p. 135.

26. Benkt Jerneck, *Folket uten frykt. Norge 1942–43* (People without Fear), Oslo: Johan Grundt Tanum, 1945, p. 30.

that the voyage would last that long. Mentioned were: "potatoes, coffee ersatz (substitutes), vegetables, macaroni, milk for the children, bread and margarine."[27]

Director Schei immediately ordered his subordinate, Lars Kaare Konsmo Salvesen, to comply with Wagner's request for provisions for the 530 Jews who were to be evacuated that day at 3:00 p.m. In the course of two hours, additional supplies of sardines, kippered herring, fishcakes, and large quantities of canned food for dinner were obtained. Kaare Salvesen testified at Wagner's trial that he went personally to the pier to make sure that all the provisions would be brought on board the S/S Donau. How the Jews were treated made a strong impression on him. They were terrorized and forced to carry the heavy packages, including potato sacks, at an accelerated tempo.[28] The Jews, however, received nothing of the food which the Norwegians had managed to assemble. The Jews were fed "bread, margarine, and some thin soup"[29] during the voyage to Stettin. During the railroad journey to Auschwitz the Jews received no food. The supplies were shipped from Auschwitz to Berlin.

Willy Brandt gave this description of what occurred on the pier prior to the deportation:[30]

> While children cried and mothers pleaded for mercy, they were thrown into cars and driven down to the German troop ship, Donau, which was laid up at the pier of the Norwegian-American Line. At the pier the most heartbreaking scenes took place. The Quisling police behaved in a most brutal way even when it concerned women and babies. The sick on stretchers were thrown on board. Even mentally deranged from Ullevål Hospital were fetched for deportation.

A notorious Nazi, Dr. Hans Engh, had arrived early in the morning, November 26, at the hospital accompanied by a group of the Hird. They were looking for the records of Jewish patients to be deported. The personnel at the hospital, however, including nurses and doctors, had cre-

27. Wagner, op. cit., "Testimony," April 30, 1947, pp. 30–31.
28. Rapport til Oslo Politikammer. Landssvikavdelingen, December 8, 1942: "Vitnet var personlig til stede på bryggen for å kontrollere at de bestilte varer virkelig kom om bord ... vaktene terroriserte jødene ved et voldsomt språk m.v. Jødene måtte selv bære de tunge matvaresekker om bord i et voldsomt tempo."
29. Wagner, op. cit., pp. 31–32: "Jødene så intet til den hermetikk som ekspedisjonssjef Schei så omsorgsfullt hadde sendt. Jødene levde på brød, margarin og litt tynn suppe."
30. Willy Brandt, "Jødepogromene i Norge, oktober–november 1942" (Jewish pogroms in Norway, October–November 1942), in Fram Norsk Magasin, London, July 24, 1943.

ated an extensive network of false records and had assisted some Jewish patients to escape. Otherwise, in spite of protests by doctors and nurses, Jews who were so ill that they had to be carried away on stretchers, were taken from the hospital.[31] An eyewitness to the November 26 deportation reported that "a German sailor watching a Jewish cripple being loaded on board was overheard muttering: 'For this the Germans will have to pay some day.'"[32]

In his written report of November 27, Marthinsen made several complaints. The Oslo police had procrastinated in providing the only suitable lodging for Jews arriving from out-of-town — the gymnasium of the Oslo police barracks. This problem was settled only after many hours of negotiation. Another complaint was that he had received a message from the German Security Police, at 8 p.m. on November 25, notifying him of a change in evacuation plans: families where a spouse was an aryan would not be evacuated at all. This caused many problems since initial lists and preparations had been based on the original instructions.[33] Furthermore, he complained that he had been given too little time to prepare such an extensive action. He should have had as many days as he had been given hours.

A survivor of Auschwitz, Kai S.J. Feinberg from Oslo, was arrested in October and brought on board the S.S. *Donau* on November 26. He has reported as follows:[34]

> On board I met my mother and father, sister and adopted brother. It came as a shock to me. I believed, of course, that they would not have permitted themselves to be arrested, because my father certainly knew what it was all about. But he told me, "As long as you were arrested, we could not think about escaping to Sweden." And he also felt responsibility for the refugees from Central Europe. He did not speak much on board the *Donau* but made me understand that he knew what was going to happen. I remember one evening when we youngsters went on deck and

31. "Jewish Persecution-Deportation from Oslo," American Legation, Stockholm, *Dispatch No. 1629*, April 9, 1943, as cited from Norwegian Press Section, Bulletin No. 204, December 4, 1942. National Archives, Washington, D.C., pp. 1–3.

32. American Legation, Stockholm, *Dispatch No. 1629*, April 9, 1943. Memorandum: "Additional Information Concerning Persecution of Jews in Norway," National Archives, Washington, D.C., p. 6.

33. *Wagner*, op. cit., October 8, 1946, pp. 76–80. "*Dette voldte oss adskillig bryderi idet forarbeidene var kommet temmelig langt, på basis av det opprinnelige grunnlag.*"

34. "*Kai Feinberg — norsk jøde i Auschwitz*" (Kai Feinberg — Norwegian Jew in Auschwitz), *Dagbladet*, Oslo, February 24, 1979.

started singing, it was quite cozy. We imagined that we were being sent
to work camps where the family could be together and survive the war.
. . . There was a certain optimism on board, especially when we arrived
at Øresund, where Sweden was fully lit up on one side and Denmark
blacked out on the other. Should we jump overboard? No one did it. Then
we arrived at Stettin. The German SS took care of us. We were called
Dreckjude and *Schmutziger Jude.* They confiscated all the food we had
with us and we received very little to eat. We were transported in cattle
cars to Auschwitz, the men and women separately. We received nothing
to eat or drink during the transportation. The trip from Stettin to
Auschwitz lasted about two days. The cars were opened, and, for the first
time we met other prisoners, Polish Jews with the hair shaven off. They
wore the striped prison uniforms. We paraded five and five for an SS officer, probably Josef Mengele. This was the "selection." Women, children
and senior citizens were transported by cars. We did not know where to.
Today we know all of them went directly to the gas chambers. My mother,
sister, adopted brother, grandmother, aunt and uncles, altogether thirty
relatives, died this way. Only two of my uncles, a cousin, and I went to
camp Birkenau where we were tattooed on the arm. My number was
79108. The lowest number I have seen in Auschwitz was 26000, the highest 230000. It was only the men capable of working who came to this camp
and received a number. In our transport it was 186 out of 532. All the others were gassed immediately. My father was beaten and brought to the
hospital. Thanks to Professor Epstein, who arrived with our transport
from Norway, I managed to be at the hospital where my father died on
January 7, 1943. I was left alone. I could not stand it any longer.

The Norwegian newspaper in London, *Norsk Tidend* (Norwegian
News) reported on December 9, 1942, that the deportation ship with
532 Jews on board had "safely reached a German Baltic port after a
stormy voyage. . . ."[35] The documents from Stettin showed that 532 Norwegian Jews had arrived on board S.S. *Donau* on November 30, and had
continued by train to Auschwitz, where they arrived at 9 p.m. the following day. The official notice of the Camp Commander had this wording: "Auschwitz, December 1, 1942. *Confirmation of receipt.* Receipt
of — 532 — [emphasis in source] Jews from Norway is hereby confirmed."[36] According to the official report, 186 men were taken into cus-

35. *"De jødiske 'passasjerer' kommet fram. Deportasjonsskipet i tysk Østersjø-havn"*
(The Jewish "passengers" have arrived. The deportation ship in German Baltic Sea harbor), *Norsk Tidend* (London), December 9, 1942, p. 5.
36. T. Friedmann, *Dokumentensammlung über "Die Deportierung der Juden aus*

tody and received numbers 79064 to 79249. Out of the 532 deported from Oslo — not from Bergen as listed in an official document — 346 were immediately killed in the gas chambers.[37]

One of the few survivors of this transport, Herman Sachnowitz, has given a detailed description of the treatment of Norwegian Jews at Auschwitz in his book *Det angår også deg* (It Also Concerns You):[38]

> The working day lasted ten hours. Again and again we were beaten and kicked because we did not work fast enough. Even the need to relieve oneself could be a problem. One had to be cool and clear in the head in order not to do anything hasty such as urinating without first asking permission. *"Bitte austreten zu dürfen!"* It was even worse if one started to run a little because the need was urgent. If one forgot oneself, one ran the risk of being shot. There were always guards nearby who kept watch on us. "If you are ordered to run, you must never run," father had said the last time we ever saw him. And he was right. I had proof of that many, many times. There could be many reasons why some poor devil starting running, but usually he was tricked into it. When an SS-man wanted to get rid of a prisoner, he might ask him to fetch something or other and spur him on with angry shouts: "Los, los!" Inexperienced prisoners would obey the order and run. For the last time. Shot attempting to escape! Living targets were very attractive to many SS-soldiers.
>
> I particularly remember this day at the Buna Works because it was the first brutal contact with the curse of slave labor. I cannot explain how I managed to survive it. Most of the time I probably worked and slaved in a state of semiconsciousness, and of the march back to the camp I can only remember that each step was a trial of strength.
>
> We were given breakfast at about five o'clock. It consisted of two to three hundred grams of bread, and sometimes we had nothing at all. If we did not get any breakfast, we did not react at all. We were so used to this. With the bread we usually received a mug of ersatz coffee, greyish brown water without any taste.
>
> After breakfast we started off for roll-call. The inhabitants from block after block used to march up to the parade ground, an enormous open

Norwegen nach Auschwitz." Stadt-Verwaltung Ramat Gan, Israel, 1963, pp. 11–13: "Auschwitz, December 1, 1942: *Die Übernahme von -532- Juden aus Norwegen wird hiermit bestätigt. Obergruppenführer Stark.*" See also *Aftenposten* (Oslo), May 2, 1961.

37. *Hefte von Auschwitz*, 1960, Vol. 3, p. 104: "December 1, 1942. RSHA Transport, Juden aus Bergen [sic!] (Norwegen), *Nach der Selection lieferte man 186 Männer als Häftlinge ins Lager ein, sie bekamen die nr. 79064–79249. Die Übrigen wurden vergasst.*"

38. Herman Sachnowitz, *Det angår også deg* (It Also Concerns You), Oslo: Cappelens, 1976, pp. 51–53; *"levende skyteskiver var fristende mål for mange SS-soldater."*

square roughly in the middle of the camp. It was here that the report-writer's lectern was placed on special occasions and it was also here that they placed the whipping block and gallows for floggings and executions.

We others had to keep going from six in the morning to six in the evening. Only then were we allowed to see to our dead and dying comrades. We had to carry them back to the camp on our shoulders and then stand for hours on the parade ground until "stocktaking" was over. If a Kommando of fifty men had marched out, fifty had to come back. Whether they were dead or alive was of no consequence, only the number mattered.

When we marched in, the Kapo's report probably went: "Kabel Kommando 2, Prisoner number 78235 back to camp with fifty prisoners of whom fourteen are dead.'"

Professor Leo Eitinger, a leading Norwegian psychiatrist and a survivor of Auschwitz, testified at the Quisling trial that it was only the Norwegian Jews who, without exception, were deported to the death camps and "that there can be no doubt that Quisling must take the main responsibility."[39] At the trial, the prosecutor noted that, "Quisling was an active participant against Jews and . . . this is the reason why the Jewish question took on a much more dreadful development in Norway than, for example, in Denmark."[40] Testimony by Supreme Court Justice Karsten Meyer from Denmark stated that "what happened in Norway must be attributed to the initiatives by Quisling. One can see that from the way they did not follow those directives, which the Germans followed in other regions[41] such as arresting Jewish women married to "Aryans. The Norwegian action differed from those in other countries. For example, during this period of "Final Solution," transportation to death camps was prepared prior to, and was ready at the time the Jews were arrested. In Norway, however, there was a delay of more than a month from the time of first deportation by ship in November, and up to three months before shipping was obtained for the second large deportation in February 1943. The leading pro-Nazi Norwegian newspa-

39. *Quislingsaken. Samlet rettsreferat*, Oslo: A.S. Bokkommisjon, 1945, p. 131. Testimony by Dr. Leo Eitinger: *"Det var bare de norske jøder som uten unntagelse ble sendt til utryddelsesleiren i Auschwitz, og det kan ikke være tvil om at det er Quisling som bærer ansvaret for dette."*
40. *Quisling*, op. cit., p. 23: ". . . *det er grunnen til at jødesaken avviklet seg på en langt forferdeligere måte her i Norge enn f.eks. i Danmark.*"
41. Ibid., pp. 129–130: ". . . *det, der skete i Norge maa skyldes 'Quisling-Initiativer,' hvilket kan sees af, at man ikke fulgte de Linier Tyskerne fulgte andre steder.*"

per, *Aftenposten* (The Evening News), published an editorial on December 17, 1942, entitled "The Jews and Us." Here the paper refuted all contentions that the persecutions of the Jews had been launched on German initiative.[42]

Paul M. Hayes surmises that Quisling did not want to pit himself against organizations which were able to resist him. Having suffered defeats in moving against civil servants and labor unions; legal and sports organizations; teachers, churches, and student groups, "Quisling moved against the small and defenseless Jewish community."[43] The Quisling *Hird* had attacked Jewish stores by 1940, smashed windows or painted them over with anti-Semitic slogans. Systematic persecution followed, including the removal of Jews from the civil service; deprivation of Jews' licenses to practice their professions; confiscation of the synagogue in Trondheim in April 1941; confiscation of Jewish stores in the fall of 1941; stamping a 'J' on identification papers of Norwegian Jews; reintroduction of Article 2 of the Norwegian Constitution, which prohibited entry of Jews into Norway; and issuance of orders for the arrest of Jews and confiscation of their properties. By November 1942, the legal persecution of Jews by forced registration of "full" and "half" Jews had been completed without pressure from the German occupying forces. The anti-Jewish laws of the various departments were "wholly independent NS initiatives."[44] The groundwork had been systematically completed for the mass arrests and deportations of about half of Norway's Jewish population.

The German reaction may be seen from a report by Admiral Boehm to Gross-Admiral Raeder on December 24, 1942, which stated that most of the Jews residing in Norway had been arrested and deported. Since the Norwegian population had not felt the Jewish problem to be part of their own experience, as Germany had, "this action has created excitement among the Norwegian population. The National Union has lost face in the eyes of the people because the party has been drawn into the implementation of the action."[45]

Quisling's attitude was revealed in a speech he made in Trondheim

---

42. American Legation, Stockholm, *Dispatch No. 1629*, op. cit., p. 6.
43. Paul M. Hayes, *Quisling: The Career and Political Ideas of Vidkun Quisling*, London: David & Charles, Newton Abbot, 1971, p. 288.
44. Kolsrud, op. cit., p. 19: "*Departementenes lovarbeider vedrørende jødespørsmålene var helt selvstendige NS-tiltak.*"
45. Tim Greve, *Bergen i krig*, op. cit., pp. 257–258.

on December 6, 1942, where he commented on the deportations: "A
Jew is not a Norwegian, not a European. He is an Oriental. Jews have
no place in Europe. They are internationally destructive elements. The
Jews create the Jewish problem and cause active anti-Semitism. . . . For
us there can be no compromise."[46]

Still, close analysis[47] raises some questions as to the way the deportation decision was reached, and who initiated the implementation. According to Marthinsen's report of November 27, he received the deportation order from Wagner on November 24 at 8 p.m. Only then did he
become aware that ship transport would be available on November 26.
Apparently he gave his orders immediately in the same evening, because it was stated that the police force of about 300 men was available
November 24–26. The actual organization of the action started the next
morning and had to be completed the following day at noon. As mentioned, Marthinsen later complained that he was given too little time
to prepare the action.

The first question arises is why was there so much haste? On November 25 at 7:15 a.m., Reinhard sent his first telegram to Stettin. In it he
stated that he had already informed the RSHA, which he saw as responsible for the completion of the action, i.e., the organization of the transportation of the Jews from Stettin to Auschwitz. Here the second question arises: Why did Reinhard give notice to the RSHA *after* the action
had been started and why did he *suppose* ("*ich nehme an*") that the necessary "further instructions" would be given from there?

We do not have Reinhard's telegram to the RSHA, but we have the
answer which was given by Eichmann's deputy, *Sturmbannführer* Rolf
Günther on the same day, November 25, at 6 p.m. in a lengthy "most
urgent" telegram (called "Blitz"). As indicated in the answer, Reinhard's
message had also been given by "Blitz," while the one to Stettin had
been an ordinary F.S. *Fernschreiben*. Thus the message to Berlin was
meant to arrive there before the other one reached Stettin. Günther's
telegram starts as follows: "I ask you, in any case, to use the possibility,
suddenly provided by the Navy, for the deportation of the Jews from
Norway. In determining the group of people who have to be evacuated,
I ask precisely to adhere to the following instructions." These instruc-

---

46. *Fritt Folk* (Free People), Oslo, December 7, 1942.
47. I am indebted to Professor Leni Yahil, Haifa University and Yad Yashem, for the
analysis on pp. 128–130.

tions are the ones which the Norwegian Police implemented, including the "new orders" concerning the families of people in mixed marriages. It thus becomes clear why those orders were received only during the night of November 25–26. Further instructions ask for the provision of food "for at least 14 days." Thus the provisioning was not Wagner's initiative. The food certainly was not intended for the deportees, but was meant to create illusions and to provide for additional material gain. It was stated that the deportees would lose their Norwegian citizenship as soon as they left the country. The Norwegian government was to have no claims regarding individual Jews. "The return of any single deported Jew to Norway is out of the question." Here the *third question* has to be asked: How did it happen that the *Sicherheitsdienst* in Norway got the instructions for the implementation of the deportation *after* the action had been started?

In Norway, Eichmann did not have a special representative, as was the case, for example, in Holland, which was also ruled by a *Reichskommissar*. Moreover, at the Wannsee Conference of January 20, 1942, Martin Luther had warned that the Germans would meet obstacles in deportation of the small Jewish populations of Scandinavia and had argued for a postponement. Therefore, Reinhard felt himself entitled to act on his own responsibility and Eichmann, confronted with a *fait accompli*, could only try to direct the action at the last moment. This Günther did in his lengthy telegram whose language, not by accident, is extremely polite. These are not the usual orders given by Eichmann to his subordinates, but are framed more as requests prefaced by "I ask" ("Ich bitte"). In addition, Eichmann had no connection with the Navy. Transportation by train over neutral Sweden and even through occupied Denmark was considered an impossibility. Deportation would not have been feasible without a ship, which only could have been provided by the Navy. It seems that Reinhard succeeded in obtaining the S.S. *Donau* on very short notice, and this explains the haste by which the action had to be performed. It may be assumed that Eichmann and Günther were rather pleased by this "suddenly" achieved and unexpected possibility of including the Norwegian Jews in the "Final Solution." They cooperated immediately and managed to hurriedly provide for the special train from Stettin to Auschwitz via Berlin. In addition, Günther enlightened Reinhard and the SP and SD in Norway concerning the procedures to be implemented, including restrictions, security, confiscation, and camouflage.

There remain several questions we cannot answer through the use of available documentation. We do not know if there had been any contact between the SD in Norway and Eichmann before November 1942, and if Berlin was informed about the arrests of October 1942. We also do not have any indications what Quisling's part was in the initiative for the deportation in November. Only the availability of additional source material may give us the answers to these questions. Still, there can be no doubt about Quisling's striving for the "solution" of the Jewish question in Norway, and about the collaboration between him and the German authorities to that end. We are certainly knowledgeable about the role of the Norwegian police. A noted Norwegian historian, Dr. H.O. Christophersen, has commented:[48]

> What was for us a most grotesque event — disregarding the Jews' own tragic fate — was that it was the *Norwegian* and not the German police that implemented the action. It is difficult to understand that the national elements within our so-called State Police did not refuse to participate out of hand. They could not be in doubt that they transferred our Jewish countrymen to an inhuman fate.

The persecutions of the Jews did not end with the November 26 deportation. During the next weeks, the search continued for Jews at liberty, including hospitals which were obligated to submit lists of Jewish patients to Nazi authorities. In a letter of December 3, 1942, from SS *Unterstürmführer* Boehm to Police Inspector Dürbeck, the former demanded a list of names of Jews interned at Bredtvedt and Berg concentration camps. Since another deportation might soon be possible, Dürbeck was asked to speed up compilations of the lists. On January 15, 1943, the German Security Police sent orders to the Norwegian police that all full Jews, including those married to Aryans, should be arrested. As of January 14, 1943, 143 additional Jews had been readied for deportation. Of these, 134 were deported aboard the S.S. *Gotenland*,[49] the

48. H.O. Christophersen, "*Aksjonen mot jødene. Okkupasjonens tyngste slag*" (The Action Against the Jews. The Heaviest Blow during the Occupation), *Aftenposten*, evening edition, October 23, 1967.

49. Frøberg and Ebeling, *Report*, October 4, 1946, pp. 4–5: "*Evakuering av jøder med D/S Gotland [sic!] den 24.2.43*" (Evacuation of Jews aboard D/S *Gotland*, February 24, 1943): "*Den 15.1.43 ble det fra det tyske sikkerhetspoliti sendt ut ordre om at alle heljøder også de som er gift med arier, skal pågripes og sikres. . . . Den 14.1.43 satt i allt arrestert 143 jøder på Bredtveit klar til avsendelse. Av disse ble sendt 134 personer med D/S Gotland [sic!] den 24.2.43.*"

others in two groups aboard the S.S. *Monte Rosa*, 21 prisoners on November 20, 1942 and 27 prisoners on November 26.[50] The second largest deportation took place in February 1943.

Dr. Eitinger testified that Quisling had stated during his 1945 trial that he did not know about the Jewish persecutions until after the first group had been deported aboard the S.S. *Donau* on November 26, 1942, and that he had wanted to help the Jews:[51]

> We were there at Bredtvedt from the day *Donau* left until the end of February. . . . The Nazi "Minister of Justice" came to Bredtvedt to look at us, and Skancke [State Councillor of Church and Education] was also there and spoke to an old man from Trondheim, Mendelsohn, who had been brutally treated at Falstad. But nothing was done to prevent us from being deported to Germany.

The deportation took place on February 25, 1942 aboard the S.S. *Gotenland*. There were 158 Jews, most of them from northern Norway and members of the Trondheim congregation.[52] These Jews had arrived in Oslo nine hours too late to be brought on board the S.S. *Donau* the previous November 26. They had all been brought to the concentration camp at Bredtvedt, where they were incarcerated and brutally treated for three months under the supervision of the Norwegian *hirdmenn*.

One of the survivors from Trondheim, Assor Hirsch, wrote a report of his experiences, which was presented in 1947 during the Wagner trial:[53]

> We were deported on February 24, 1943 on the ship *Gotenland* from

50. Leiba Wolfberg, *"Mannen som spilte for livet"* (The Man Who Played for his Life), Interview, Norwegian Broadcasting, Oslo, February 9, 1965, Tape No. 51500/1, and November 25, 1966, Tape No. 50966. Wolfberg worked as violinist in Birkenau. As musician he received somewhat better clothing and food, but was not exempted from selection to the gas chambers.

51. *Quisling*, op. cit., p. 159: *"Jeg leste i avisene at Quisling hadde uttalt seg at han ikke visste om jødeforfølgelsene før de var blitt sendt av gårde med 'Donau,' og at han gjerne ville ha hjulpet dem. 'Donau' ble sendt i slutten av november og vi var fra den dag 'Donau' gikk helt til slutten av februar anbrakt på Bredtveit. . . . Den nazistiske justisminister var på Bredtveit og så på oss, og Skancke var der og snakket med en gammel mann fra Trondheim, Mendelsohn, som var blitt slått forferdelig på Falstad, men det ble ikke gjort noe for at vi skulle reise til Tyskland."*

52. Telex from Oslo Gestapo by SS-*Hauptsturmbannführer* Wagner, February 26, 1943, regarding transportation from Oslo of 158 Jews, 74 men, and 84 women and children, on board the troop ship S/S Gotenland. Signature, Wagner.

53. Assor Hirsch, *Wagner*, op. cit., p. 56: *"Ad forklaring angående sak mot gestapist Wagner"* (Regarding declaration concerning the case against the Gestapo person, Wagner). See *Wagner*, R.07701, 1947.

Oslo. . . . We were taken by buses to the harbor, guarded by Norwegian State Police and civilian Norwegians, who behaved brutally and impudently both against the aged, and the women and children. At the harbor we were received by German guards. On board, women and men were separated, men kept in the back cargo hold, the women and children in the front. Some of us were ordered to carry on board provisions which had probably been supplied by the Red Cross. It was a sizable amount of good food, intended for us. However, we received almost none of it. When we arrived at Stettin, I was among those who brought the provisions ashore and into the railroad cars. I cannot say what happened to the provisions, but we did not benefit from them. One day, as I was shining shoes for the guards, I started talking to some of them. I asked where we were going and how it was there. The answer was *"Nicht gut."* . . . The transportation from Stettin to Auschwitz via Berlin in locked freight cars was as inhuman as one can imagine.

In a letter of May 12, 1947 to Marcus Levin of Oslo, Dr. Leo Eitinger gave further details about the deportation:[54]

While the ship was still in the harbor at Oslo, an elderly lady [Mrs. Klein from Trondheim] fell ill. As I had been a doctor for my fellow prisoners at Bredtvedt, I was called upon and I went to the transport leader. . . . I asked what our destination would be. He said it was strictly forbidden to mention the place of destination, but he could state that we would come to a camp where the young and strong would obtain work. . . . If you behaved properly you would receive good positions. When I asked what would happen to the old, the weak and the small children, he said "You will see that in time." Another fellow prisoner [Gunst] asked whether it was certain that he would meet his wife and children. He could confirm that we would come to the same place where the first deportation had been sent. . . . Before the ship reached Germany, a razzia was undertaken. All flashlights were confiscated . . . as well as all documents, especially identity cards, border permits and travel passes, especially the latter. It was threatened that if any document was found upon the prisoners, he would be shot on the spot. . . . A young girl who had been a teacher for the children at Bredtvedt asked if she could have permission to sing with the children. "Yes," was the answer. "Just sing as long as you are alive." At that time we thought such statements were talk only, but after I had been to Auschwitz . . . I remembered these statements and it has become clear to me that these officers knew exactly what would happen to us.

---

54. *Wagner*, Case 11210, R.I. 05634/1947: *"Reservelæge Leo Eitinger, Rønvik Sykehus, Bodø."* Letter of May 12, 1946 to Marcus Levin, Waldemar Thranesgt, Oslo.

The 158 Norwegian Jews, 68 men and 90 women and children, arrived at Stettin on February 27, 1943. This was confirmed by transfer documents signed by SS *Untersturmführer* Grossmann, who delivered the Jews to the State Police in Stettin.[55] Upon receipt of an order from Adolf Eichmann in a telex of February 25, 1943, the 158 Norwegian Jews were sent to Berlin from Stettin to join a larger group of Jews destined for Auschwitz,[56] where they arrived on March 3, 1943.

Dr. Leo Eitinger reported on June 15, 1946:[57]

> Our Norwegian transport, which consisted of 186 persons of both sexes ranging from half-a-year to 85, was sent from Berlin, March 2, 1943, together with a large German transport. We were sent in cattle cars, stowed together fifty persons in each car with no consideration given to old or sick people. We arrived in Auschwitz late at night after a 36-hour journey. The station was surrounded by SS men carrying weapons.

About 130 of the group of 158, mainly from the districts of Nordland, Trøndelag, Møre, and Romsdal were sent to the gas chambers immediately upon arrival. Those fit to work received numbers 1048090–1055424. One hundred forty-five women from the total group received numbers 36935–37079 and were sent to camp Buna-Monowitz after having been tattooed on the left forearm. One of the prisoners, Julius Paltiel from Trondheim, received No. 1055362. "The others were gassed to death."[58] Among them was a baby boy, 14 months old, Harry Shotland from Harstad (b. Aug 20, 1940). The oldest was Mendel Beck-

---

55. Transfer Document verifying arrival at Stettin of 158 Jews (68 men and 90 women and children) from Norway on February 27, 1943, with SS *Untersturmführer* Grossmann as the one who handed over the prisoners (*Übergebender*). Yad Vashem Archives. Signed by Grossmann as "Deliverer" and Schapols as "Receiver."

56. Telex from Adolf Eichmann dated February 25, 1943, from Berlin to Gestapo in Stettin asking that the 158 Norwegian Jews be transported from Stettin to Berlin where they would join a larger group of Jews destined for Auschwitz. Signed, Eichmann.

57. "Rettslige Forklaringer" (Legal Depositions), L. Eitinger, *Wagner*, op. cit., p. 59: "*Protokoll over mine opplevelser i Auschwitz. Vår norske transport som bestod av 186 mennesker av begge kjønn i aldre fra ½ år til 85 år ble sendt fra Berlin 2. mars 1943 til Auschwitz sammen med en stor tysk fangetransport. Vi ble sendt i kuvogner stuet sammen i en vogn uten hensyn til gamle eller syke. Vi kom til Auschwitz etter 1½ døgns reise sent om kvelden. Stasjonen var omgitt av bevebnede SS menn.*" *Rettsbok for Salten forhørsrett*, Document 18, June 25, 1946, Bodø: "*Vitnet la frem en skriftlig beretning over sine opplevelser i fangeleiren Auschwitz, datert 15. juni 1946.*"

58. Julius Paltiel, "*Seks ganger på dødens terskel*" (Six times on the threshold of death), in Hans Melien, ed., *De kjempet for var frihet* (They fought for our freedom), Oslo: Aschehoug, 1979, p. 57: "*Die übringen wurden vergast.*"

er, 80 years old (b. October 15, 1862).[59] Out of this group of 158 deported Jews only six returned alive to Norway.[60]

A publication for the leaders of the Norwegian Nazi party, *Hirdspeilet*, (The Mirror of the Hird) wrote in its monthly summary for October 1942, in regard to the mass arrests of Jews, that one of the old aims had been realized. "The arch-enemy, the Jews, had been deprived of the opportunity to remain in Norway. Their fortunes had been confiscated "to the great chagrin of our opponents. In the end, however, it was *our money* that these people had at their disposal and now it has come to an end."[61] The next issue, covering major events from November 1942, commented on the Jewish deportation by stating that the cleaning up of the Norwegian Jewish world had progressed satisfactorily:[62]

> All male Jews have been sent some time ago to a faraway place at a temporary destination. The females and their offspring (*barnlige avleggere*) have these days been sent the same way. At the same time all non-desirable Jewish enterprises have been discontinued. The Jewish possessions are being confiscated in stages. Thus the Ministry of Interior published on November 10 a list of Jews whose properties had been confiscated.

An assessment of the crucial role played by the Norwegian Nazi party

---

59. *Våre falne norske jøder* (Our fallen Norwegian Jews), *Det Mosaiske Trossamfund* (The Mosaic Religious Society, Mimeographed), Oslo, n.d., pp. 2, 36, in Vad Vashem Archives B/28-1.

60. Jahn Otto Johansen, *Det hendte også her* (It Happened Also Here). Oslo: J.W. Cappelens Forlag, 1984, p. 69.

61. "Kringsjå — *Innenrikspolitisk månedsoversikt, oktober måned 1942,*" in *Hirdspeilet. Arbeidsplan for Hirdførere*, Vol. 1, No. 1, November 30, 1942, p. 47: "Et av Hirdens gamle mål ble realisert i denne måned, idet den store argefienden jøden no endelig er blitt fratatt myndigheten til fortsatt opphold i Norge. Deres formue er blitt beslaglagt til stor be og ynk for våre motstandere. Til syvende og sist var det imidlertid våre penger menneskene formidlet, og no er det altså slutt for godt."

62. Ibid., No. 2, December 31, 1942, "Kringsjå — *Innenrikspolitisk månedsoversikt, november måned 1942,*" p. 46: "Opprenskingen i den norske jødeverden skrider nå sikkert framover. Alle mannlige jøder er forlengst på god veg til sitt fjerne, og foreløpige bestemmelsessted. De kvinnelige og barnlige avleggere går i disse dager samme veg. Samtidig avvikles all jødeforetagender som ikke anses ønskelige i fortsatt drift. De jødiske formuer inndras videre etter hvert. Således bekjentgjorde Innenriksdepartementet den 10. ds. en liste over jøder hvis formuer er inddratt."

was made by a resistance fighter and survivor of Auschwitz, Herman
Steinfeldt of Bergen:[63]

> I cannot stress too strongly the importance of the Norwegian *collabora-*
> *tors*, 40-50,000 N.S. members, a direct and most important source of in-
> formation for the Gestapo. . . . The somber chapter in this history of the
> Jews in Norway could have been avoided. It is difficult to understand why
> historians have not acknowledged the *enormous* role of the *local N.S.*
> members. . . . Without the assistance of these . . . traitors, the Gestapo
> could not have succeeded as they did. . . . Many of these collaborators go
> around today, employed in the civil service — right here in Bergen.

---

63. Gerd Gordon, op. cit., p. 485.

XI.

In Retrospect

1. What Was Known about Hitler's "Final Solution"?

The German anti-Nazi movement, through such prominent individuals as Theodor Stelzer, Carl Friedrich Goerdler, and Helmuth James von Moltke, had given forewarnings to the Norwegian Resistance Movement about forthcoming arrests or round-ups of resistance groups.

As to the Jewish arrests and deportations, Count von Moltke, transmitted the first information in September 1942, but he knew "neither the precise plan, nor a definite time. He did not know at that time what 'die Endlösung' really meant."[1]

The official correspondence between the Norwegian Government-in-Exile and the Home Front does not cover the many anti-Semitic actions in Norway during the occupation, or make any mention of policies to be followed to rescue Jews or assist those in hiding. Were there any such policies? When and how much did the Government-in-Exile know about the destruction of Jews? Was there any cooperation between the Resistance Movement, the Home Front, and the attempted rescues of Jews condemned to death solely because they were Jews?

The official publication, *Regjeringen og Hjemmefronten under Krigen* (The Government and Home Front During the War), throws no light on these issues and mentions Jewish persecutions in only two brief documents. One is a letter of December 2, 1942, from the Home Front to the Governmet-in-Exile in London, stating:[2]

---

1. Brodersen, *Mellom Frontene*, p. 68: "... *Moltke under sitt annet besøk i Oslo i september 1942 advarte oss om at en aksjon ville komme, men han visste intet om de presise planer eller om noe bestemt tidspunkt. Han var den gang ennå ikke klar over hva 'die Endlösung' i virkeligheten gikk ut på.*"

2. *Regjeringen og Hjemmefronten under krigen. Aktsykker utgitt av Stortinget* (The Government and the Home Front during the War. Documents published by the Storting)

The all overshadowing event, has, of course, been the Jewish pogroms. People have little by little become careful about talking loudly in the streets, but in these days this rule has been broken. All of this has been so revolting that people have not been able to resist expressing their feelings. It looks so completely meaningless."

The other document, dated Oslo, June 28, 1944, is also from the Home Front to the Government-in-Exile:[3]

> We may remind you about the brilliant work done by the transport organizations when it was important, upon the shortest possible notice, to get the Jews out, and later the students.

One of the rescue actions took place in December, 1942, when about 40 Jews were escorted to Sweden by two border pilots, Ole Burås and Torkel Fornes. Burås was shot at Kroksund north of the lake of Rödeness, but Fornes escaped, and continued his dangerous work until the end of the war.[4]

When did the Norwegian Government-in-Exile learn about the Holocaust? The leaders of the allied governments had detailed information about the Holocaust by the summer of 1942. The London *Daily Telegraph* reported in June, 1942, that 700,000 Jews had been gassed. Walter Laqueur has asserted that by December 1942, "every European government had heard the news, if not necessarily most of its citizens."[5] What did the Norwegian government do with this informaion? Did the civil or military resistance movement in Norway disseminate informa-

Oslo: Aschehoug & Co., 1948, p. 139. Some of the Home Front's leaders were: Paal Berg, Arvid Brodersen, Gunnar Jahn, Olaf Gjerløv, Hans Halvorsen, Ferdinand Schjelderup, Didrik Arup Seip, Jens Christian Hauge, Einar Gerhardsen, Paul Hartmann, Tor Skjønsberg, Eivind Berggrav. For a more complete presentation, see Rolf Kluge, *Hjemmefrontledelsen tar form. Kretsen dannes sommeren 1941* (The Leadership of the Home Front takes form. The Circle is formed summer 1941) Oslo-Bergen-Tromsø: Universitetsforlaget, 1970, 96 pp.

3. Ibid., pp. 422–423: "Bull til Trygve Lie, dat. Stockholm 8. juli 1944 (Brev fra Hjemmefronten dat. Oslo 28 juni 1944) Vedlegg: Ad Frihetsrådet; p. 423: "Vi kan minne om det strålende arbeid som ble gjort av transportorganisasjonene da det gjaldt på kortest mulig varsel å få ut jødene og senere studentene ..." The official Norwegian representative in Stockholm was Minister (Sendemann) Jens Bull. Trygve Lie was Norway's Minister of Foreign Affairs of the Government-in-Exile, London.

4. Arild Haaland, "Splittelse og Samhold," (Division and Cohesion) in *Norges Kulturhistorie* (Cultural History of Norway), Vol. 6, Oslo: H. Aschehoug & Co., 1980, p. 312. See also, Ulstein, op. cit., v. III, p. 415.

5. Walter Laqueur, *The Terrible Secret. Suppression of the Truth About Hitler's "Final Solution"*," Boston: Little, Brown and Co., 1980, p. 6.

tion about Jewish extermination through the underground press? Why
were only a relatively few notices about Jewish persecutions published
in the free press? In September 1942, a report appeared on the general
European Jewish situation in the illegal paper, *Norsk Ungdom* (Norwegian Youth), followed by a half-dozen brief notices from October 26 to
November 26 in *Norwegian News*, London *(Norske Nyheter)*, *Fri
Fagbevegelse* (Free Trade Unions), *For Konge og Fedreland* (For King
and Fatherland), and *Friheten* (Freedom).[6] In September 1942, *Norsk
Ungdom* stated that "at this time, 700,000 Jews had been killed through
wholesale murder.[7] A widely-read illegal paper, edited by Eyvind John-
son, published in Sweden but distributed in Norway, *Håndslag. Fakta
og Orientering for Nordmenn* (Handshakes. Facts and Orientation for
Norwegians), gave on December 3, 1942, under the heading
"Jødeforfølgelsene" (Persecutions of the Jews)[8] a somewhat misleading
information:

> The Jews in Oslo were, at first, taken to Bredtvedt, and from there a few
> days later to the new prison camp at Sem, near Tønsberg, which shall only
> be a temporary place of residence. Later on, all will be sent for forced la-
> bor, either to Northern Norway or to Poland.

The illegal newspaper *Fritt Land* (Free Land) stated that the Germans
occupied Lvov on June 29, 1941, where 160,000 Jews lived. During the
fall of 1943, not one was left alive. "They were all dead, executed, killed
or succumbed to epidemics. Every day ten or a hundred were executed,
but larger 'actions' also took place when tens of thousands of Jews were
killed in the course of a few days."[9]

London Radio, another of the approximately 250 illegal news releases

---

6. Kaare Haukaas, *Faktaregister for Okkupasjonen*, Oslo, 1947, pp. 32–33 (mimeo).
7. Terje Halvorsen, *"Holocaust og de illegale avisene,"* *Dagbladet*, Oslo, July 18, 1977.
He quotes from the illegal paper *Hjemmefronten* (The Home Front) which, in January
1944, stated that, "No one knows how many Jews have been murdered by the Hitler regime. The guess varies from 2.5 to 4 millions." *(Gjetninger varierer mellom 2.5 til 4
millioner.)*
8. *Håndslag* (Handshakes, Facts and Orientations for Norwegians), No. 14, December
3, 1942, p. 23: *"I Oslo ble jødene først ført till Bredtvedt, og herfra ble de et par dager
senere sendt til den nye fangeleiren i Sem ved Tønsberg. Her samles nå jøder fra hele
landet. Det er meningen at leiren i Sem bare skal være et foreløbig oppholdsted. Senere
skal alle videre på tvangsarbeid, enten i Nord-Norge eller i Polen."*
9. *Fritt land*, No. 43, Vol. 1, June 21, 1944, as cited in *"Noen visste om Holocaust!"*
(Some one knew about the Holocaust!) by Gunnar Jermann, *Dagbladet*, Oslo, October
7, 1979.

during the German occupations,[10] gave the following account on December 4, 1942, under the heading "The Fate of the Jews in Occupied Countries":[11]

> The constantly increasing strong measures against the Jews in Norway is part of the systematic policy of extermination which the Third Reich has, over a long period of time, perpetrated against Europe's Jewish population. The English sector of the World Jewish Congress reported on August 6, this year (1942), that out of the seven million Jews living in occupied countries, one million have already lost their lives.

This report gave a detailed description of the fate of the Jewish population in Poland:

> In the concentration camp Oswiecim (Auschwitz) in Southern Poland, where Poles and Jews are incarcerated together, 50 persons die every day. There is really no reason to disbelieve that the total number of Jewish victims now adds up to 700,000.

However, a more correct figure of the Jews murdered by the end of 1942 was four million, according to Dr. Richard Korherr's report to Heinrich Himmler of March 23, 1943, "The Final Solution" of the European Jewish Question."[12]

Although the destruction of European Jewry was to be kept absolutely secret, the systematic extermination of Jews had become known both in Europe and the United States by the fall of 1942. Complete ignorance about the massacres could not be claimed by the Allied governments.[13] The first report about the "Final Solution" was published in the *London Times* on April 2, 1942, referring specifically to the massacre of Dutch Jews in Mauthausen. The London *Daily Telegraph* reported on June 25 and 30, 1942 that "poison gas was used to kill Jews in Chelmno, etc."[14] This was six months before the massacres were condemned in a

---

10. *Tor Dagre, Nytt fra Norge,* (News from Norway) Oslo, November 23, 1981: "20,000 Norwegians worked in 250 illegal newspapers during the war." (*20,000 nordmenn arbeidet med krigstidens 250 illegale aviser*).

11. *London Radio,* December 4, 1942, p. 1.

12. Yitchak Arad, Yisrael Gutman, Abraham Margaliot, eds., *Documents on the Holocaust. Selected sources on the Destruction of the Jews of Germany and Austria, Poland and the Soviet Union,* Jerusalem: Yad Vashem, 1981, pp. 332–334: "SS Statistics on the 'Final Solution' of the Jewish Question, March 23, 1943," prepared by Richard Korherr, head of the Statistics Department in Himmler's office.

13. Walter Laqueur, *The Terrible Secret,* op. cit. p. 6.

14. Walter Laqueur, *The First News of the Holocaust,* The Leo Baeck Memorial Lec-

joint statement from London by Allied governments, including Norway
on December 17, 1942. The news had emanated from Poland, neutral
countries such as Sweden or Switzerland, from the International Red
Cross, or from the World Jewish Congress in Geneva.[15] The various intelligence services of the Allied Forces, including Norway, had undoubt-
edly received news about the systematic killing of Jews. It was spread
by the BBC all over Europe by the early summer of 1942, but either
was not believed or suppressed as *"greuel"* (atrocity) propaganda," and
therefore not to be believed. The Vatican and the International Red
Cross as well as the World Jewish Congress through Dr. Gerhardt
Riegner in Geneva were all well informed about the Jewish catastrophe,
and this information was transmitted to the Allied countries. The first
public disclosure, however, was made by the noted Nobel Prize winner
Thomas Mann over the BBC in December 1941 and January 1942. By May
1942, the "Bund," the Jewish Socialist Party of Poland, had transmitted
detailed reports to its Government-in-Exile in London from where the reports were broadcast over BBC on June 2 and 26, 1942. The Allies under-
took no effective measures to save the Jews of Europe, employing the
empty slogan: "Rescue through Victory." At the end of World War II, very
few Jews were left to be rescued. The Jews had been abandoned.

2. Reactions and Protests against Jewish Persecutions in Norway

Within Norway, public opinion had been aroused by the brutal treatment, arrests, and deportation of Jews. A nationwide sense of agony was
best articulated by the heads of the Norwegian Lutheran Church.[16]
Since the aim of the German occupation forces was to consistently nazify
the Norwegian way of life, the Norwegian people fought not only on a
military front but also on cultural and religious fronts.

Important in this respect was the non-violent resistance or
"holdningskamp," i.e. opposing nazification "through a policy of shunning and the use of *paroles* or directives."[17] During the occupation, the

ture No. 23, New York: Leo Baeck Institute, 1979, pp. 26–29. See also G. P. Harbitz, "Hva
man visste om Holocaust," (What one knew about Holocaust) *Morgenbladet*, Oslo, August
1, 1979.

15. Laquuer, *The First News*, op. cit., pp. 16–17.

16. Einar Molland, "Kirkens Kamp," in Sverre Steen, op. cit., Vol. III, p. 36.

17. Gerd Gordon, op. cit., p. VI: *"Holdningskamp:* A struggle for a right attitude fo-
cused against Nazification; a policy of shunning and use of *paroles* or directives to guide
the people's resistance actions."

struggle of the Norwegian Church concentrated mainly on moral values: justice, humanity, and freedom of conscience. The Church became a focal organization in guiding the Norwegian Resistance Movement. The role of the Church became crucial; it was to protect the Christian values which the Nazis aimed at destroying. The Nazis had proved to be experts at transforming their own society and made a determined effort to do the same in Norway. They knew exactly what their aim was and how to achieve it: by controlling all institutions through terrorism and by nazifying the population through schools, youth and trade organizations, and the churches. Little had the Quisling party leaders or the Nazi occupying power realized that Norwegian clergymen would insist on speaking their own minds. Time and again we find that the clergy expressed opinions which were completely contrary to Nazi edicts. The views of the Church were instantaneously approved by the majority of the Norwegian population. Throughout the occupation, it was the pulpit that became the most commonly utilized means of communication in opposing Nazism. On some occasions, the Church was the main institution protesting against brutalities, such as the deportation of the Norwegian Jews in the fall of 1942. The leaders of the Church, who had resigned from their offices, were fighting a crucial battle against nazification. The seven bishops Eivind Berggrav, Andreas Fleischer, Henrik Hille, Wollert Krohn-Hansen, James Maroni, Gabriel Skagestad and Johan Støren, who had resigned on Feb. 24, 1942, strongly protested the Jewish persecutions. In a letter of November 10, 1942, to Minister-President Quisling, the bishops stated that Jews had had a legal right for 91 years to reside and earn a livelihood in Norway, but now they were being deprived of their properties without warning.[18] Furthermore, they were being punished as the worst criminals, wholly and solely because they were Jews. The bishops pointed out that the Minister-President Quisling had on various occasions emphasized that his party would protect the basic Christian values, and one of them was now being endangered: the Christian commandment to "love thy neighbor," the most elementary legal right for any human being. "When we now appeal to you, Mr. Minister-President, it is not to defend whatever wrongs the Jews may have committed. If they have committed crimes, they shall

18. *Norsk Tidend*, London (published by the Information Office, Royal Norwegian Government), November 28, 1942, as printed in Johan M. Snoek, *The Grey Book*, The Hague: Van Gorcum & Co., pp. 116–118.

be tried, judged, and punished according to Norwegian law just as all
other citizens. But those who have committed no crime shall enjoy the
protection of our country's justice."

The letter went on to say that this appeal was caused by the deepest
dictates of conscience, because silence in view of this legalized injustice
against Jews would make the Church co-guilty in this injustice:[19]

"The Church has God's call and full authority to proclaim God's law
and God's Gospel. Therefore, it cannot remain silent when God's com-
mandments are being trampled underfoot. And now it is one of Christianity's basic values which is being violated; the commandment of God
which is fundamental to all society. . . . Stop the persecution of Jews and
stop the race hatred which, through the press, is being spread in our
land."

The bishops emphasized in closing that this appeal had nothing to do
with politics. Before worldly authorities the Church maintained that
obedience in temporal matters must follow God's word.

This protest was courageous, but prior to the declaration, little had
been done by the Church to stem the rising tide of nazification and anti-
Semitism in Norway. During the fall of 1940, the leadership of the
Church acquiesced to a German demand to omit mention of Norway's
King in the Church Prayer (Kirkebønnen).[20] When the National Union
Party in *Fritt Folk* of March 9, 1942, accused the Jews and other ethnic
groups of "poisoning the soul of the Norwegian people," the Church had
been silent.[21]

The Church's November protest was supported by many respected
theologians, nineteen church organizations, and six non-state church religious societies. A total of over sixty signatures from all sections of Norway's Protestant communities endorsed the protest. On two consecutive
Sundays, November 15 and 22, 1942, prayers were said for the Jews from

---

19. Samuel Abrahamsen, "The Relationship of Church and State during the German
Occupation of Norway, 1940–1945," in *Holocaust Studies Annual*, Vol. II, *The Churches'
Response to the Holocaust*, The Penkevill Publishing Company, Greenwood, Florida,
1986, p. 16.

20. *Norges Kulturhistorie*, Oslo: H. Aschehoug & Co., 1980, Vol. 6, p. 310.

21. Torleiv Austad, "Fra statskirke til selvadministrert folkekirke. Den norske kirken
under krigen" (From State Church to Self-Administered Folk Church. The Norwegian
Church during the War), in Stein Ugelvik Larsen and Ingun Montgomery, eds., *Kirken,
Krisen og Krigen* (The Church, Crisis and War), Oslo-Bergen-Tromsø: Universitetsforlaget, 1982, p. 346.

the pulpits and in most cases the text of the protest letter was read. The pulpits of the Protestant churches had become a most effective means of anti-Nazi communication during the occupation.

The Catholoic Church, however, did not participate in the official protest against the Jewish persecutions. Bishop Jacob Mangers, who was in charge of the Catholic Church in Norway during the occupation, had on November 10, 1942 sent a letter to *Innenriksdepartementet*[22] (the Norwegian Ministry of the Interior) pleading that Jews who had been baptized and become members of the Catholic Church should be exempted from Quisling's Jewish law of October 26, 1942. The Bishop asked especially that this favor should be extended to Mr. Hans Huszar of Bergen because "this young man had become a Catholic some years ago, and had always shown himself as a real Norwegian. He has completed his military and neutrality services, and has also proven his un-Jewish mentality by assuming the debt of his deceased father, although he could have easily gotten rid of the debt by declaring bankruptcy. He supports his mother who is now alone, and he is without property." Bishope Mangers also pleaded exemptions for other baptized Jews: Dr. Ernst Adler, who had arrived from Vienna in 1939 and "was already then a Catholic. He is a good Christian, completely unpolitical, and he has devoted himself completely to literature and philosophy." As to the family of Samuel B. Jaffe of Maridalsveien 46, Oslo, "the husband is not Catholic, but his wife and daughter are. We ask that these two must, at any rate, retain that part of the property that is rightly theirs so that they shall not become homeless."[23] Adolf Neumann, Briskebyveien 2, Oslo, had become a Catholic some years ago. As to the family Neubauer, Strømsborgveien 25, Bygdø, the husband, mother, and two children had become members of the Catholic Church in 1939. Bishop Mangers concluded the letter by expressing his confidence that the Department of the Interior would comply with his request since other countries, especially Slovakia, had not included baptized Jews in the general laws for Jews.

On the same day, November 10, 1942, that Bishop Mangers had mailed the letter to the Department of the Interior, he was approached by Professor Ole Hallesby, chairman of the Temporary Church Leadership *(Den Midlertidige Kirkeledelsen)* to sign a church protest against

---

22. Letter of November 10, 1942, from Bishop Jacob Mangers, *Det Apostoliske Vikariat* to the Ministry of Interior, Oslo. Hamar Bishopric Archives, Hamar.
23. Ibid., p. 1.

the Jewish persecutions in Norway. Bishop Mangers declined. In a letter to Professor Hallesby dated November 10, 1942, Bishop Mangers explained in detail why he could not sign the protest:[24]

> Since I have sent this morning a request to the Department of the Interior and asked that the baptized Jews must be liberated, I find, after exacting deliberations, not to send a new request before an answer has been received to the first. A new request on my part will undoubtedly cause the first one to not be considered and as such may harm the Christians of Jewish ancestry. As soon as I have received an answer, I shall see whether I can send a new request. It would undoubtedly look strange now if the authorities received two from me dated the same day. I hope that Herr Professor will understand this, and will not construe this as if I would keep myself completely outside this important cause.

Bishop Manger's request to the Department of the Interior for release of baptized Jews remained "unanswered and without any result."[25]

While the protests and prayers of the Norwegian Lutheran Church did not stop the deportation of the Jews, the vigorous protest made a deep impression in Norway and abroad. The fight of the Lutheran Church to resist nazification had become identical with the fight for national freedom in Norway. The Church struggled, not on the periphery, but in the center of the battle for the nation's soul. The majority of the population realized, as as expressed by Ferdinand Schjelderup, a leading member of the Home Front, that resistance would pay off "cost what it may — to the bitter end!"[26]

The Germans tried to minimize the effectiveness of the protest. For example, in the daily reports of December, 1942, it was mentioned that the Norwegian churches had pleaded for the Norwegian Jews, but "the radical solution of the Jewish question will be forgotten by the egoistic Norwegians."[27] The Quisling "Bishop" in Bergen, G'eorg Falch Hansen,

24. Letter of November 10, 1942, from Bishop Mangers to Professor Hallesby, Archives, Hamar Bishopric, Hamar: ". . . jeg finner etter nøyere overveielse ikke å kunne sende noen ny henstilling før det er kommet svar på den første. En ny henstilling fra min side vilde uten tvil bevirke at den første ikke blir tatt hensyn til og slik bli til skade de kristne av jødisk herkomst." See also Gottlieb W. Rieber-Mohn, "Vi var med. Glimt fra den katolske kirke under okkupasjonen" (We participated. Glimpses from the Catholic Church During the Occupation), St. Olav, No. 57, 1945, p. 94.

25. Personal communication to the author from Pastor Johs. J. Duin, Hamar Bishopric, February 22, 1982, p. 2.

26. Ferdinand Schjelderup, På Bred Front (On a Wide Front), Oslo: Grøndahl & Søns Forlag, 1947, p. 301.

showed his reaction against Jews by declaring that "Jews are pest bacilli on the body of society."[28]

The reactions in Sweden to the deportation of Norway's Jews were strong. The Swedish bishops quoted the protest of Norway's bishops and added their own comments. The noted theologian Natanael Beskow stated on the occasion of a large protest meeting in Stockholm:[29]

> A ship that left Oslo harbor had a freight of anguish on board. We can not imagine how much these human beings, men, women and children, are suffering. . . . We can not call them back. They go to their death or to slavery. . . . If we can do nothing else we can try to be the voice of the condemned. . . . let them through us call forth their anguish and accusations. . . .

Domprost Olle Nystedt stated on Sunday, November 22, 1942, at the Gothenburg Cathedral, that "the churches in Sweden cannot remain silent when such things happen on our borders. If we are silent the stones will cry out. We are shaken to our innermost, thinking of the suffering of the unfortunates. This is a breaking of God's law and a violation of the basic values of our civilization,"[30] and appealed to the Swedish government to increase all efforts to rescue Norway's Jews.

The Swedish press was almost unanimous in condemning the brutal treatment of Norway's Jews. Ture Nerman, editor of *Trots Allt* (In Spite of Everything), wrote that "the bestialities which Nazism commits in Norway are nothing new, but it is shocking that it is happening so close by. We protest against the treatment of Norway's Jews."[31] In addition, the Swedish women's organizations published a protest expressing their

27. *Anlage 120 zum Tätigkeitbericht December 1942 Abt Ic Niederschrift über die Ic-Besprechung beim AOK Norwegen in der Zeit vom 8.–11.12 1942: 1. Tag 8.12.1942:* "3. *Einzelnes. Die Gesamtkirche Norwegens hat für die Juden Interpelliert, als bekannt wird, dass die Juden zum Osten transportiert wurden. Die radikale Lösung der Judenfrage wird jedoch der egoistische Norweger vergessen."* ·
28. Willy Brandt, *Krigen i Norge,* op. cit. II, p. 137. *"Quisling-biskopen Falch Hansen i Bergen. . . . konkluderte med at 'jødene er pestbasiller på samfunnslegemet.'"*
29. Protest Meeting, Stockholm, December 2, 1942, Yad Vashem Archives, 0/54/38: *"Ett skepp löpte ut från Oslo hamn med en last av kval ombord. Jag tror knappast någon av oss riktigt kan sätta sig in i vad de har lidit och lider ock kommer at lida, dessa män, kvinnor, barn och åldringar. . . . Vi kan inte kalla dem tillbaka. . . . De går till döden eller till slaveriet. . . . Kan vi inte göra något annat, så kan vi försöka att vära röst åt de dömda. . . . låta dem genom oss ropa ut sin ångest och sin anklagelse."*
30. *Nordiska Röster mot Judeförföljelse och Vald. Dokument och Kommentar.* Stockholm: *Judisk Tidsskrift,* 1943, p. 14. *Yad Vashem Archives,* 85.2952: *"Det finns situationer, då det ordet gäller: om dessa tiga, skola stenarna ropa."* (If these keep silent, the stones will shout).
31. Ture Nerman, *Trots Allt,* Stockholm, December 4, 1942.

anger at the persecutions of Jews in Norway: "Persecutions of people belonging to another race is against the Nordic concept of justice and has,
until now, been unknown in Nordic countries."[32]

There was protest even within Quisling's party. An article in the party
journal, *N. S. Månedshefte* (National Union Monthly Journal) of December 15, 1942, stated:[33]

> ... we must not forget that this [Jewish] problem is not only a racial one,
> but also a national and, above all, a human one. The Norwegian people
> have never regarded Jews as countrymen ... since our people is too
> healthy-minded for that, but they have always been regarded as human
> beings, and, at that, as unfortunate human beings. Our movement must
> be held responsible to the Norwegian people for the way it solves the
> problem. Above all we have to guard ourselves against the destruction
> of feelings of justice within ourselves. It does not help to win the world
> if one harms one's own soul.

The Oslo Bishop Lars Frøyland, a non-member of NS, but appointed
by Quisling, wrote in 1943, that there was something that is a disgrace
to the Norwegian people:[34]

> ... our behavior toward people of another race and another belief within
> our own borders. I feel bound by my conscience to say this. And I do this
> even if it shall cost me ever so much. Is it correct to judge everyone the
> same way, and to punish the innocent with the guilty? We are, after all,
> Norwegians! We are, after all, Christians!

---

32. *Norsk Tidend*, London, December 9, 1942: *"Forfølgelsen av folk tilhørende en
annen rase er i strid med den nordiske rettsoppfatning og har hittil vært ukjent i nordiske
land."*

33. In *N. S. Månedshefle*, December 15, 1942, as quoted by Johan Scharffenberg in
Morgenbladet (Morning Journal), Oslo, September 15, 1952: *"Protester mot Quislings
jødeforfølgelse" (Protests against Quisling's Jewish persecutions): "Vårt land løser idag et
av tidens største problemer, jødespørsmålet. Måtte vi da ikke glemme, at dette problem
ikke bare er et raseproblem, men også et nasjonalt, og fremfor alt et menneskelig. Det
norske folk har aldri betraktet jødene som landsmenn, dertil er folket for sunt. Men det
har alltid betraktet dem som mennesker, og som ulykkelige mennesker. Vår bevegelse må
stå til ansvar for det norske folk for den måte det løser problemet på. ... fremfor alt må
vi være på vakt mot å ødelegge rettferdighetsfølelsen i oss selv. Det hjelper lite å vinne
hele verden hvis man tar skade på sin sjel."*

34. Lars Frøyland, *I Korsets Tegn* (By the Sign of the Cross), Oslo, Viking Forlag, 1943,
pp. 43–44: *"Til slutt lyt eg nemna ting som eg tykkjer er syrgjeleg og som skjemmer folket
vårt: Framferdi vår mot folk av ei onnor rase og ei onnor tru, innom våre eigne grenser.
Eg kjenner meg bunden av samvitet mitt til å segje dette. Og eg gjer det um det so skal
kosta meg aldri so mykje. Er det rett å skjere all yver ein kam og straffa dei uskuldige med
dei skuldiga? Me er då nordmenn! me er då kristne!"*

The reaction of the Norwegian Government-in-Exile to persecution of Jews in Norway was expressed by the Prime Minister, Johan Nygaardsvold, in *The Jewish Bulletin*, London in 1942.[35] He stated that in "democratic Norway there was never any question of distinction between the class, race, or creed of Norwegian citizens. But when the German hordes forced their way into our peace-loving country, they had to find a Jewish problem. Anti-Jewish demonstrations were staged by the Germans, windows were smashed, and insulting remarks were painted on the walls and windows of Jewish properties. Their livelihood was taken from them, their citizenship revoked; they were oppressed and starved. But they still fight on as staunchly as other patriotic Norwegians." The P.M. went on to state that all these wrongs would be righted when Norway was once more to be a free land.

3. Statistics of the Destruction of Norway's Jews

Having escaped to Sweden from Norway in the fall of 1942, Marcus Levin, chairman of the Oslo Joint Distribution Committee, started to keep reliable statistics on deported Norwegian Jews as well as on Jews escaping to Sweden. His work was supported, in part, by the Royal Norwegian Legation in Stockholm and by the Refugee Section of the Stockholm Jewish Community.

The first statistical report submitted to the Norwegian Legation on July 6, 1943, was divided into three categories and included deportees on board the *Monte Rosa, Donau,* and *Gotenland:*[36]

1. Norwegian citizens . . . . 469 persons
2. Norwegian stateless . . . . 174 persons
3. Foreign stateless . . . . 82 persons

This report gave a total of 725 deported persons. Group 2 (stateless Jews) included persons who for many years had lived in Norway, having obtained work permits and other rights, but who had never obtained Norwegian citizenship. Group 3 included persons of foreign citizenship

35. *The Jewish Bulletin*, London, No. 13, September 1942/5702 p. 1, "A Message from the Norwegian Prime Minister Professor Nygaardsvold," *Yad Vashem Archives*, 054/38.
36. Marcus Levin, Stockholm, July 6, 1943, J. No. 16015, "Report to the Norwegian Legation, Stockholm," pp. 102, Archives, Norwegian Department of Foreign Affairs, Oslo (NDFAO).

who had left their countries and arrived in Norway after Hitler had come to power in Germany in 1933.

A corrected table of statistics was submitted on May 5, 1944, by Minister Jens Bull, Royal Norwegian Legation, Stockholm, to the Royal Department of Foreign Affairs, London. The report stated that in addition to the main deportations of November 26, 1942, and February 24, 1943, several minor deportations had taken place resulting in a total of 740 persons deported:[37]

Norwegian citizens	471 persons
Norwegian stateless	177 persons
Foreign stateless	92 persons

A further breakdown of foreign nationalities were:

German	53
Austrian	20
Czechoslovakian	14
Hungarian	2
British	1
Dutch	1
Polish	1

Out of the 740 persons deported, 410 were men, 268 women, and 62 children under 15 years of age. Of the deported men, 134 were below age 30; of the deported women, 55 were below 30. A tabulation of the deportation lists at *Yad Vashem Archives* show 761 Jews were deported from Norway. Of these twenty-four survived.[38] Twenty-two had lost their lives through other war-related actions.[39]

4. The Homecoming of the Few

As World War II was coming to an end, the Nazi atrocities against the European Jews became known. It was then hoped that an end to anti-Semitism had taken place, and that the survivors would be welcomed

37. Jens Bull, Stockholm, May 5, 1944, J. No. 13210 NDFAO: *Jøder fra Norge i tysk fangenskap: "Tidligere oversikter er nå blitt korrigert. Foruten de to store hovedtransporter som avgikk den 26.11.42 og den 24.2.1943 er det avgått flere småtransporter."*
38. *Yad Vashem*, B/28-1 and 28/10; NDFAO, U. 251/5, "Jødespørsmålet," Bind II, 1 juni 1943–30 april 1956."
39. *News of Norway*, Washington D.C., Vol. 22, No. 37, November 22, 1965.

back to their native countries. On their homecoming the resistance fighters against the German occupiers were received as heroes. Not so the Jews. Ragnar Kvam related the homecoming of a tailor, Israel Klein to Dybdal, Norway in May 1945:[40]

> Dybdal a spring day in 1945. Everyone is assembled at the railroad station to welcome home a couple of freedom-fighters. The teacher lifts his baton. The choir sings patriotic songs. Everyone hails the freedom- fighters. None of the expected heroes alight from the train. But finally a door opens in the middle of the train. Out comes a small man, a very small man. A man who everyone in Dybdal had forgotten and still do not remember. The teacher lowers his baton. The little man jumps smilingly down from the platform with his traveling bag. A boy's voice: "Mother, it is the Jew!"
>
> And through the enormous assembly of good Norwegians who are expecting their freedom-fighters — a shout in unison: "The Jew!"
>
> No freedom-fighters, no one with the Norwegian flag on his sleeves, none of "the boys from the forest." Only — the Jew!
>
> There he stands fumbling with his cap when the train departs. Everyone had forgotten that the Jew had disappeared when the other Jews further south in the country had been apprehended. But — righteousness deserves justice. *(Rett skal være rett.)* The Jew was also a human being. He did not receive any patriotic songs. . . . The Jews have killed Christ. But the Jew also received a hurrah. It was really a feeble hurrah, because the disappointment was so great. When would the freedom-fighters come, when would the boys from the forest arrive?

A different description of the only survivor of a family of seven members is recorded by Herman Sachnowitz:[41]

> One day, more wonderfully bright than any other day in my life, I descended from the train at the station in Larvik, the town of my childhood. A crowd of people had come to meet me, and there were flags, hundreds of Norwegian flags. The youth band which I had once played in was lined up and a welcome celebration had been arranged in one of the hotels. . . . I went through the house which the Germans had vandalized. The rooms were empty, stripped of everything, like me. Nobody awaited me here. In a way, however, they were nearer to me now, my dear ones, nearer than they had been for a long time. It was here I had said farewell to all of them. Goodbye, father, goodbye, Frank, goodbye, all my family! . . . Life had

---

40. Ragnar Kvam, *Den siste Ghetto* (The Last Ghetto), Oslo: H. Aschehoug & Co., p. 55.

41. Sachnowitz, *op. cit.*, pp. 227-228.

meaning and I, too, had to fight on. Life would be a struggle but a *good* struggle from now on, I had to believe that. I had to fight my way out of the darkness until one day I could cast off my burden, to tell the truth about all my dead ones, six to seven million Jews who had been systematically exterminated in German concentration camps.

In December, 1976, Sachnowitz was honored by Yad Vashem, the Martyrs' and Heroes' Remembrance Authority, by the Israeli Ambassador to Norway, David Rivlin. He stated that Sachnowtiz's book, *It Also Concerns You*, was "a powerful reminder of the fate of European Jews, and of the Jews in Norway in particular."[42] The author died on March 5, 1978, 57 years old. That same month his publisher, Aschehoug & Co., established the "Herman Sachnowitz Scholarship." It would be distributed every year to a high school student who had written the best essay on a theme related to the Holocaust.[43] The first competition took place in 1979 with over 200 students participating.

The twenty-four Norwegian Jews who returned from Nazi concentration camps and those other Jews returning from Sweden or overseas faced serious psychological and emotional problems in rebuilding their lives in a free Norway. Throughout the ages, close family relationships had been a precondition for survival. During the war, families were isolated for years. Upon returning they found what they had not expected: their nuclear families had been wiped out. There was hardly one family that had not suffered severe losses of loved ones. In addition, the Nazi and Quisling authorities had confiscated, stolen, or sold by public auctions properties or personal belongings of Jews. The Norwegian government in London, however, had on December 18, 1942, issued a provisional decree "concerning the invalidity of legal transactions connected with the occupation."[44] The pre-war owners were guaranteed restitution of homes, stores, apartments, personal belongings and communal properties. Thus, the two Jewish communities in Trondheim and Oslo were reconstituted with great effort and sacrifice.[45] With financial

42. "Yad Vashem Honors Oslo Author," New York: *Jewish Journal*, December 31, 1976, p. 29.

43. *"Cappelen har opprettet et Sachnowitz-stipend,"* (Cappelen Has Established a Scholarship in Memory of Sachnowitz) *Nytt fra Norge* (News from Norway), Oslo, March 7, 1978, page 14.

44. Nehemiah Robinson, *Indemnification and Reparations. Jewish Aspects*, New York: Institute of Jewish Affairs of the American Jewish Congress and World Jewish Congress, 1944, p. 129.

45. *"Det mosaiske gudshus gjenreist. Gjeninnvielse ay synagogen i Trondheim igår."* (Rededication of the Synagogue in Trondheim yesterday). Trondheim: *Adresseavisen*, Oc-

assistance from the Conference on Jewish Material Claims and the American Joint Distribution Committee, both communities were reconstituted and continued to function. The synagogue in Trondheim was rededicated on October 14, 1947, with Rabbi Abraham Israel Jacobsohn and the chief rabbi from Denmark conducting the service. In attendance were also Rabbi Elias Berlinger of Finland; Rabbi Isaac Grünewald of Malmö, Sweden; Rabbi Emil Kronheim of Stockholm, and Cantor Leo Grabowski of Copenhagen. The President of the Congregation, Oskar Mendelsohn, thanked everyone for helping restore the synagogue.

Already in 1946 the Norwegian government had initiated a program to assist European refugees and displaced persons (DPs) by extending money and trade credits to UNRRA (United Nations Relief and Rehabilitation Administration) and by regularly contributing to the office of the U. N. High Commissioner for Refugees. Temporary camps for the millions of DP's scattered throughout Europe were established in Germany, Austria, Sweden & Italy right after World War II. In July, 1946, the government agreed to give 300 Jewish refugees the opportunity to emigrate from Germany and 300 from Poland. In February, 1947, a Norwegian commission headed by Minister of Social Affairs, Haslaug Aasland, was sent by the Ministry of Social Affairs to Germany to select the prospective immigrants. Under the chairmanship of Major Alf Volckmar and Wilhelm Böe, secretary-general of the Norwegian Refugee Council, the potential immigrants were chosen. On May 10, 1947, four hundred Jewish refugees arrived in Norway on board the S/S *Svalbard*.[46] The refugees consisted of one hundred families with children and about one hundred single persons.[47] Those who were married and had children were placed at a camp at Ystehede on the banks of Iddefjord near the Swedish border in southern Norway.[48] Others were placed at Mysen. The local Jewish communities and organizations participated in the resettlement and acculturation of the refugees. The Jewish Women's Organization in Trondheim contributed money and clothing for each newborn baby at Ystehede.[49] The government offered full

---

tober 15, 1947.

46. Alf Volckmar, "Jewish Immigration to Norway," a Report to Secretary Banger, Ministry of Social Affairs, Oslo: January 8, 1948, p. 1.

47. *Stortingsmelding nr. 11, 1952, Norges hjelp til flyktninger,* Oslo: Sosialdepartementet, 1952, p. 4 (Parliamentary Report Number 11, 1952, Norway's Aid to Refugees).

48. Philip Singer and Gilbert Cranberg, "Some of the Homeless and Tempest-Tossed Continental Jews Start Life Anew in Norway," *Nordisk Tidende,* Brooklyn: October 16, 1947.

civil rights, adequate housing, social security, medical services, free language instruction, counseling, professional services, and wage-and-
working conditions on par with those of other Norwegians in order to
facilitate adjustment to Norwegian society. After seven years they could
apply for Norwegian citizenship. Mr. Böe explained that "our main problem is that so many refugees must take jobs below those they held in
Poland."[50] In general it should be stated that refugees in Norway had
received rights going beyond the 1951 U.N. Convention Related to the
Status for Refugees. They were resettled not in order to gain manpower
for Norway, but solely out of humanitarian considerations.[50A] This was
in trend with the unselfish work of Fridtjof Nansen who in 1920 had been
appointed High Commissioner by the League of Nations. Nansen succeeded in repatriating over half a million prisoners of war from over thirty different nationalities.

In 1952, a group of three hundred refugees arrived, including about
one hundred tubercular or former TB patients as well as 50 blind persons. These were known as "hard core cases."[51] Under the leadership
of Norway's Minister of Social Affairs, Aaslaug Aasland, the handicapped
were either taken care of by specialists in rehabilitation, or were placed
in social institutions or sanatoria. Starting in 1952, all these activities
were coordinated by the Norwegian Relief council, a successor to Aid
to Europe (Europahjelpen). In 1949 this organization brought two hundred Jewish children from North Africa to Norway for a stay of eight
months of rehabilitation before emigrating to Israel. One group of 28
children crashed in a Dutch airplane outside Oslo. Only one child, Isaac
Allal, survived.[52] The reaction of the Norwegians was generous when
private organization and labor unions contributed $40,000 to establish

49. Jødisk Kvinneforening, Trondheim, 1919–1969. En oversikt over foreningens virke
gjennom 50 år. (Jewish Women's Association, Trondheim, 1919–1969. A Survey of the Association's Work through 50 Years.) Trondheim: Adresseavisens Boktrykkeri, 1969, p. 7.
50. Sidney Du Broff, "The Viking Jews," Hadassah Magazine, The Women's Zionist Organization of America, New York: January 1973, p. 31.
50A. Wilhelm S. Bøe, "The Spirit of Nansen. Norwegian Aid to Refugees Around the
World," The Norseman, No. 2, 1962, pp. 4, 5.
51. Jacques Vernant, The Refugee in the Post-War World. London: George Allen and
Unwin Ltd., 1953, p. 372.
52. Odd Hølaas, Norge under Haakon VII 1905–1952. Tidsrommet 1945–1952 ved
Asbjørn Barlaup og Henning Storm (Norway under Haakon VII 1905–1952. The Period
1945–1952 edited by Asbjørn Barlaup and Henning Storm), Oslo: J. W. Cappelens Forlag,
1952, p. 566.

in Israel a "Kibbutz Norway," and provided thirty Norwegian-built pre-fabricated houses.[53]

Norway's strong humanitarian inclinations found expression in assisting needy people. The refugees and DPs were accepted as friends, affectionately referred to as "our new Norwegians."[54]

An opinion poll taken on July 5, 1947, by the publication *Hvem, Hva, Hvor* (Who, What, Where)[55] regarding Displaced Persons revealed the following attitudes in the population:

Question: "Norway has agreed to rescue 600 Jewish DPs. Do you think this is right or wrong?"

Answer: "Right." (68 percent male, 78 percent female). "Wrong." (32 percent male, 22 percent female).

In spite of these favorable attitudes not all of the DPs remained in Norway. In the period 1948–1952, following the establishment of the State of Israel, about three hundred left for countries overseas. Many of the DPs and refugees had been placed outside the Jewish communities at Trondheim or Oslo in order to find better housing and employment opportunities. However well- meaning this policy was intended, the Jews felt isolated in these rural communities with little incentives for integration into Norwegian society.

5. Epilogue

The first postwar census of Norway's Jews took place in November 1946, showing a total of 559. In spite of the severe losses of relatives and friends there was a common determination to rebuild the congregations. A memorial service for all Norwegian Jews killed during the German occupation took place in the Oslo synagogue at Bergstien on Friday August 31, 1945 (22nd day of the Hebrew month Elul, 5705.) The service was conducted by Cantor Leo Grabowski from Copenhagen and by the Chief Rabbi of Denmark Dr. Max M. Friediger, who had survived internment in Theresienstadt from August, 1943, to April, 1945.[56] In at-

53. Samuel Abrahamsen, "The Saga of Norway's Jews," New York: *Congress Weekly*, vol. 18, no. 25, October 8, 1951, p. 10.

54. Fred M. Hechinger, "700 Reich DP's Find New Life in Norway," *New York Post*, August 15, 1948, p. 8.

55. *Hvem, Hvad, Hvor* (Who, What, Where), Oslo: *Aftenpostens Oppslagsbok 1947*, p. 121.

56. Max M. Friediger, *Theresienstadt*: København, J. Fr. Clausens Forlag, 1946, pp. 20; 142.

tendance at the service were His Royal Highness Crown Prince Olav, Dr. Johan Scharffenberg, Odd Nansen, two cabinet members, as well as governmental and church representatives. A special prayer for the Royal House was said in Hebrew:

> He who gives victory to the Kings and power to the annointed, and whose Kingdom is the eternal Kingdom, he, who saved his Servant David from the threatening sword, who forged a Road through the Ocean and Path through the powerful Waters, He will bless, keep, preserve, protect, elevate and exalt to Glory and Honour
>
> KING HAAKON VII
> CROWN PRINCE OLAV
> CROWN PRINCESS MÄRTHA
> and
> THE WHOLE ROYAL HOUSE
> So be the Will of God:
>
> Amen.

To commemorate the murdered Norwegian Jews two memorials were erected after the war. A memorial for the small Jewish community at Trondheim was unveiled on October 14, 1947 with 131 names[57] the same year as the rededication of the synagogue took place. The base of this memorial bears the inscription:[58] "The Mosaic Religious Society of Trondheim erected this monument in memory of its members who were shot, deported, and murdered during the German reign of terror during the war years 1940–45."

The murder of the Jews at Auschwitz from Northern and Central Norway had taken place on March 3, 1943, which, according to the Hebrew calendar was the first month of Adar Rishon. 1942/43 was a leap year in the Hebrew calendar. The Jewish community in Trondheim had set aside the 26th day of Adar Rishon to commemorate the Jews deported and killed from Trøndelag, neighboring counties as well as from Northern Norway.

The Oslo Congregation established the Sabbath of Chanukkah (Re-

---

57. Ole-Einar Andersen, "Fra jernbanestasjon til jødisk synagoge, Det mosaiske trosamfunn i Trondheim er 70 år," (From Railroad Station to Jewish Synagogue. The Mosaic Congregation in Trondheim is 70 years). *Adresseavisen*, Trondheim, October 25, 1975.

58. The inscription of the Trondheim memorial of Jews killed during the Holocaust reads as follows: *"Det Mosaiske Trossamfund i Trondheim reiste dette monumentet til minne om de trosfeller som ble skutt, deportert, myrdet under det tyske voldsherredømme i krigsårene 1940–1945."*

dedication or The Feast of Light), which occurs on the 24th day of Kislev
(i.e., usually the month of December) to commemorate the victims from
Southern Norway. The Oslo monument at Helsfyr Cemetery, unveiled
on November 1, 1948, was executed by the Danish sculptor Harald
Isenstein. Eight of the Norwegian Jewish concentration camp survivors
formed the guard. Among those who attended were His Royal Highness
Crown Prince Olav and his adjutant; the president of the *Storting*,
Fredrik Monsen; Dr. Gerhard Fuchs, representing the State of Israel;
president of the Oslo Jewish Community, Harry M. Koritzinsky; pres-
ident of Oslo University, Professor Otto Lous Mohr; members of the
Committee on Arrangements, Mendel Bernstein, Leon Jarner, and M.
L. Milner; representatives from the Norwegian churches and from the
diplomatic corps. The chief rabbi from Denmark, Marcus Melchior, and
Cantor Grabowski conducted the service. Professor Didrik Arup Seip,
who was also present, had prepared the Norwegian and Hebrew texts.[59]
The English translation reads:[60]

> Erected in memory of the 620 Jews who during the German occupation
> of Norway 1940–1945 were killed here in this country or deported and
> perished in concentration camps in Germany. An urn with ashes of those
> who perished in Auschwitz was deposited in this place on December 7,
> 1952.

Following these ceremonies a memorial meeting was held at the venera-
ble Old Festival Hall at the University of Oslo. The noted author Johan
Borgen was the keynote speaker. He reminded the audience about the
many harsh years of the German occupation and, especially, the tragic
fate of Norway's Jews. On that same day, November 1, 1948, a Norway-
Israel Association was established through the initiative of the author
Odd Bang-Hansen. The association has been actively involved in fur-
thering cultural exchanges between Norway and Israel. These activities
became formalized through a cultural agreement in 1956, leading to scientific and artistic exchanges between the two countries.

In 1961 Thomas Chr. Wyller and Egil A. Wyller proposed to give the

---

59. "Wergelands og Nansens ånd fremdeles levende i Norge." *Morgenposten*, Oslo, November 2, 1948. (The Spirit of Wergelands and Nansens still alive in Norway.)

60. The inscription of the Oslo monument is: "*Reist til minne om de 620 jøder som under
den tyske okkupasjon av Norge 1940–1945 ble drept her i landet eller deportert og omkom
i konsentrasjonsleir i Tyskland. En urne med aske etter omkomne i Auschwitz er satt ned
på dette sted 7. desember 1952.*" The number of 620 Jews on the monument is wrong.
A more correct figure is about 730 Jews.

Norwegian Jews a national gift of honor. They said, "Let our sympathy with our Jews be expressed in a concrete way. Every surviving Norwegian Jew is the successor to the dead Jews. At any rate the memory of the dead will live on; and that is the duty of the Norwegian people to preserve."[61] This commitment was implemented on May 6, 1986, when a memorial by the Norwegian sculptor Svein M. Havartstein was unveiled over the prominent Jewish community leader, Moritz Rabinowitz in the city of Haugesund in Southern Norway.[62] Rabinowitz was born in Rajgrod, Poland on September 20, 1887, went to Norway in 1909, and stayed at first in Bergen before settling in Haugesund. Here he became very well known as a prolific anti- Nazi writer and was very much beloved for his philanthropic and humanitarian activities. His fight against world-wide anti-Semitism was reflected in numerous articles and in his book *Verden og vi* (We and the World). He was arrested in December 1940, released, re-arrested, and deported to the Sachsenhausen concentration camp, where he was murdered in February, 1942.[63]

On another occasion a distinct Norwegian honor was bestowed upon the world renowned author and Holocaust survivor Elie Wiesel in Oslo on December 10, 1986. The chairman of the Norwegian Nobel Committee, Egil Aarvik, presented the Nobel Peace Prize to Professor Wiesel for being a messenger to mankind, not of hatred, but of brotherhood and reconciliation. He had become a most eloquent spokesman for the view that mankind must not forget the lessons of the Holocaust,[64] and that the human spirit must conquer brute force. The Nobel Committee's selection of Wiesel for this high honor was received with the greatest acclaim throughout the world. In his acceptance speech at the University of Oslo Ceremonial Hall, Elie Wiesel thanked the Nobel Prize Committee and the people of Norway for "declaring on this singular occasion that our survival has meaning for mankind."[65]

61. Thomas Chr. Wyller, Egil A. Wyller, *"Gi våre jøder en æresgave,"* (Let's give our Jews a Gift of Honor). *Dagbladet,* Oslo, May 16, 1961.

62. Ole Oddenes, *"Første minnestein over norsk jøde avduket,"* (The First Memorial to a Norwegian Jew Unveiled), *Haugesund Avis,* May 7, 1986, p. 9.

63. *"Rabinowitz minnet på Holocaust-dagen,"* (Rabinowitz Remembered on the Day of the Holocaust), *Haugesund Avis,* May 7, 1986, p. 1

64. Finn Jor, *"Nobels fredspris til Elie Wiesel. Han preker forsoning og fred,"* (Nobel's Peace Prize to Elie Wiesel. He preaches Atonement and Peace), *Aftenposten Ukens Nytt,* Oslo, Vol. 797, no. 120, October 16, 1986, p. 1.

65. "Wiesel Accepting the Nobel, Asks Living to Remember," *The New York Times,* December 11, 1986, pp. 1A; 12A.

King Haakon's Courageous Reply "NO!" to the German demand for surrender by Dr. Curt Bräuer April 10, 1940.

Courtesy: Royal Norwegian Information Service in the United States.

Monument in Oslo over HENRIK WERGELAND (1808–1845), the emancipator of Norway's Jews. On front is inscribed: "Henrik Wergeland — the tireless Champion of men's and Citizens' Freedom and Rights."

On the back: "Grateful Jews outside of Norway erected this in his Memory."

Trygve Halvdan Lie (1896–1968), Norway's Minister of Foreign Affairs 1940–1946, worked indefatigably for his plan to rescue deported Norwegian Jews in exchange for wounded German prisoners-of-war held by the Allies.

Courtesy: Guri Lie Zeckendorf.

Two leading Norwegian Jewish musicians: Ernst Glaser (violin) and Rovert Levin (piano).

Photos of the interior and exterior of Trondheim Synagogue.

Unveiling of monument at Helsfyr Cemetery November 1, 1948, attended by His Royal Highness Crown Prince Olav. An urn with ashes from Auschwitz was deposited on December 7, 1952.

Unveiling of a memorial on October 14, 1947 at the Trondheim Jewish Cemetery over Jews killed during World War II.

Anti-Semitic slogan painted on display windows in Oslo, March 1941: "Jewish Parasites gave Norway April 9th."

Rabbi Abraham Israel Jacobsohn, leader of the Trondheim Jewish Community, examining the clothing in June 1947 of three Jews murdered in the Falstad Forest.

Identification made in June 1947 of three Jews murdered at the Falstad Concentration Camp in November 1942. At the center, in beret, Jacob Abrahamsen Ilevik, D.D.S., brother of the author.

Watching exhumation in July 1947 of three bodies: Moritz Nevesetsky Abrahamsen, Kalman Glick and Herman Schidorsky, murdered by the German occupying forces in the Falstad Forest, November 1942. In front, Police Officer Thomassen; to the right, Rabbi A. I. Jacobsohn.

King Haakon VII and Crown Prince Olav pursued by German bombers running for shelter in the small town of Nybergsund in south-eastern Norway, April 11, 1940.
Courtesy: Norwegian Information Services, New York, N.Y.

Bibliography

Aano, Jakob. *"Norge et ren-rase-samfunn"* (Norway a Pure Racial Society), *Norway Times* (Nordisk Tidende), New York, February 19, 1981

Aarflot, Andreas. *Norsk kirkehistorie* (Norwegian Church History). Oslo: 1967.

Aasen, Elizabeth. *"Vår nasjonale kulturarv"* (Our National Cultural Heritage). In: *"Er skolen kunnskapssentral eller kulturformidler?"* Samtiden, Oslo: Aschehoug, vol. 90, no. 1, 1981, pp. 74–80.

Aberle, Ernst. *Vi må ikke glemme* (We Must Not Forget). Oslo: J. W. Cappelens Forlag, 1980.

Abrahamsen, David. "Quisling: Abnormal Messiah." In: *Men, Mind and Power*, pp. 95–113. New York: Columbia University Press, 1945.

Abrahamsen, David. *Jeg er jøde. En norsk jøde om jødene i Norge og om folket uten landegrenser* (I Am a Jew. A Norwegian Jew about the Jews in Norway, and about the People without Frontiers). Oslo: Johan Grundt Tanum, 1935. New and revised edition, 1985.

Abrahamsen, Samuel. "Norway." In: *The Universal Jewish Encyclopedia*, Vol. 8, pp. 242–244. New York: Universal Jewish Encyclopedia Co. Inc., 1942.

Abrahamsen, Samuel. "The Exclusion Clause of Jews in the Norwegian Constitution of May 17, 1814." *Jewish Social Studies* XXX: 2 (April 1968), pp. 67–88.

Abrahamsen, Samuel. "The Holocaust in Norway." In: Randolph L. Braham, ed. *Contemporary Views on the Holocaust*. Chap. V., pp. 109–142. Boston-London-The Hague: Kluver-Nijhoff Publishing Co., 1983.

Abrahamsen, Samuel. "Norwegian Jewry in the Holocaust," *Encyclopedia of the Holocaust*, Macmillan Publishing Company, New York & London, vol. 3, 1990 pp. 1067-1068.

Abrahamsen, Samuel. "The Relationship of Church and State during the German Occupation of Norway, 1940–1945." In: *Holocaust Studies Annual, Volume II, The Churches' Response to the Holocaust*, pp. 1–27. Greenwood, FL: The Penkvill Publishing Company, 1986.

Abrahamsen, Samuel. "The Rescue of Denmark's Jews." *The American- Scandinavian Review* LX: 2 (June 1972), pp. 157–164.

Abrahamsen, Samuel. "The Saga of Norway's Jews." *Congress Weekly* 18: 25 (October 1951), pp. 8–10.

Abrahamsen, Samuel. "Wergeland and Article 2 of the Norwegian Constitution." *Scandinavian Studies* 38: 2 (1966), pp. 102–123.

Abrahamsen, Samuel. *Sweden's Foreign Policy.* Washington D.C.: Public Affairs Press, 1957.

Abrahamsen, Samuel, "The Role of the Norwegian Lutheran Church during World War II," in *Remembering for the Future Jews and Christians during and after the Holocaust. Papers presented at the International Scholars'*

Conference, Oxford and London, Pergamon Press, New York, 1988, pp. 3-17.

Abrahamson, Irving, (ed.), *The Voice and Vision of Elie Wiesel*, Holocaust Library, New York, 1985, 3 vols.

Ackerman, Nathan, and Marie Jahida. *Antisemitism and Emotional Disorder.* New York: 1950.

Adler, Rudel S. "A Chronicle of Rescue Efforts." In: *Yearbook of the Leo Baeck Institute of Jews from Germany,* Vol. XI, pp. 213–241. London: Secker and Warburg, 1966.

Aikio, Matti. *Hebræerens Søn* (The Son of the Hebrew). Christiania: 1911.

American Legation, Stockholm, *Dispatch No. 1629*, April 9, 1943. Memorandum: "Additional Information Concerning Persecution of Jews in Norway," National Archives, Washington, D.C.

Amundsen, Leif. *"Henrik Wergeland og Universitetsbiblioteket"* (Henrik Wergeland and the University Library). *Edda* XLV (1945), pp. 120–121, 131.

Amundsen, Leif, ed. *Brev til Henrik Wergeland* (Letters to Henrik Wergeland). Oslo: 1956.

Andenæs, Johs. *"Var hjemmefrontens kamp folkerettsstridig?"* (Was the Fight of the Home Front Contrary to International Law?) In: *Festskrift til J. H. Andresen*, pp. 1–12. Oslo: 1948.

Andenæs, Johs. *Det vanskelige oppgjøret. Rettsoppgjøret etter okkupasjonen. De offentlige tjenestemenn* (The Difficult Accounting: Legal Accounting after the Occupation. The Public Servants). Oslo: Tanum Nordli, 1979.

Andenæs, Johs., O. Riste, and M. Skodvin. *Norway and the Second World War.* Oslo: Johan Grundt Tanum Forlag, 1966.

Andenæs, Tønnes. *Grunnloven vår. 1814 til idag* (Our Constitution. 1814 unto Today). Oslo-Bergen-Tromsø: Universitetsforlaget, 1966.

Andenæs, Tønnes, ed. *The Constitution of Norway.* Oslo: Norwegian University Press, 1962.

Arad, Yitchak, Yisrael Gutman, and Abraham Margaliot, eds. *Documents on the Holocaust.* Jerusalem: Yad Vashem, 1981.

Arnli, Jon Arild. *Det norske politi: Perioden 1938–våren 1941* (The Norwegian Police: Period from 1938 to Spring 1941), Hovedoppgave #4918, M. A. Thesis, University of Oslo, 1941.

Aronsfeld, Caesar C. "The Ghosts of 1492. Jewish Aspects of the Struggle for Religious Freedom in Spain, 1848–1976." *Jewish Social Studies*, Monograph Series No. 1. New York: Columbia University Press, 1979.

Assman, K. "The Invasion of Norway." *United States Naval Institute Proceedings* (April 1952), pp. 401–413.

Assman, Kurt. *Deutsche Schicksaljahre* (The German Years of Fate). Wiesbaden: Eberhard Brookhaus, 1950.

Austad, Torleiv. *"Fra Statskirke til selvadministrert folkekirke. Den norske kirken under krigen"* (From State Church to Self-Administered Folk Church. The Norwegian Church During the War). In: Stein Ugelvik Larsen and Ingun Montgomery, eds. *Kirken, Krisen og Krigen* (The Church, Crisis and War). Oslo-Bergen-Tromsø: Universitetsforlaget, 1982.

Austad, Torleiv. *Kirkens Grunn. Analyse av en kirkelig bekjennelse fra okkupasjonstiden 1940–45* (The Foundation of the Church. Analysis of an Ecclesiastical Confession from the Occupation 1940–45). Oslo: Luther Forlag, 1974.

"*Avstamningserklæring*" (Declaration of Descent), November 11, 1942. Statsarkivet, Oslo, I.D. No. 00886 II, February 2, 1943.

Baron, Salo W. *A Social and Religious History of the Jews.* Vol. XIII. New York: Columbia University Press, 1969.

Bauer, Yehudah. *The Holocaust in Historical Perspective.* Seattle: University of Washington Press, 1978.

Bauer, Yehudah and Nili Keren. *The Holocaust: A History.* New York: New Viewpoints, 1982.

Bekker, Harald. "*Jødene i skolens lærebøker*" (Jews in the School's Textbooks). *Kirke og Kultur* (Church and Culture) 82 (1977), pp. 130–140.

Benkow, Jo. *Fra Synagogen til Løvebakken* (From the Synagogue to the Parliament). Oslo: Gyldendal Norsk Forlag, 1985.

Berg, Arthur. *Med Israel i kamp for fred* (With Israel in the Fight for Peace). Oslo: Lunde Forlag, 1979.

Bergfald, Odd. *Gestapo i Norge* (Secret State Police in Norway). Oslo: Hjemmenes Forlag, 1978.

Bergfald, Odd. *Helmuth Reinhard, Soldat eller Morder?* (Helmuth Reinhard, Soldier or Murderer). Oslo: Chr. Schibsteds Forlag, 1967.

Bergfald, Odd. "*Hoaas — Jeg er rasist — en hedersbetegnelse*" (Hoaas — I am a Racist — an Honorary Designation). *Aftenposten*, Oslo, August 18, 1976.

Berggrav, Eivind. "*Paroler høsten 1940*" (Directives, Fall 1940). *Morgenbladet*, Oslo, July 31, 1945.

Berggrav, Eivind. *Da kampen kom. Noen blad fra startåret* (When the War Came, Some Notes from the First Year). Oslo: Land og Kirke, 1945.

Bergsgård, Arne. *Fra 17. mai til 9. april* (From May 17 to April 9). Oslo: 1958.

Berlin, Isaiah. *Dictionary of the History of Ideas.* Vol. II. New York: Charles Scribner's Sons, 1973.

Bernadotte, Folke. *The Curtain Falls, Last Days of the Third Reich.* New York: Alfred A. Knopf, 1945.

Berulfsen, Bjarne. "*Antisemitisme som litterær importvare*" (Anti-Semitism as a Literary Import). *Edda — Nordisk Tidsskrift for litteraturforskning*, Oslo LVIII: 2 (1958).

Berulfsen, Bjarne. "*Jøder og Island*" (Jews and Iceland). In: *Kulturhistorisk Leksikon for nordisk Middelalder: fra vikingetid til reformasjonen* (Cultural Historical Dictionary) Vol. VIII, pp. 76–78. Copenhagen: Rosenkilde and Bagger, 1963.

Berulfsen, Bjarne. "*Jødehatet immportert til Norge gjennom kirkelig og geistlig litteratur*" (Jew-hatred imported to Norway through ecclesiastical and clerical literature). *Dagbladet*, Oslo, October 10, 1958.

160   SAMUEL ABRAHAMSEN

Beyer, Harald. *Henrik Wergeland, Thi Friheden ere Himmelens Sag* (Henrik Wergeland, Liberty is the Cause of Heaven). Oslo: Lunde Forlag, 1979.
Beyer, Harald. *Norsk Litteraturhistorie* (Norwegian History of Literature). Oslo: Aschehoug, 1952. English edition: *A History of Norwegian Literature*. New York: New York University Press and the American- Scandinavian Foundation, 1956.
"*Bibelskolelærer Jørgensen har bedt om unnskyldning for radioandakt*" (Bible Teacher Jørgensen Asks Pardon for Radio Sermon). *Aftenposten*, August 29, 1980.
Biering, Aage. "*I dekning og på flukt*" (In Hiding and on the Run). In: Sverre Steen, ed. *Norges Krig, 1940–1945* (Norway's War, 1940–1945). Vol. III, pp. 401–438. Oslo: Gyldendal Norsk Forlag, 1948.
Birkeland, Bjarte, and Stein Ugelvik Larsen. *Nazismen og norsk litteratur* (Nazism and Norwegian Literature). Oslo: Universitetsforlaget, 1975.
Bjercke, Eilert. *Judea drømmer* (Judea Dreams). Christiania: 1913.
Bjørnsen, Bjørn. *Det utrolige døgnet — 9. april 1940* (The Unbelievable 24 Hours — April 9, 1940). Oslo: Gyldendal, 1977.
Blackbook of Localities Whose Jewish Population Was Exterminated by the Nazis, Jerusalem: Yad Vashem Martyrs' and Heroes' Remembrance Authority, 1965.
Blindheim, Svein. "*Hvorfor sloss 7000 nordmen under Hitlers fane på østfronten?*" (Why did 7000 Norwegians fight under Hitler's banner on the Eastern Front?). *Nordisk Tidende*, Brooklyn, N.Y., June 9, 1977.
Blindheim, Svein. *Nordmenn under Hitlers Fane. Dei norske frontkjemparane* (Norwegians under Hitler's Banner). Oslo: Noregs Boklag, 1977.
Boehm, H. "*Die Politische Entwicklung in Norwegen 1941–43 unter Gross- Admiral Raeder*" (The Political Development in Norway). *Nation Europa* (July 1952), pp. 24–311.
Borgen, Johan. *Dager på Grini* (Days at Grini). Oslo: Gyldendal, 1945.
Bostrup, Bjørn. *The Foreign Policy of Norway.* Oslo: 1968.
Braham, Randolph L. *The Eichmann Case: A Source Book*. New York: World Federation of Hungarian Jews, 1969.
Brandt, Willy. "*Jødepogromene i Norge oktober–november 1942*" (The Jewish Pogroms in Norway, October–November 1942). *Fram Norsk Magasin*, London (July 24, 1943).
Brandt, Willy. *Krigen i Norge* (The War in Norway), Vols. I & II. Oslo: Aschehoug, 1945.
Branzeg, Nils. "*Det er vi som er problemet*" (We are the Problem), *Dagbladet*, November 6, 1954, p. 4.
Braunaas, Nils. "*Jødehat på Eidsvold — og i København*" (Jew-hatred at Eidsvold and in Copenhagen), "Dagbladets Kronikk," *Dagbladet* (Oslo), December 29, 1964, pp. 3–4.
Bredsdorff, Elias, Brita Mortensen, and Ronald Popperwell. *An Introduction to Scandinavian Literature*. Copenhagen and Cambridge, 1951; reprinted Westport, Conn.: Greenwood, 1970.
Broberg, Gunnar, Runblom, Harald, & Tyden, Mattias, (Eds.). *Judiskt Liv i*

Norden (Jewish Life in the Northern Countries), Center for Multiethnic Research, Uppsala University: Uppsala, Sweden, 1988.

Brockendorff, Werner. *Kollaboration oder Widerstand. Die Zusammenarbeit mit den Deutschen in den besetzten Ländern während des zweiten Weltkrieges und deren schrecklische Folgen.* München: Verlag Welsermui, 1968.

Brodersen, Arvid. *Fra et nomadeliv. Erindringer* (From the Life of a Nomad. Remembrances). Oslo: Gyldendal Norsk Forlag, 1982.

Brodersen, Arvid. *"Norsk kontakt med mennene bak Hitler-attentatet"* (Norwegian Contact with the Persons Behind the Attack on Hitler). *Farmand*, Oslo 80: 10 (March 8, 1975), pp. 38–43.

Brodersen, Arvid. *Mellom Frontene* (Between the Fronts). Oslo: J. W. Cappelens Forlag, 1979.

Browning, Christopher. *The Final Solution and the German Foreign Office: A Study of Referat DIII of Abteilung Deutschland, 1940–43.* New York: Holmes and Meier, 1978.

Bruknapp, Dag O. *"Idéene splitter partiet. Rasespørsmålets betydning i NS's utvikling"* (The Ideas split the party. The significance of racial questions in the development of the National Union Party). In: Rolf Danielsen and Stein Ugelvik Larsen, eds. *Fra idé til dom. Noen trekk fra utviklingen av Nasjonal Samling* (From Idea to Sentencing. Some Aspects of the Development of the National Union Party). Oslo: Universitetsforlaget, 1978.

Bryn, Halfdan. *Menneskerasene og deres utviklingshistorie* (The Human Races and Their History of Development). Oslo, 1925.

Bull, Francis. *Norsk Litteraturhistorie fra Reformasjonen til 1814* (Norwegian Literary History from the Reformation to 1814). Oslo: H. Aschehoug & Co., 1985.

Bull, Francis. *Tretten Taler på Grini* (Thirteen Speeches at Grini). Oslo: Gyldendal, 1945.

Bull, Francis and Fredrik Paasche. *Norsk Litteraturhistorie.* Vol. III. Oslo: H. Aschehoug & Co. 1959.

Carlgren, W. M. *Swedish Foreign Policy During the Second World War.* New York: St. Martin's Press, 1977; London and Tonbridge: Ernest Benn, 1977.

Carlsen, Ingvald B. *Kirkefronten i Norge under okkupasjonen 1940–1945* (The Church Front in Norway during the Occupation 1940–1945). Oslo: H. Aschehoug and Co., 1945.

Carlsen, Ingvald B. *Kirkens kamp i Norge under Besættelsen, 1940–1945* (The Fight of the Church of Norway During the Occupation). København: P. Haase Forlag, 1946.

Castberg, Frede. *Norge under okkupasjonen, 1940–1943* (Norway during Occupation, 1940–1943). Oslo: 1945.

Castberg, Frede. *The Norwegian Way of Life.* London: 1954.

Christensen, Chr. A. R. *Vårt Folks Historie, Okkupasjonsår og Etterkrigstid* (Our People's History, Years of Occupation and Postwar Times). Vol. 9. Oslo: Aschehoug, 1961.

Christie, K. C. *Den norske kirken i kamp* (The Norwegian Church in Battle). Oslo: Land og Kirke, 1945.

Christophersen, H. O. *"Aksjonen mot jødene. Okkupasjonens tyngste slag"* (The Action Against Jews. The Heaviest Blow During the Occupation). *Aftenposten*, evening edition, October 23, 1967.

Christophersen, H. O. *Av nød til seir* (From Distress to Victory). Oslo: Grøndahl & Søn Forlag A. S., 1977.

Clarkson, Peter C. "Luther and Hitler: A Controversy Renewed." *Journal of Ecumenical Studies* XVII: 3 (1980).

Cohen, S. Ralph. "Scandinavia's Jewish Communities." *The American- Scandinavian Review* LVI:2 (June 1968), pp. 125–135.

Conway, J. S. *The Nazi Persecution of the Churches 1933–1945*. New York: Basic Books, 1968.

Cruickshank, Charles, *SOE in Scandinavia*. Oxford, New York: Oxford University Press, 1986.

Curtis, Monica, ed. *Norway and the War, September 1939–December 1940*. London: Oxford University Press, 1941.

Dagre, Tor. "20,000 Norwegians Worked in 250 Illegal Newspapers during the War." *Nytt Fra Norge* (News From Norway), November 23, 1981.

Dahl, Hans Fredrik. "The Scandinavian Right. An Elementary Introduction." *Scandinavian Review* 70: 2 (June 1982), pp. 21–26.

Dahl, Hans Fredrik. *Dette er London, NRK i krig, 1940–1945* (This is London, Norwegian Broadcasting at War, 1940–1945). Oslo: J. W. Cappelen, 1978.

Dahl, Hans Fredrik, Bernt Hagtvet, and Guri Hjeltnes. *Den norske nasjonalsocialismen. Nasjonal Samling 1933–1945 i tekst og bilder* (The Norwegian National Socialism. National Union Party 1933–1945 in Text and Pictures). Oslo: Pax Forlag, 1982.

Danielsen, R., and Stein Ugelvik Larsen, eds. *Fra idé til dom: Noen trekk fra utviklingen av Nasjonal Samling* (From Idea to Sentencing: Some Aspects of the Development of the National Union Party). Bergen: Universitetsforlaget, 1976.

Dawidowicz, Lucy S. *A Holocaust Reader*, New York: Behrman House, 1976.

Dawidowicz, Lucy S. *The Holocaust and the Historians*. Cambridge: Harvard University Press, 1981.

Dawidowicz, Lucy S. *The War Against the Jews 1933–1945*. New York: Holt, Rinehart and Winston, 1975.

Den norske regjerings virksomhet under krigen fra 9. april 1940 til 22. juni 1945. Departementenes meldinger. Utgitt av Stortinget (Activities of the Norwegian Government during the War from April 9, 1940 to June 22, 1945. Reports by the Departments. Published by the Parliament). Oslo: H. Aschehoug & Co. (W. Nygaard), 1948.

Den Norske Tilskuer (The Norwegian Observer), Nos. 41, 42 (October 8, 1817), pp. 334–336.

Den Nye Verdenskeiser (The New World Emperor; i. e., The Protocols of the Elders of Zion). Christiania: 1920, another edition, 1944.

Derry, T. K. *A History of Modern Norway 1814–1972.* Oxford: Oxford University Press, 1973.

Derry, T. K. *A History of Scandinavia — Norway, Sweden, Denmark, Finland and Iceland.* Minneapolis: University of Minnesota Press, 1979.

Derry, T. K. *A Short History of Norway,* 2nd edition. London, 1968.

Derry, T. K. *The Campaign in Norway, History of the Second World War.* Butler, J. R. M., ed. United Kingdom Military Series. London: Her Majesty's Stationery Office, Sanders, Phillips and Co. Ltd., 1952.

Derry, T. K. "Norway." In: J. Woolf, ed. *European Fascism,* pp. 217–230. New York: Random House, 1968.

des Pres, Terence. *The Survivor: An Anatomy of Life in the Death Camps.* New York: Oxford University Press, 1976.

Ditleff, N. Chr., *Da tysklandsfangene ble reddet* (When the Prisoners in Germany Were Rescued) Oslo: Johan Grundt Tanum, 1955.

Drinan, Robert F. "The Christian Response to the Holocaust." *Annals of the American Academy of Political and Social Sciences,* vol. 450. Philadelphia (July 1980), pp. 179–189.

Duker, Abraham G., and Meir Ben-Horin. *Emancipation and Counter- Emancipation.* New York: Ktav Publishing Co., 1974.

Dyrhaug, Tore. *Norge okkupert! Tysk etterretning om Norge og nordmenn 1942–1945* (Norway Occupied! German Reports about Norway and Norwegians 1940–1945). Oslo: Universitetsforlaget, 1985.

Eckstein, Harry. *Division and Cohesion in a Democracy. A Study of Norway.* Princeton: Princeton University Press, 1966.

Egeland, Erik. "Ulstein's Saga," *Aftenposten,* Oslo, January 24, 1978.

Eide, Asbjørn. *Kyrkjestriden, okkupasjonsmakta og Nasjonal Samling. Hovedoppgave i historie* (The Church Struggle and the Rulers of the Occupation). Oslo: University Library, 1971.

Eitinger, Leo. "Concentration Camp Survivors in the Post-War World." *American Journal of Orthopsychiatry* XXXII (1962), pp. 367–375.

Eitinger, Leo. *Concentration Camp Survivors in Norway and Israel.* Oslo: Universitetsforlaget; and London: Allen & Unwin, 1964.

Eitinger, Leo. "On Being a Psychiatrist and a Survivor." In: Alvin H. Rosenfeld and Irving Greenberg, eds. *Confronting the Holocaust: The Impact of Elie Wiesel.* Bloomington and London: Indiana University Press, 1978.

Eitinger, Leo. *"Overlevende fra konsentrasjonsleirer i judaistisk sikt"* (Concentration Camp Survivors from the Perspective of Jewish Studies), *Nordisk Judaistik* (Scandinavian Jewish Studies) I: 1 (December 1975), pp. 41–48.

Eitinger, Leo. *Psykiatriske undersøkelser blant flyktninger i Norge* (Psychiatric Investigations among Refugees in Norway). Oslo: Universitetsforlaget, 1958.

Eitinger, Leo. "Preliminary Notes on a Study of Concentration Camp Survivors in Norway." *Israel Annals of Psychiatry and Related Disciplines* I: 1 (April 1963), pp. 59–67.

Eitinger, Leo (Ed.), *The Antisemitism in Our Time. A Threat Against Us All. Pro-*

ceedings of the First International Hearing on Antisemitism Oslo, 7–8 June 1983. Oslo: The Nansen Committee, 1984.

Eitinger, Leo, and Oskar Mendelsohn. *"Ni av 530 på "Donau" overlevde"* (Nine out of 530 onboard the *Donau* Survived), *Aftenposten*, Oslo, May 8, 1985.

Eitrem, Hans. "En Situasjon i Wergelands Liv" (A Situation in Wergeland's Life). *Samtiden*, Oslo, 1970.

Elberling, Emil. *"Skildring af jøder i Dansk (og Norsk) Digtning"* (Description of Jews in Danish (and Norwegian) Poetry). *Tidsskrift for Jødisk Historie og Literatur* III (1925), pp. 261–284, Copenhagen.

Eliot, Thomas, and Arthur Hillman. *Norway's Families*. Philadelphia, 1959.

Embassy of the United States, London. Document No. 5559. Subject: Position of Norwegian Government. Washington, D.C.: National Archives No. 730032, July 8, 1940.

Encyclopedia Judaica. "Holocaust," Vol. 8, Columns 828–916. Jerusalem: Keter, 1971 (reprinted in separate paperback by Keter as *Holocaust*, Israel Pocket Library).

Encyclopedia Judaica. "Norway: Holocaust Period." Vol. 12, p. 1224. Jerusalem-New York: Macmillan Publishing Co., 1971.

Fasting, Kåre. *Musikkselskabet, "Harmonien" gjennom to hundre år* (The Musical Society, The Harmony, During Two Hundred Years). Bergen: Johan Grieg, 1965.

Fein, Helen. *Accounting for Genocide. National Responses and Jewish Victimization During the Holocaust*. New York: The Free Press, 1979.

Findahl, Theodor. *Jøde* (Jew). Oslo: 1933.

Fjellbu, Arne. *Memoirs from the War Years*. Minneapolis: Augsburg Publishing House, 1947.

Fjellbu, Arne. *Minner fra Krigsårene* (Memoirs from the War Years). Oslo: Land og Kirke, 1945.

Flint, Johan T. "The Church in Relation to Family Life." In: T. D. Eliot, A. Hillmann, et al., eds. *Norway's Families*. Philadelphia, 1960.

Flint, Johan T. "The Secularization of Norwegian Society." *Comparative Studies in Society and History*, Den Haag VI: 3 (1964), pp. 325–344.

Flønes, Olav, and Ole Skirstad,. *Partisaner, Soldater, og S.D.* (Partisans, Soldiers and S.D.). Trondheim: A. Holbæk Eriksen and Co., 1945.

Förhandlingarna 1945 om svensk intervention i Norge, och Danmark (Negotiations in 1945 Regarding Swedish Intervention in Norway and Denmark). Stockholm: Kungl. Utrikesdepartementet, Ny serie II: 11, 1957.

Forskrifter i medhold av lov av 26 oktober 1942 vedrørende inndragning av formue som har tilhørt jøder (Regulations in Reference to the Law of October 26, 1942 Concerning Confiscation of Properties Which Have Belonged to Jews). *Norwegian Law Gazette* (January 8, 1943).

Fra Oslo Byrett. *Dom 22.12 1948 over Halldis Neegaard Østbye, "Tiltalens post 3"* (From the Court Record of Oslo Municipality, December 22, 1948.)

Franzen, I. N. *"For Jøderne"* (For the Jews). *Den Constitutionelle, 7de Aargang*. No. 135 (15. mai 1842).

Friediger, Marcus. *Den Jødiske rituelle Schächtning* (The Jewish Ritual Slaughtering). København, 1926.

Friedman, Philip. *Roads to Extinction. Essays on the Holocaust.* Ada A. J. Friedman, ed. Philadelphia: The Jewish Publication Society of America, 1980.

Friedman, Philip. *Their Brothers' Keepers.* New York: Crown Publishers, 1957.

Friedman, Saul. *No Haven for the Oppressed. United States Policy Towards Jewish Refugees.* Detroit: Wayne State University Press, 1973.

Friedmann, Tuwiah. *Dokumentsammlung über "Die Deportierung der Juden aus Norwegen nach Auschwitz"* (Documentary Collection on the "Deportation of Jews from Norway to Auschwitz"). Ramat Gan, Israel: Stadt-Verwaltung, 1963.

Friis, Erik J. "The Norwegian Government-in-Exile, 1940–1945." In: Carl F. Bayerschmidt and Erik J. Friis, eds. *Scandinavian Studies,* pp. 422–444. Seattle: University of Washington Press, 1965.

Fritt Folk, January 14, 1939. *"Vekk med det jødisk marxistiske diktatur i Norge."* (Abolish the Jewish-Marxist Dictatorship in Norway).

Fritt Folk, March 18, 1939. *"Jakobs røst. Hvem råder over den engelske presse?"* (Jacob's Voice. Who Rules the English Press?).

Fritt Folk, February 11, 1939. *"Overfylt hus til Quislings foredrag tirsdag. Resolusjon mot jødeinvasjonen vedtatt med overveldende majoritet."* (Full House at Quisling's lecture Tuesday. Resolution against Jewish Invasion accepted by overwhelming majority).

Frøyland, Lars. *I Korsets Tegn* (By the Sign of the Cross). Oslo: Viking Forlag, 1943.

Gabrielsen, Bjørn Vidar. *Menn og Politikk. Senterpartiet 1920–1970* (Men and Politics. The Center Party 1920–1970). Oslo: H. Aschehoug & Co. (W. Nygaard), 1977.

Galtung, Johan. "Norway in the World Community." In: Natalie Rogoff Ramsøy, ed. *Norwegian Society,* pp. 395-398. New York: Humanities Press, 1974.

Giertsen, Børre. R. (ed.), *Norsk Fangeleksikon. Grinifangene.* (Norwegian Encyclopedia of Prisoners. The Grini Prisoners), Oslo, 1946.

Gilbert, Martin. *Atlas of the Holocaust.* Jerusalem: Steimatsky, 1982.

Gilbert, Martin. *Final Journey. The Fate of the Jews in Nazi-Europe.* New York: Mayflower Books, 1979.

Gilbert, Martin. *The Holocaust. A History of the Jews of during the Second World War.* New York: Holt, Rinehart and Winston. Philadelphia: The Jewish Publication Society of America, 1985.

Gjelsvik, Tore. *Hjemmefronten: Den sivile motstand under okkupasjonen 1940–1945* (The Civil Resistance during the Occupation 1940–1945). Oslo: J. W. Cappelens Forlag, 1977.

Gjelsvik, Tore. *Norwegian Resistance 1940–1945.* London: C. Hurst and Co., 1979.

Gordon, Gerd Stray. *The Norwegian Resistance during the German Occupation, 1940–1945: Repression, Terror and Resistance, the West Country of Norway.* Ph.D. Thesis, University of Pittsburgh. Ann Arbor: University Microfilms International, 1978.

Greve, Tim. *Bergen i Krig 1940–1942* (Bergen at War 1940–1942). Bergen: J. W. Eide Forlag, 1979.

Greve, Tim. "Norsk forsøk på å redde jødene i 1942–1943. Britene sa nei" (Norwegian Attempts to Rescue Jews during 1942–1943. The British Said No). *Verdens Gang*, Oslo, October 4, 1983.

Grimnes, Ole Kristian. *Et flyktingesamfunn vokser fram. Nordmenn i Sverige 1940–1945* (A Society of Refugees Grows Forth. Norwegians in Sweden). Oslo: Universitetsforlaget, 1969.

Grimnes, Ole Kristian. "The Beginnings of the Resistance Movement." In: Henrik S. Nissen, ed. *Scandinavia during the Second World War*, pp. 182–220. Minneapolis: University of Minnesota Press, 1983.

Gutman, Yisrael and Livia Rothkirchen, eds. *The Catastrophe of European Jewry; Antecedents, History, Reflections.* Jerusalem: Yad Vashem, 1976.

Haaland, Arild. *"Nazisme, Litteratur og Knut Hamsun"* (Nazism, Literature and Knut Hamsun). In: Bjarte Birkeland and Stein Ugelvik Larsen, eds. *Nazismen og norsk litteratur* (Nazism and Norwegian Literature). Bergen-Oslo-Tromsø: Universitetsforlaget, 1975.

Haaland, Arild. *"Splittelse og Samhold"* (Division and Cohesion). In: *Norges Kulturhistorie* (Cultural History of Norway). Vol. 6, pp. 291–312. Oslo: H. Aschehoug & Co., 1980.

Haave, Carl, and Sverre J. Herstad. *I Quislings Hønsegård, Berg interneringsleir* (In Quisling's Chicken Coop, Berg Internment Camp). Oslo: Alb. Cammermeyers Forlag, 1948.

Hale, Frederick. "An Embattled Church." *Scandinavian Review* 69;1 (March 1981), pp. 52–60.

Helliesen Lund, Sigrid. *Alltid Underveis. I samarbeid med Celine Wormdal* (Always on the Road. In cooperation with Celine Wormdal). Oslo: Tiden Norsk Forlag, 1981.

Halvorsen, Terje. *"Holocaust og de illegale avisene"* (Holocaust and the Illegal Newspapers). *Dagbladet*, Oslo, July 18, 1977.

Hambro, Carl J. *I Saw it Happen in Norway.* New York: Appleton-Century, 1940.

Hambro, Johan. *C. J. Hambro, Liv og Drøm* (C. J. Hambro, Life and Dream). Oslo: Aschehoug, 1984.

Hamerow, Theodore S. "The Hidden Holocaust," *Commentary* 79: 3 (1985), p. 274.

Hammar, Thomas. *Sverige åt Svenskarna. Innvandringspolitik, utlänningskontroll och asylrätt 1900–1932* (Sweden for the Swedes. Policy of Immigration, Control of Foreigners and Right to Asylum, 1900–1932). Stockholm: Caslon Boktryckeri, 1964.

Handeland, Oscar. *Kristent Samråd i Kirkekampen* (The Christian Common Council in the Church Conflict). Bergen: Lunde, 1945.

Handlingar rör. Sveriges politik under andra världskriget. Förspelet till det tyske angreppet på Danmark och Norge den 9. april 1940 (Acts Regarding Sweden's Policies During World War II. Prelude to the German Attack on

Denmark and Norway, April 9, 1940). Stockholm: Kungl. Utrikesdepartementet, 1947.

Håndslag (Handshake. Facts and Orientation for Norwegians), No. 14, December 3, 1942.

Hansen, Thorkild. *Prosessen mot Hamsun* (The Process against Hamsun). Oslo: Gyldendal Norsk Forlag, 1978.

Hartmann, Sverre. *Bak fronten* (Behind the Front). Oslo. 1955.

Hartmann, Sverre. *Fører uten folk. Forsvarsminister Quisling — hans bakgrunn og vei inn i norsk politikk* (Leader without Followers. Minister of Defense Quisling — his background and path into Norwegian politics). Oslo: Tiden Norsk Forlag, 1970.

Hartmann, Sverre. *"Topphemmeligheter på svøm i Drøbaksundet"* (Top Secrets Afloat in the Drøbak Sound). *Aftenposten*, Oslo, Morning Edition, June 16, 1983.

Hartmann, Sverre, and Johan Vogt, eds. *Aktstykker om den tyske finanspolitikk i Norge 1940–1945* (Documents regarding the German Finance Policy in Norway) German edition: *Akten über die deutsche finanzpolitik in Norwegen 1940–1945*. Oslo: Universitetsforlaget, 1958.

Hauge, Jens Christian. *Frigjøringen* (The Liberation). Oslo: Gyldendal, 1970.

Haukaas, Kaare. *Faktaregister for Okkupasjonen*. Oslo, 1947. (mimeo).

Hausner, Gideon. *Justice in Jerusalem*. New York: Harper and Row, 1966.

Hayes, Paul M. *Quisling, the Career and Political Ideas of Vidkun Quisling, 1887–1945*. London: Newton Abbott, David and Charles, 1971.

Hechinger, Fred M. "700 Reich DP's Find New Life in Norway." *New York Post, August 15, 1948*.

Heiberg, Hans. *Så stort et hjerte. Henrik Wergeland* (Such a Big Heart. Henrik Wergeland). Oslo: Aschehoug, 1972.

"Hemmelig jødisk synagoge på loftet" (Secret Jewish synagogue in the attic). *Adresseavisen*, Trondheim, November 6, 1981.

Hewins, Ralph. *Quisling: Prophet Without Honor.* New York: The John Day Company, 1966.

Hilberg, Raul. *The Destruction of the European Jews*. Chicago: Quadrangle Books, 1961.

Hilberg, Raul. *The Destruction of the European Jews*. Revised and Definitive Edition. 3 Vols. New York-London: Holmes and Meier, 1985.

Hilger, Gustav and Alfred G. Meyer. *The Incompatible Allies. A Memoir- History of German-Soviet Relations 1918–1941*. New York: The Macmillan Company, 1953.

Hinsley, F. H. *British Intelligence in the Second World War*. Vol. I. London: Her Majesty's Stationery Office, 1978.

Hoberman, John M. "The Psychopathology of an Abortive Leadership: The Case of Vidkun Quisling." In: Robert S. Robins, ed. *Psychopathology and Political Leadership*, pp. 175–201. New Orleans: Tulane University, n.d.

Hoberman, John M. "Vidkun Quisling's Psychological Image." *Scandinavian Studies* 46: 3 (1974), pp. 242–264.

Hoess, R. *Commandant of Auschwitz*. New York: Popular Library, 1961.

Hoffman, Peter. *The History of the German Resistance.* Cambridge: Massachusetts Institute of Technology Press, 1977.

Høidal, Oddvar. "Hjort, Quisling and Nasjonal Samling's disintegration." *Scandinavian Studies* 47: 4 (1975), pp. 467–497.

Høidal, Oddvar. *"Quislings stilling ved den norske legasjon i Moskva juni 1927–desember 1929"* (Quisling's Position at the Norwegian Legation in Moscow, June 1927–December 1929). *Historisk Tidsskrift* (Oslo) 53:2 (1974).

Høidal, Oddvar, Quisling. *A Study in Treason.* Oslo: Norwegian University Press, 1989.

Holberg, Luvig. *"Epistola CDLXXV: Jøder lyver for at lyve"* (Jews lie in order to lie). In: F. J. Jansen, ed. *Epistler.* Vols. V, VII, VIII. København: H. Hagerup, 1953.

Holm, Laila. *"Familien Mahlers tragiske skjebne"* (The Tragic Fate of the Mahler Family). *Arbeider-Avisa*, Trondheim, March 30, 1983.

Holmboe, Haakon. *"De som ble tatt"* (Those Who Were Caught). In: Sverre Steen, ed. *Norges Krig* (Norway's War). Vol. 3, pp. 439–494. Oslo: Gyldendal Norsk Forlag, 1950.

Hovde, B. J. *The Scandinavian Countries, 1720–1865 — The Rise of the Middle Classes.* 2 Vols. Ithaca: Cornell University Press, 1948.

Høye, B., and T. M. Ager. *The Fight of the Norwegian Church Against Nazism.* New York: The Macmillan Company, 1943.

Hubatsch, Walter, *Die Deutsche Besetzung von Dänemark und Norwegen,* Göttingen: Musterschmidt, 1952.

Hubatsch, Walter. *"Weserübung": Die Deutsche Besetzung von Dänemark und Norwegen.* Göttingen: Musterschmidt Wissenschaftlischer Verlag, 1960.

Hurum, Hans Jørgen. *"Musikk under okkupasjonen"* (Music during the Occupation). *Kultur-Nytt* Oslo 7 (1981).

Hurum, Hans Jørgen. *Musikken under okkupasjonen 1940–1945* (Music during the Occupation, 1940–1945). Oslo: Aschehoug, 1946.

Ihlen, and Kugelberg. *Frendefolk: Streiflys Mellem Norge Og Sverige* (Neighbors: Sidelights Between Norway and Sweden). Oslo: Aschehoug, 1945.

Iltelegram fra Statspolitisjefen den 25. oktober 1942 kl. 10:30 (Urgent Telegram from Chief of State Police, October 25, 1942, at 10:30 A.M.). National Archives, Oslo.

Innstilling VI fra Undersøkelseskommisjonen av 1945. Regjeringen Nygaardsvolds virksomhet fra 7. juni 1940 til 25. juni 1945 (A Report from the Commission of Investigation of 1945. Activities of the Government of Nygaardsvold from June 7, 1940 to June 25, 1945). Oslo: 1947.

International Military Tribunal. Vol. 28, p. 406, Soc. 1809-PS; Vol. 34, Doc. 065.

Jacobsen, Elsa. *"Antisemittisme og kristendomsundervisning"* (Anti-Semitism and Instruction in Christianity). *Dagbladet*, Oslo, August 23, 1956.

Jæger, Henrik. *Illustrert Norsk Litteraturhistorie* (Illustrated History of Norwegian Literature), Kristiania: 1896.

Jameson H., and J. Sharp. "Non-Violent Resistance and the Nazis: The Case of

Norway." In: M. Q. Sibley, ed. *The Quiet Battle*. New York: Doubleday, 1963.

Jansen, F. J. Billeskov, ed. *Ludvig Holberg Værker i Tolv Bind*. Vol. III: *Jødiske Historie fra Verdens Begyndelse, fortsatt til disse Tider*. København: Rosenkilde og Bagger, 1970.

Jarner, Leon. *"Antisemittismen i norsk hverdagsliv"* (Anti-Semitism in Norwegian Daily Life). *Verdens Gang*, Oslo, November 29, 1947

Jensen, Magnus. *Norges Historie fra 1905 til våre dager* (History of Norway from 1905 until Today). Oslo: Universitetsforlaget, 1971.

Jerneck, Bengt. *Folket uten frykt*. *Norge 1942–43* (The People Without Fear. Norway 1942-43). Oslo: Johan Grundt Tanum, 1945.

Jewish Bulletin, The. London. No. 13, September 1942/5702: "A Message from the Norwegian Prime Minister Professor Nygaardsvold." Yad Vashem 054/38.

"Jewish Persecution-Deportation from Oslo," American Legation, Stockholm, No. 1629, April 9, 1943. Norwegian Press Section, Bulletin No. 204, December 4, 1942. National Archives, Washington D.C.

Jewish Telegraphic Agency News, June 10, 1941.

"Jøder" (Jews). In: *Kulturhistorisk Leksikon for nordisk Middelalder* (Cultural-Historical Encyclopedia of the Nordic Middle Ages), Vol. VIII. København: Rosenkilde & Bagger, 1963, pp. 74–78.

Johansen, Jahn Otto. *"Anti-semittismen idag"* (Anti-Semitism Today). *Kirke og Kultur*, Særtrykk (Special Reprint), lecture at the Theological Faculty, University of Oslo, January 27, 1981.

Johansen, Jahn Otto. *Anti-semitismens spøkelse* (The Ghost of Anti-Semitism). Oslo: Ansgar Forlag, 1985.

Johansen, Jahn Otto. *Det hendte også her* (It Also Happened Here). Oslo: J. W. Cappelens Forlag, 1984.

Johansen, Jahn Otto. *Min jødiske krig* (My Jewish War). Oslo: J. W. Cappelens Forlag, 1983.

Johansen, Jahn Otto. *Min jødiske reise* (My Jewish Journey). Oslo: J. W. Cappelens Forlag, 1982.

Johansen, Jahn Otto. *Min Yiddische mamma* (My Yiddish Mother). Oslo: J. W. Cappelens Forlag, 1980.

Johansen, Per Ole. *"Kampen om Menstadslaget"* (The Fight over the Battle at Menstad). *Tidsskrift for arbeiderbevegelsens historie* 1 (1982), pp. 147–162.

Johansen, Per Ole. *Oss selv nærmest* (We Are Closest to Ourselves). *Norge og jødene 1914–1943*. Oslo: Gyldendal Norsk Forlag, 1984.

Jødisk Kvinneforening, Trondheim, 1919–1969. En oversikt over foreningens virke gjennom 50 år. (Jewish Women's Association, Trondheim, 1919–1969. A Survey of the Association's Work through 50 years.), Trondheim: Adresseavisens Boktrykkeri, 1969, 15 pp.

Jonassen, Christen T. *Value Systems and Personality in a Western Civilization: Norwegians in Europe and America*. Columbus, OH: Ohio State University Press, 1983.

Jørgensen, Jens Peter. "*Gud er både god og streng*" (God is both good and strict), *Vårt Land* (Our Land), August 12, 1980.

Kabell, Aage. *Wergeland*. Vol. 1: *Barndom og Ungdom*, (Childhood and Youth). *Skrifter utgitt av Det Norske Videnskapsakademi i Oslo, Historisk-Filosofisk Klasse* (Volumes published by the Norwegian Academy of Science Historical-Philosophical Faculties) Oslo: Aschehoug, 1956.

Karlsen, Thorleif. *Lang dag i politiet* (Long Day in the Police). Oslo: Gyldendal Norsk Forlag, 1979.

Katz, Fred E. "A Sociological Perspective to the Holocaust." *Modern Judaism* (October 1982), Baltimore: The Johns Hopkins University Press, vol. 2, No. 3, October 1982, pp. 273–296.

Katz, Fred E. "Implementation of the Holocaust: the Behavior of Nazi Officials." *Comparative Studies in Society and History* 24 (July 3, 1982).

King Christian V Law of 1683. Vol. 3, Chapter 20, Articles 1 and 2 "*Om Jøder og Tatere.*" (Regarding Jews and Gypsies).

Kirken i sentrum. Trondheim Methodistmenighet 100 år, 1881-6, november, 1981 (The Church in the Center. The Trondheim Methodist Congregation through 100 years. 1881–November 6, 1981). Oslo: Norsk Forlagsselskap, 1981.

Kjellstadli, Sverre. "*Den norske militære motstand og SOE*" (Norwegian Military Resistance and SOE [SOE = Special Operations Executive). In: *Norge og den 2. Verdenskrig, 1940 Fra Nøytral til Okkupert* (Norway in in the Second World War. From Neutrality to Occupation), pp. 241–264. Oslo: Universitetsforlaget, 1969.

Kjellstadli, Sverre. *Hjemmestyrkene. Hovedtrekk av den militære motstand under okkupasjonen.* Vol. I. Oslo: Aschehoug, 1959.

Kjellstadli, Sverre. "Milorg 1940–45". *Heimevernsbladet*, May, 1955.

Kjellstadli, Sverre. "The Resistance Movement in Norway and the Allies, 1940–45," In: *European Resistance Movements, 1939–1945, pp. 324–339. Second International Conference on the History of Resistance. New York: Pergamon Press, 1964.*

Klausen, Arne Martin, ed. *Den norske væremåten. Antropologiske søkelys på norsk kultur* (The Norwegian Ethos. Anthropological Investigations of Norwegian Culture). Oslo: J. W. Cappelens Forlag, 1984.

Klausen, Arne Martin. "*Sosial organisasjon i et norsk dissentersamfunn*" (Social Organization in a Norwegian Society of Dissent). *Tidsskrift for samfunnsforskning* Oslo (1960), pp. 153–176.

Knudsen, Harold Franklin. *Jeg var Quisling's sekretær* (I was Quisling's Secretary). København: Eget Forlag, 1951.

Koblik, Steven, ed. *Sweden's Development from Poverty to Affluence,1750–1970*. Minneapolis: University of Minnesota Press, 1975.

Koblik, Steven, "No Truck with Himmler." The Politics of Rescue and the Swedish Red Cross Mission, March–May 1945," *Scandia. Tidsskrift för historisk forskning* Vol. 51, Nos. 1–2, 1985, pp. 173–195.

Koht, Halvdan. *Norsk Utanrikspolitikk fram til 9. april 1940* (Norwegian Foreign Policy to April 9, 1940). Oslo: 1947.

Koht, Halvdan. *Norway: Neutral and Invaded.* New York: Macmillan. 1941.
Koblik, Steven, *The Stones Cry Out. Sweden's Response to the Persecution of the Jews 1933-1945* New York: Holocaust Library, 1988.
Koht, Halvdan. *Henrik Wergeland. Ei Folkeskrift* (A Popular Edition) Kristiania: H. Aschehoug & Co., 1908.
Kolsrud, Ole. *"For 40 år siden — Da nordmenn jaget jøder: Rød "J" i alle pass,"* (Forty years ago — When Norwegians Persecuted Jews: Red "J" in All Passports"), *Dagbladet, Oslo,* October 16, 1982.
Kongeriget Norges Grundlov Given I Rigsforsamlingen paa Eidsvold den 17de mai 1814. Oslo: H. Aschehoug & Co., 1964.
Koritzinsky, Harry. *"Jødene i Norge 1940–1942, — Redegjørelse avgitt i Stockholm, 30. november 1942"* (The Jews in Norway, 1940–1942. A report given in Stockholm, November 30, 1942). *Yad Vashem Archives,* Jerusalem.
Koritzinsky, Harry M. *Jødernes historie i Norge. Henrik Wergelands kamp for jødesaken* (The History of the Jews in Norway. Henry Wergeland's Fight for the Jewish Cause). Kristiania: 1922.
Kraglund, Ivar. *Narvik-Planen; tanker om en demarkasjonslinje i Nord-Norge, 1940* (The Narvik Plan; Thoughts about a Line of Demarcation in Northern Norway, 1940). Hovedoppgave i historie, høsten 1981, Universitetet i Oslo (M.A. Thesis, Institute of History, University of Oslo), Fall 1981.
Kramish, Arnold. *The Griffin. The Greatest Untold Espionage Story of World War II.* Boston: Houghton Mifflin Company, 1986.
Krausnik, Hermut, Hans Buckheim, Martin Broszat and Hans Adolf Jacobsen. *Anatomy of the SS State.* New York: Walker and Company, 1968.
Kren, George N., and Leon Rappaport. "Resistance to the Holocaust: The Idea and the Act." In: Yehuda Bauer and Nathan Rotenstreich, eds. *The Holocaust as Historical Experience.* New York: Holmes & Meier, 1981.
"Kringsjå — Innenrikspolitisk månedsoversikt, oktober måned 1942" (Monthly Survey of Domestic Affairs). *Hirdspeilet. Arbeidsplan for Hirdførere* 1:1, November 30, 1942.
Kunngjøring, Reservepolitiet, Nr. 222/1944, Stockholm, den 22. aug. 1944: Fra Sjefen for Reservepolitiet.
Kunngjøring, Staatspolitet, Oslo- og Aker Avdeling, Riksarkivet, Oslo, STAPO-O.A.Arv. 5000/42.
Kvam, Ragnar. "Among Two Hundred Survivors from Auschwitz." *Judaism* 28: 2 (Summer 1979), p. 285.
Kvam, Ragnar. *Den siste Ghetto* (The Last Ghetto). Oslo: H. Aschehoug & Co., 1975.
Lange, August, and Johan Schreiner, eds. *Griniboken* (The Book About Grini). 2 Vols. Oslo: Gyldendal Norsk Forlag, 1946.
Laqueur, Walter. *The Terrible Secret Suppression of the Truth About Hitler's "Final Solution."* Boston: Little, Brown & Co., 1980.
Larsen, Karen. *A History of Norway.* Princeton: Princeton University Press; and New York: The American-Scandinavian Foundation, 1948.
Larsen, Stein Ugelvik. *"Det angår også Norge: Vanlige politifolk offer for farlig kobling."* (It also concerns Norway). *Bergens Tidende,* March 31, 1979.

Larsen, Turid. "*Norge — Verdens største lokalsamfunn*" (Norway–The World's Largest Local Society). Reviewing Arne Martin Klausen, ed. *Den norske væremåten* (The Norwegian Ethos). *Arbeiderbladet*, Oslo, March 29, 1984.

Lehmkuhl, Herman. *Hitler Attacks Norway*, Montreal-London-Washington: Norwegian Information Services, 1943.

Levin, Marcus. *Rapport til Oslo Politikammer (Landssvikavdelingen)* (Report to Oslo Police Precinct, Department for Treason), August 31, 1946.

Levin, Nora. *The Holocaust: The Destruction of European Jewry 1933–1945*. New York: Thomas Y. Crowell, 1968.

Levin, Robert. *Med Livét i hendene* (With My Life at Stake). Oslo: J.W. Cappelens Forlag, 1983.

Lie, Trygve. *Hjemover* (Homeward). Oslo: Tiden Norsk Forlag, 1958

Lie, Trygve. *Leve eller dø, Norge i Krig* (Live or Die, Norway at War). Oslo; Tiden Norsk Forlag, 1955.

Lindström, Ulf. *Fascism in Scandinavia 1920–1940*. Stockholm: Almquist & Wiksell International, 1985.

Lindvald, Axel. "*Af Jødernes Frigørelseshistorie. Den danske Regering og Jøderne omkring 19. hundredes Begyndelse.*" (From the History of the Emancipation of the Jews. The Danish Government and the Jews at the Beginning of the 19th century). *Tidsskrift for Jødisk Historie og Literatur*. København: Levin og Munksgaard, vol. III, 1925.

Lislegaard, Othar, and Torbjørn Børte. *Skuddene som reddet Norge: Senkningen av "Blücher" 9. april, 1940* (The Shots That Saved Norway: The Sinking of the "Blücher," April 9, 1940). Oslo: Aschehoug, 1975.

Lødrup, Hans P. *Det store oppgjør* (The Great Accounting). Oslo: Dreyer, 1945.

Loock, Hans-Dietrich. *Quisling, Rosenberg und Terboven, Zur Vorgeschichte und Geschichte der National Sozialistichen Revolution in Norwegen*. Stuttgart: Deutsch Verlags-Anstalt, 1970.

Loock, Hans-Dietrich. "Support for *Nasjonal Samling* in the Thirties." In Stein Ugelvik Larsen, Bernt Hagtvet, Jan Petter Myklebust, eds. *Who Were the Fascists? Social Roots of European Fascism*. Bergen-Oslo-Tromsø: Universitetsforlaget, 1980.

"*Lov av 26 oktober 1942 om inndraging av formue som tilhører jøder*" (Law of October 26, 1942 Regarding Confiscation of Jewish Properties). *Norges Handels-og Sjøfartstidende*, October 27, 1942.

Lov av 13. juni 1969, nr. 25 om trudomssamfunn og ymist anna (Law of June 13, 1969, No. 25, Regarding Religious Societies and Other Items).

Ludlow, Peter. "Britain and Northern Europe, 1940–1945." *Scandinavian Journal of History* 4 (1979), pp. 123–162.

Lund, Sigrid Helliesen. *Alltid Underveis. I samarbeid med Celine Wormdal;* (Always on the Road. In cooperation with Celine Wormdal), Oslo: Tiden Norsk Forlag, 1981.

Luihn, Hans. *De illegale avisene* (The Illegal Newspapers). Oslo: Universitetsforlaget, 1960.

Luther, Martin. "On the Jews and Their Lies." In: *Luther's Works: T he Chris-*

tian Society IV, Vol. 47. Philadelphia: Concordia Publishing House and Fortress Press, 1972.

Marrus, Michael R., and Robert O. Paxton. "The Nazis and the Jews in Occupied Western Europe, 1940–1944 (France, Belgium, Holland, Denmark, Norway and Italy)." *Journal of Modern History* 54 (December 1982), pp. 687–714.

Masur, Norbert. *En Jude talar med Himmler* (A Jew Talks With Himmler). Stockholm: Albert Bonniers, 1945.

Matheson, Peter Clarkson. "Luther and Hitler: A Controversy Renewed." *Journal of Ecumenical Studies* XVII: 3 (Summer 1980), pp. 445–453.

Melchior, Marcus. "*Jødiske Typer i Holbergs Komedier*" (Jewish Types in Holberg's Comedies). In: *Tænkt og Talt* (Thought and Spoken) København: H. Hirschsprungs Forlag, 1967, pp. 216–223.

Melsom, Odd. *På Nasjonal Uriaspost* (On National Post as Urias). Oslo: Institutt for Norsk Okkupasjonhisstorie, 1975.

Mendelsohn, Oskar. "Actions Against the Jews in Norway during the War." *Nordisk Judaistik* (Scandinavian Jewish Studies) 3: 2 (March 1981), pp. 27–35.

Mendelsohn, Oskar. "*De norske jødenes martyrium*" (The Martyrdom of the Norwegian Jews). *Judisk Krönika*, Stockholm (February 1961).

Mendelsohn, Oskar. "*Holocaust-litteraturen på norsk*" (The Literature on the Holocaust in Norwegian). *Nordisk Judaistik* (Scandinavian Jewish Studies) 4: 1 (October 1982), pp. 15–22.

Mendelsohn, Oskar. "*Inntrykk av undervisning og undervisningsmateriale i norske skoler*" (Impressions of Instruction and Material of Instruction in Norwegian Schools). *Nordisk Judaistik* (Scandinavian Jewish Studies) 4: 1 (October 1982), pp. 43–47.

Mendelsohn, Oskar. "*Jødeforfølgelsene i Norge — Norsk motstand — Hjelp til Flukt*" (Jewish Persecutions in Norway — Norwegian Resistance — Help to Escape.) *Jødisk Menighetsblad* 2:3 (Oslo) Kislev 5738, December, 1977.

Mendelsohn, Oskar. "Jødene i Norge" (The Jews in Norway). In: Hallvard Rieber-Mohn and Leo Eitinger, eds. *Retten til å overleve. En bok om Israel, Norge og antisemittismen* (The Right to Survive, A Book About Israel, Norway and anti-Semitism). pp. 71–85. Oslo: J.W. Cappelens Forlag, 1976.

Mendelsohn, Oskar. "Jødene i Norge" (The Jews in Norway). In: Egil A. Wyller, and Terje Gudbrandson. eds. *Jødene og Jødedommen* (The Jews and Judaism), pp. 73–87. Oslo: Universitetsforlaget, 1977.

Mendelsohn, Oskar. *Jødenes historie i Norge gjennom 300 å. Bind I* (The History of Jews in Norway Over 300 Years. Vol. I). Oslo: Universitetsforlaget, 1969. Vol. II, 1986.

Michel, Henri. *The Shadow War: European Resistance 1939–1945*. Translated from the French by Richard Barry. New York: Harper and Row, 1972.

Milgram, Stanley. *Obedience to Authority. An Experimental View.* New York: Harper and Row, 1968.

Milward, Alan S. *The Fascist Economy in Norway.* Oxford: Clarendon Press, 1972.

Mjøen, Jon Alfred. *Det norske program for rasehygiene* (The Norwegian Program for Racial Hygiene). Oslo: 1932.

Molland, Einar. *"Kirkens Kamp"* (The Fight of the Church). In: Sverre Steen, ed. *Norges Krig, 1940–1945* (Norway's War, 1940–1945). Vol. III, pp. 35–72. Oslo: Gyldendal Norsk Forlag, 1950.

Monneray, Henry, ed. *La Persécution des Juif en France et dans les autres pays de l'ouest presentée par la France à Nuremberg.* Paris: 1947.

Mordal, Jacques. *La Campagne de Norvége.* Paris: Self, 1949.

Næss, Harald. "Review of Torkild Hansen, *Prosessen mot Hamsun*". *Scandinavian Studies* 51: 3 (1979).

Nansen, Odd. *Fra dag til dag* (From Day to Day). Oslo: Dreyer, Vols. I–III, 1946.

Nansen, Odd. *From Day to Day.* New York: G. P. Putnam's Sons, 1949.

Narrowe, Morton H. "Action or Assimilation? A Jewish Identity Crisis." *Scandinavian Review,* New York 66: 1 (March 1978), pp. 47–52.

Nelson, George R. *Freedom and Welfare, Social Patterns in the Northern Countries of Europe.* The Ministries of Social Affairs of Denmark, Finland, Norway and Sweden, 1953.

Nerman, Ture. *Norsk Front. Det norske folkets frihetskamp.* Stockholm: Federative, 1941 (Norwegian Front. The Fight for Liberty of the Norwegian People).

News of Norway, Washington D.C., Vol. 22, No. 37, November 22, 1965.

Nilus (pseudonym). *Jødefaren* (The Jewish Danger), n.p., n.d.

1945 Års Svenska Hjälpexpedition till Tyskland. Førspel och Förhandlingar (The Aid Expedition in 1945 to Germany. Prelude and Negotiations). Stockholm: Kungl. Utrikesdepartementet Ny serie II: 8, 1956.

Nissen, Bernt A. *Året 1814* (The Year 1814) Oslo: Aschehoug, 1964.

Nissen, Henrik, ed. *Scandinavia During the Second World War.* Minneapolis: The University of Minnesota Press, 1983.

Nøkleby, Berit. *"Fra november til april — Sendemann Bräuers personlige politikk"* (From November to April — Minister Bräuer's personal policy). In: *Norge og den 2. verdenskrig. Fra nøytral til okkupert. Studier i norske samtidshistorie.* Oslo-Bergen-Tromsø: Universitetsforlaget, 1969.

Nordiska Röster mot Judeförföljelse och Vald. Dokument och Kommentar. Stockholm: *Judisk Tidsskrift,* 1943.

Norge och den norske exil regeringen under andra Världskriget. Statens offentliga utredningar (Norway and the Norwegian Government-in-Exile during World War II. Public Investigations by the State). Stockholm: Justitiedepartementet, 1972.

Norge — Høyesterett (Norwegian Supreme Court) kjennelse den 18. februar 1977 i sak L.nr. 10B/1977, S.nr. 293/1976. (Verdict of February 18, 1977).

Norges Forhold til Sverige Under krigen 1940–45. Aktstykker utgitt av Det Kongelige Utenriksdepartment (Norway's Relationship to Sweden during the War, 1940–45. Documents published by the Royal Department of Public Affairs). 3 Vols. Oslo: Gyldendal Norsk Forlag, 1950.

Norges Offisielle Statistikk, Vol. IX, 26, p. 13: *"Stortingsvalget 1933"* (Parliamentary elections, 1933). *Norges Offisielle Statistikk*, Vol. IX, 107.

Norland, Andreas. *Harde tider. Fedrelandslaget i norsk politikk* (Hard Times. The Patriotic League in Norwegian Politics). Oslo: Dreyers Forlag, 1973.

Norsk Tidend, London (published by the Information Office, Royal Norwegian Government), November 28, 1942, and December 9, 1942.

"Norway." In: *Black Book of Localities Whose Jewish Population Was Exterminated by the Nazis*. Yad Vashem, 1965.

Nygaard, Knut. *"Hva visste vi?"* (What did we know?) *Bergens Tidende*, "Kronikk," June 29, 1983.

Nygaardsvold, Johan. *Beretning om den norske regjerings virksomhet fra 9. april 1940 til 25. juni 1945*. Utgitt av Stortinget (Activities of the Norwegian Government During the War from April 9, 1940 to June 22, 1945. Published by the Parliament). Oslo, H. Aschehoug & Co. (W. Nygaard), 1948.

Nyrønning, Sverre M. "Reddet jøder fra nazistenes Helvede" (Saved Jews from the hell of the Nazis). *Forsvarets Forum* (The Forum of the Defense), No. 5, March 31, 1980.

Nytt fra Norge, (News from Norway) October 24, 1978. and December 20, 1982.

Oberkommando der Wehrmacht, Kampf um Norwegen (The Battle Over Norway). Berlin: Zeitgeschichte-Verlag, 1940.

Office of Strategic Services. No. 32746 A-4457. Washington D.C.: National Archives, April 23, 1943.

Øksendal, Asbjørn. *Operasjon Oleander, Gestapo Trondheim og Leksvikaffæren, 1942–44 (Operation Oleander). Trondheim: Det Nordenfjeldske Forlag, 1968.*

Olson, Ted. "Death at Skrikerud Pond." *Harper's Magazine* 206: 1236 (May 1953), pp. 65–71.

Ørvik, Nils. *the Decline of Neutrality 1914–1945*. Oslo: Johan Grundt Tanum, 1953.

Palmstrøm, Finn, and Rolf Nordmann Torgersen. *Preliminary Reports on Germany's Crimes against Norway*. Oslo: Grøndahl og Søn. 1945.

Paltiel, Julius. *"Seks ganger på dødens terskel"* (Six Times on the Brink of Death). In Hans Melien, ed. *De kjempet for vår frihet* (They Fought For Our Freedom). pp. 55-68. Oslo: Aschehoug, 1979.

Paulsen, Helge. *"Antisemittisk handelsspionasje i Norge"* (Anti-Semitic Commercial Espionage in Norway). *Dagbladet*, Oslo, May 18, 1965.

Paulsen, Helge. *"Litt om forholdet mellom NS og Reichskommissariat i Norge 1940–45."* (Something of the Relationships between NS and Reichskommissariat). In: Rolf Danielsen and Stein Ugelvik Larsen, eds. *Fra idé til dom. Noen trekk fra utviklingen av Nasjonal Samling* (From Idea to Conviction. Some Aspects of the Development of the National Union Party), pp. 196–214. Bergen-Oslo-Tromsø: Universitetsforlaget, 1976.

Paulsen, Helge. *"Reichskommissariat og 'motytelsen' under riksrådsforhandlingene"* (Reichskommisariat and "reciprocity" during negotiations for a National Council), In: *Norge og den 2. Verdenskrig, 1940. Fra*

Nøytral til Okkupert (Norway in the Second World War. From Neutral to Occupied Country), pp. 287–356. Oslo: Universitetsforlaget, 1969.

Pearlman, Moshe. *The Capture and Trial of Adolf Eichmann.* New York: Simon and Schuster, 1963.

Petrow, Richard. *The Bitter Years. The Invasion and Occupation of Denmark and Norway, April 1940–May 1945.* New York: William Morrow and Co., 1974.

Poliakov, Leon. *Harvest of Hate. The Nazi Program for the Destruction of the Jews of Europe.* New York: Syracuse University Press, 1954.

Public Record Office (London), FO 371/33063 xc/A/5356, from British Legation, Stockholm, October 15, 1942.

Quisling, Vidkun. *Kampen mellem arier og jødemakt. Tale i Frankfurt, 28. Mars 1941 om jødeproblemet* (The fight between Aryan and Jewish power. Speech in Frankfurt about the Jewish problem, March 28, 1941). Oslo: *Nasjonal Samlings Rikstrykkeri,* 1941.

Quislingsaken. Samlet rettsreferat (The Case Against Quisling — Complete Legal Report). Oslo: A/S Bokkommisjon, 1945.

"Racial Questions and Persecution of the Jews in Norway," U.S. Legation, Stockholm, December 23, 1942, NND 730032.

Raeder, Erich. *Mein Leben* (My Life). Tübingen-Neckar, 1957. Vol. I, 1956; Vol. II, 1967.

Ramsøy, Natalie Rogoff, ed. *Det norske samfunn* (The Norwegian Society). Oslo: Gyldendal Norsk Forlag, 1968. English edition, Norwegian Society, New York: Humanities Press, 1974. Third edition, Lars Allden, Natalie Rogoff Ramsøy, Mariken Vaa, eds., Oslo: Gyldendal Norsk Forlag, 1986, 424 pp.

Rapport til Oslo Politikammer Landssvikavdelingen, avgitt av Kriminalassistene Thorbjørn Frøberg og Knut Ebeling (Report to Oslo Police Precinct) *Aksjonene mot jødene* (The Actions Against Jews). Oslo, October 4, 1946.

Rasmussen, Sigurd. *Barmhjertighetsfronten. Norges Røde Kors under krigen 1940–45* (The Charity Front. Norwegian Red Cross during the War 1940–45). Oslo, 1950.

Regjeringen og Hjemmefronten under Krigen. Aktstykker utgitt av Stortinget (The Government and the Home Front during the War. Documents Published by the Parliament). Oslo: H. Aschehoug & Co., 1948.

Reitlinger, Gerald. *The Final Solution: An Attempt to Exterminate the Jews of Europe 1939–1945.* New Jersey: Yoseloff, 1968.

Popperwell, Ronald G. *Norway.* London & Tonbridge: Ernst Benn Limited, 1972. "Proclamation from the Norwegian Government, agreed to by the King in Council." April 17, 1940.

"Proklamasjon fra Høysterett." Bestemmelser av Administrasjonsrådet (Announcement by the Supreme Court. Regulations by the Administrative Council). No. 1, May 8, 1940.

Protest Meeting, Stockholm, December 2, 1942, Yad Vashem Archives, 0/54/38.

Protokoll for møter i det Administrasjonsråd som er oppnevnt av Høyesterett mandag den 15 April, 1940. "År 1940 den 16. mai" (Protocol of Meetings of the Administrative Council Appointed by the Supreme Court, Monday, April 15, 1940).

Prytz, Carl Frederik. "Jødene og kirkebønnen" (The Jews and the Church Prayer). *Dagbladet*, Oslo, February 28, 1961.

Public Record Office (London), FO371/42752, from Foreign Office, Refugee Department to Sir Herbert Emerson, Inter-governmental Committee, 11D Regent Street, London, W. 1.

Public Record Office, FO371/2263, Dispatch No. 57 (1170/A), April 23, 1940; and PRO No. 883, British Consul General, Rotterdam, April 26, 1940.

Public Record Office, FO371/23653 XC/A/5356Public Record Office, FO371/24815/N37776263 and N3990/2/63. Reports from the British Naval Attaché/

Public Record Office, FO371/3286 XC/A/5321, November 19, 1942, British Embassy to Norway, Part I.

Public Record Office, FO371/3286, November 19, 1942, British Embassy to Norway, Part I, pp. 2–3.

Rautkallio, Hannu. *Finland and the Holocaust. The Rescue of Finland's Jews*. New York: Holocaust Library, 1987.

Rettslige forklaringer fra hjemvendte norske fanger (Legal depositions by returning Norwegian Jews). Testimony, February 26, 1946, Oslo: Tinghus.

Rieber-Mohn, Hallvard, and Leo Eitinger, eds. *Retten til å overleve. En bok om Israel, Norge og antisemittismen* (The Right to Survive. A Book About Israel, Norway and Anti-Semitism). Oslo: J.W. Cappelens Forlag, 1977.

Ringdal, Nils Johan. *Mellom Barken og Veden. Politiet under okkupasjonen* (Between the Bark and the Wood. The Police during the Occupation), Oslo: Aschehoug, 1987.

Riste, Olav, and Berit Nøkleby. *Norway 1940.-45: the Resistance Movement*. Oslo: Johan Grundt Tanum Forlag, 1970.

Robinson, Jacob, and Philip Friedman, eds. *Guide to Jewish History Under Nazi Impact*. Yad Vashem and YIVO Joint Documentary Project, Bibliographical Series No. 1. New York: St. Martin's Press, 1960.

Robinson, Nehemiah. *Indemnification and Reparations. Jewish Aspects*. New York: Institute of Jewish Affairs of The American Jewish Congress and World Jewish Congress, 1944.

Rolfsen, Wilh. *Usynlige veier. Blad av Edderkoppens og Flyktningseksportens Saga* (Invisible Roads. Chapters from the Saga of the Spider and the Transport of Refugees). Oslo: 1946.

Rødder, Sverre. *Bergen Politi under okkupasjonen* (The Police in Bergen during the Occupation). Bergen: Bergen Politikammer, 1974.

Rose, Arnold. *The Roots of Prejudice*. Paris: UNESCO, 1958.

Rosenberg, A. *Das Politische Tagebuch Alfred Rosenbergs 1934/35 und 1939*. München, 1964.

Ross, Robert W. *So It Was True. The American Protestant Press and the Nazi Persecution of the Jews*. Minneapolis: University of Minnesota Press, 1980.

Rubenstein, R. I. *The Cunning of History. The Holocaust and The American Future*. New York: Harper and Row, 1975.

Sachnowitz, Herman. *Det angår også deg* (It Also Concerns You). Oslo: Cappelens, 1976.

"*Sammenslutning mellem de to jødiske menigheter i Oslo. Men begge synagoger bibeholdes*" (Unification of the two Jewish congregations. But both synagogues remain). *Aftenposten*, Oslo, October 2, 1939.

Savosnick, Robert, *Jeg ville ikke dø!* (I did not want to die!) Oslo: Cappelen, 1986.

Saxlund, Eivind. *Jøder og Gojim* (Jews and Non-Jews). Christiania: 1910. Second Edition, 1911.

Scharffenberg, Johan. "*Jødehatet og jødeforfølgelsene*" (Jewish Hatred and Jewish Persecution). In: August Schow, ed. *Frihet og Menneskeverd* (Freedom and Human Worth), pp. 69–77. Oslo: H. Aschehoug & Co., 1972.

Scharffenberg, Johan. *Norske aktstykker til okkupasjonens forhistorie* (Norwegian Documents Regarding the Prehistory of the Occupation). Oslo: 1950.

Schjelderup, Ferdinand. *På Bred Front* (On a Broad Front). Oslo: Grøndahl and Søns Forlag, 1947.

Schleunes, K. A. *The Twisted Road to Auschwitz: Nazi Policy Toward German Jews, 1933–39.* Urbana, IL, 1970.

Schübeler, Ludwig. *Kirkekampen slik jeg så den* (The Church Struggle As I Saw It). Oslo: Lutherstiftelsen, 1946.

Seeskin, K. R. "The Reality of Radical Evil." *Judaism* 29: 4 (Fall 1980), pp. 440–453.

Seip, Didrik Arup. "Henrik Wergeland og jødene i Sverige" (Henrik Wergeland and the Jews in Sweden). *Edda* (1927).

Seip, Didrik Arup. *Hjemme og i fiendeland, 1940–1945* (At Home and in Enemy Country, 1940–1945). Oslo: Gyldendal, 1946.

Selznick, G. J., and S. Steinberg. *The Tenacity of Prejudice. Anti-Semitism in Contemporary America.* New York: Harper and Row, 1969.

Senje, Sigurd. *Ekko fra Skriktjenn. En dokumentarroman basert på Feldmannsaken 1942–47* (Echo from Skrik Pond. A documentary novel based on the Feldman Case). Oslo: Pax Forlag A. S., 1982.

Sharp, Gene. *Exploring Non-Violent Action.* Boston: Porter Sargent, 1974.

Shirer, William L. *Berlin Diary, The Journal of a Foreign Correspondent.* New York: Alfred A. Knopf, 1941.

Shirer, William L. *The Rise and Fall of the Third Reich.* New York: Simon and Shuster, 1960.

Simpson, Allen. "Knut Hamsun's Anti-Semitism." *Edda*, Oslo, No. 5 (1977), pp. 373–393.

Sinding, Ernst. "*Andres og eget i Ludvig Holbergs 'Den Jødiske Historie.'*" *Edda* 43: 4 (1959).

Singer, Philip, and Gilbert Cranbery. "Some of the Homeless and Tempest-Tossed Continental Jews Start Life Anew in Norway." *Nordisk Tidende*, Brooklyn, October 16, 1947.

Skard, Sigmund. *Bøker om Norges Kamp* (Books About the Fight of Norway). Oslo: Bibliografiske Samlinger, 1945.

Skodvin, Magne. "Det store fremstøt" (The Great Offensive) In: Steen, Sverre, ed. *Norges Krig, 1940–1945* (Norway's War, 1940–1945). Vol. II, pp. 573–734. Oslo: Gyldendal Norsk Forlag, 1948.

Skodvin, Magne. *Kampen om Okkupasjonsstyret i Norge*. Oslo: Det Norske Samlaget, 1956.

Skodvin, Magne. *"La Presse Norvégienne sous l'occupation Allemande"* (The Norwegian Press during the German Occupation). *Revue d'Historie de la Deuxième Guerre Mondiale* VIII (1970), pp. 69–86.

Skodvin, Magne. *"Norge i stormaktsstrategien: Fra Finlandsfreden til 'Wilfred'"* (From Finland's Peace to 'Wilfred'") In: Norge og den 2. Verdenskrig, 1940 Fra Nøytral til Okkupert (Norway in World War II. From Neutrality to Occupation), pp. 89–126.

Skodvin, Magne. *"Norsk okkupasjonhistorie i europeisk samanheng"* (Norwegian History of Occupation in European Context). *Nordisk Tidsskrift* 6 (1951), pp. 308–320.

Skodvin, Magne. *"Om bakgrunnen for Führer-Erlass av 24. april 1940"* (Regarding the Background for Hitler's Order of April 24, 1940). *Norsk Historisk Tidsskrift*, 35, No. 2, pp. 97–131.

Skodvin, Magne. *Som seilene fylles av stormen* (As the Sails Are Filled by the Storm). Oslo: Gyldendal Norsk Forlag, 1982.

Skodvin, Magne. *Striden om okkupasjonsstyret i Norge fram til 25de sept. 1940* (The Fight about the Rule of Occupation in Norway). Oslo: Det Norske Samlaget, 1956.

Skouen, Arne. *"Ytring"* (Remarks). *Dagbladet*, Oslo, August 20, 1973; April 6, 1979.

Snoek, Johan M. *The Grey Book: A Collection of Protests against Anti-Semitism and the Persecution of the Jews. Issued by Non-Roman Catholic Churches and Church Leaders during Hitler's Rule.* Assen, The Netherlands: Van Gorcum, 1969.

Sørhaug, Hans Christian *"Totemisme på norsk — betraktninger om den norske social-demokratismes vesen"* (Totemism in Norway — Considerations of the Essence of the Norwegian Social Democracy). In Arne Martin Clausen, ed. *Den norske væremåten* (The Norwegian Ethos), Oslo: J.W. Cappelens Forlag, 1984, pp. 61–87.

Steen, Sverre, ed. *Norges Krig 1940–45* (Norway's War 1940–45) 3 Vols. Oslo: Gyldendal, 1948–1950.

Steen, Sverre. *"Riksrådsforhandlingene"* (Negotiations for a Settlement). In: *Norge og den 2. Verdenskrig, 1940 Fra Nøytral til Okkupert* (Norway in World War II. From Neutrality to Occupation), pp. 127–283. Oslo: Universitetsforlaget, 1969.

Stemland, Terje. *"Jøder i Norge. Men vår drøm er like levende"* (Jews in Norway. But Our Dream is Still Alive). *A-Magasinet Uketillegg til Aftenposten*, No. 48, December 4, 1982.

Stempling av jøders legitimasjonsbevis from the Chief of Security Police, January 10, 1942. National Archives, Oslo, Ref. No 5289/41A.

Storing, James A. *Norwegian Democracy.* Boston: Houghton Mifflin Co., 1963.

Stortingsforhandlinger. Vol. 5, Document No. 18, 1927.

180

SAMUEL ABRAHAMSEN

Stortingsmelding nr. 11, 1952, Norges hjelp til flyktninger, Oslo: Social-departementet, 1952 (Parliamentary Report number 11, 1952, Norway's Help to Refugees).

Strafsache gegen Hellmuth Reinhard, Baden-Baden, February 1, 1967. (mimeographed)

Straffesak mot Vidkun Abraham Lauritz Jonssøn Quisling (Court Proeedings against Quisling). Oslo: Utgitt på offentlig bekostning av Eidsivating lagstols landssviksavdeling, 1946.

Strøm, Axel. Norwegian Concentration Camp Survivors. Oslo: Universitetsforlaget, 1968.

Strøm, Axel. "Rasisme og antisemittisme i Norge" (Racism and Anti-Semitism in Norway). In: Leo Eitinger, Mennesker blant mennesker. En bok om antisemittisme og fremmedhat. Med et tillegg av Axel Strøm (Men among Men. A book about Anti-Semitism and Xenophobia. With an Addition by Axel Strøm). Oslo: J.W. Cappelens Forlag A/S, 1985.

Strøm, Axel, et al. "Examination of Norwegian Ex-Concentration Camp Prisoners." Journal of Neuropsychiatry IV (1962), pp. 43–62.

Sundell, Olaf. 9. April (The Ninth of April), Stockholm: Sohlmans.

Suominen, Elina. Kuolemanlaiva S/S Hohenhörn. Juutalaispakolaisten kohtalo Suomessa (The Ship of Death S/S Hohenhörn. The Fate of the Jewish Refugees in Finland). Helsinki: Werner Söderström Osakeyhtiö, 1979.

Sverd, Irene, alias Halldis Neegard Østbye. Jødeproblemet og dets løsning (The Jewish Problem and its Solution). Oslo: Eget Forlag, Gjærder og Co., Boktrykkeri, 1939, 128 pp.

Sverd, Irene, alias Halldis Neegard Østbye. Jødenes Krig (The War of the Jews). Oslo: 1943.

Sveri, Knut. "Landssvikoppgjørets merkeligste rettsak" (The Strangest Case in the Legal Accounting for Treason). In: Anders Bratholm, Helge Olav Bugge, Nils Christie and Terkel Opsahl, eds. Lov og frihet. Festskrift til Johs. Andenæs, på 70-årsdagen 7. september 1982. Oslo: Universitetsforlaget, 1982.

Sveriges förhållande till Danmark och Norge under krigsåren. Redogörelser avgivna til utrikesnämnden av ministern for utrikesärendena 1941–45 (Sweden's Relationship to Denmark and Norway during the War Years. Reports Given to the Committee on Foreign Affairs by the Minister of Foreign Affairs, 1941–45). Stockholm: P. A. Nordstedt & Söners Förlag, 1945.

Sylten, Mikal P. O.. Hvem er hvem i Jødeverden, samt fortegnelse over fremmedes forretninger i Norge 1932 (Who's Who in the Jewish World, Including a Register of Businesses Owned by Foreigners in Norway, 1932). Oslo: Nationalt Tidsskrift, 1932, 1940.

Tangen, Dag. "Norges Krystallnatt, 1942: 10 jøder i hver konvolutt" (Norway's Crystal Night: 10 Jews in every envelope). Dagbladet, Oslo, April 4 and May 28, 1979.

Tenenbaum, Joseph. "The Crucial Year 1938." Yad Vashem Studies, Jerusalem II (1958), pp. 49–77.

Torgersen, R. N., and F. Palmstrøm. *Preliminary Report on Germany's Crimes Against Norway.* Oslo: Grøndahl og Søn, 1945.

Trommer, Aage. "Scandinavia and the Turn of the Tide." In: Henrik S. Nissen, ed., *Scandinavia During the Second World War.* Minneapolis: University of Minnesota Press, 1983.

Udgaard, Nils Morten. *Great Power Politics and Norwegian Policy.* Oslo: Universitetsforlaget, 1973.

Ugelvik Larsen, Stein "The Social Foundations of Norwegian Fascism, 1933–1945. An Analysis of Membership Data." In: Stein Ugelvik Larsen, Bernt Hagtvet, Jan Petter Myklebust, eds. *Who Were the Fascists? Social Roots of European Fascism.* pp. 595–620, Bergen-Oslo-Tromsø: Universitetsforlaget, 1980.

Ugelvik Larsen, Stein, Bernt Hagtvet, and Jan Petter Myklebust, eds. *Who Were The Fascists? Social Roots of European Fascism.* Bergen-Oslo-Tromsø: Universitetsforlaget, 1980.

Ulateig, Egil. "*Verre enn Auschwitz. De jødiske fangenes skjebne, Historien om Falstad — en konsentrasjonsleir i Norge*" (Worse than Auschwitz. The Fate of the Jewish Prisoners. The History of Falstad — a Concentration Camp in Norway). *Vi Menn*, Oslo, No. 24 (June 14, 1983), pp. 10–13.

Ulstein, Ragnar. *Englandsfarten. Vol. I: Alarm i Ålesund* (The Transport to England. Volume I: Alarm in Ålesund). Oslo: Det Norske Samlaget, 1967.

Ulstein, Ragnar. *Svensketrafikken I. Flyktninger til Sverige 1940–43* (The Swedish Traffic. Refugees to Sweden 1940–43). Oslo: Det Norske Samlaget, 1974.

Valentin, Hugo. "Rescue and Relief Activities on Behalf of Jewish Victims of Nazism in Scandinavia." In: *YIVO Annual of Jewish Social Science*, Vol VIII, pp. 224–251. New York: Yiddish Scientific Institute. 1953.

Valentin, Hugo. "The History of the Jews in Sweden." In: Herman Bary, ed. *European Jewish Yearbook*, pp. 290–294. Frankfurt and Paris: 1953.

Valentin, Hugo. *Antisemitism Historically and Critically Examined.* New York: The Viking Press, 1943.

Valentin, Hugo. *Judarna i Sverige* (The Jews in Sweden). Stockholm: Bonniers, 1964.

Valentin, Hugo. *Judarnas Historia i Sverige* (History of the Jews in Sweden), Stockholm: Bonniers, 1924.

Våre falne norske jøder — utarbeidet avd Det Mosaiske Trosamfund, Oslo (Our Fallen Norwegian Jews, as listed by The Mosaic Religious Society of Oslo.) Yad Vashem Achives B/28-1, n.d.

Vogt, Benjamin. "Quisling. The Man and the Criminal." *The American- Scandinavian Review* XXXV: 3 (September 1947), pp. 201–209; XXXVI; 1 (March 1948), pp. 37–46.

Vogt, Benjamin. *Mennesket Vidkun og forræderen Quisling* (The Human Being Vidkun and The Traitor Quisling). Oslo: Aschehoug, 1965.

Vogt, Johan. "*En korrespondanse med Mr. Hewins*" (A Correspondence with Mr. Hewins). In: *Speil for tidens ansikt* (Mirrors of the Face of Our Time), Oslo: J.W. Cappelens Forlag, 1970.

Vogt, Johan. *Det store brennoffer. Jødenes skjebne under den andre verdenskrig* (The Holocaust. The Fate of the Jews during World War II). Oslo: Universitetsforlaget, 1966.

Volckmar, Alf. "Jewish Immigration to Norway," a Report to Secretary Banger, Ministry of Social Affairs. Oslo: January 8, 1948.

Våre falne 1939–1945, utgitt av den norske stat (Our Fallen 1939–1945). Vol. 1–4. Oslo: Published by the State of Norway, 1949–50.

Wachsman, Z. H. *Jews in Post-War Europe, the Governments in Exile and Their Attitude Towards the Jews.* New York: H. H. Glanz, 1944.

Wasberg, Gunnar. *Historien om 1814. En beretning i dokumenter, sitater og illustrasjoner* (History of 1814. An account through documents, quotations, and illustrations). Oslo: Dreyers Forlag, 1964.

Weis, Aharon. "Quantitative Measurement of Features of the Holocaust: Notes on the Book by Helen Fein." *Yad Vashem Studies* XIV (1981), pp. 319–334.

Wergeland, Henrik. *Indlæg i Jødesagen til Understøttelse for Forslaget om Ophævelse af Norges Grundlovs Paragraph 2. Sidste Passus* (Plea for the Jewish Cause in Support of the Proposal to rescind Article 2, Last Paragraph of Norway's Constitution, Christiania, 1841.

Wergeland, Henrik. *Samlede Skrifter* (Collected Works). Edited by Hartvig Lassen. Christiania: Chr. Tønsberg Forlag, 1852–57.

Werner, Alfred. "Henrik Arnold Wergeland." *The Universal Jewish Encyclopedia.* Vol. 10. New York: Universal Jewish Encyclopedia Co., Inc. 1948, p. 503.

Wiehrmyhr, J. "*Registrering av jøder i Norge*" (Registration of Jews in Norway). Letter of October 27, 1942. Ref. No. 1205/42B, p. 1. National Archives, Oslo.

Wiesel, Elie, *Night,* New York: Hill and Wang, 1960.

Wiesel, Elie, *Dawn,* Jason, Aronson, New York, 1985.

Wiesel, Elie, *The Gates of the Forest,* Schocken, 1966.

Wiesel, Elie, *Against Silence: The Voice and Vision of Elie Wiesel,* Irving Abrahamson (Ed.), Holocaust Library, New York, 1985.

Wiesener, A. *Nordmenn for tysk krigsrett* (Norwegians Facing German Court Martial). Oslo: Dreyer, 1954.

Wisløff, Carl Fr. *Norsk Kirkehistorie.* Vol. III. Oslo: Lutherstiftelsen, 1971.

Wolfberg, Leiba. "*Mannen som spilte for livet*" (The Man Who Played for his Life). Interview, Norwegian Broadcasting Co., Oslo, February 9, 1965, Tape No. 51500/1, and November 25, 1966, Tape No. 50966.

Wormdal, Celine. *Kvinner i krig* (Women at War). Oslo: Aschehoug, 1979.

Wyller, Thomas Christian. *Nyordning og motstand: Organisasjonenes rolle under okkupasjonen* (New Order and Resistance: The Role of Organizations during the Occupation). Oslo: J.W. Cappelens Forlag, 1948.

Wyller, Thomas Christian, "*Vidkun Quisling og Rettsoppgjøret,*" (Vidkun Quisling and the Legal Accounting). *Samtiden,* Oslo, vol. 75, (1966) pp. 216 ff.

Wyller, Trygve. *Fangeliv og fri tanke* (Prison Life and Free Thought). Oslo: J.W. Cappelens Forlag, 1948.

Yad Vashem Archives, Doc. B/28-1. "*Yad Vashem-medalje til våre redningsmenn*" (Yad Vashem Medal to our Rescuers). *Jødisk Menighetsblad for Det Mosaiske Trosamfund, Oslo og Trondheim* (Jewish Journal for the Mosaic Religious Community, Oslo and Trondheim) 2: 3 (December 1977), pp. 13–32.

Yahil, Leni. "Raoul Wallenberg — His Mission and His Activities in Hungary." *Yad Vashem Studies*, Jerusalem, XV (1983), pp. 7–53.

Yahil, Leni. "Scandinavian Countries to the Rescue of Concentration Camp Prisoners." *Yad Vashem Studies*, vol. VI Jerusalem, 1967, pp. 181–220.

Yahil, Leni. *The Rescue of Danish Jewry*, Philadelphia: Jewish Publication Society, 1969.

Yahil, Leni. "Methods of Persecution. A Comparison of the 'Final Solution' in Holland and Denmark." *Scripta Hierosolymita* 23 (1972).

Zimmels, H. J. *The Echo of the Nazi Holocaust in Rabbinical Literature*. New York: Ktav Publishing Co., 1977.

Bibliographies

Guide to Jewish History under Nazi Impact, compiled by Jacob Robinson and Philip Friedman. Yad Vashem & YIVO Joint Documentary Project, Bibliographical Series No. 1. Martin Press, New York, 1960. 425 pp.

The Holocaust and After; Sources and Literature in English, compiled by Jacob Robinson, assisted by Mrs. Philip Friedman. Yad Vashem and YIVO Joint Documentary Project, Bibliographical Series No. 12. Jerusalem, Israel Universities Press, 1973. 353 pp.

Documents

DOCUMENT 1

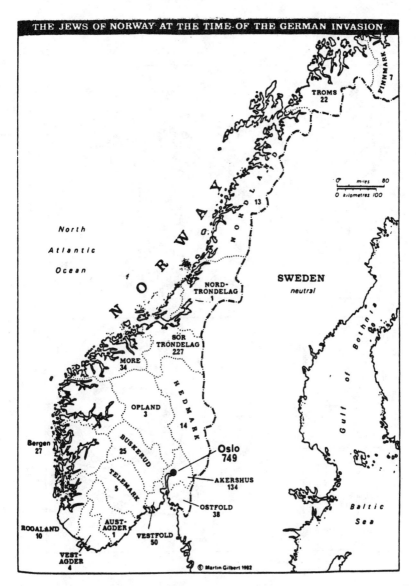

THE JEWS OF NORWAY AT THE TIME OF THE GERMAN INVASION

North Atlantic Ocean

NORWAY

SWEDEN
neutral

FINNMARK 7

TROMS 22

NORDLAND 13

NORD-TRONDELAG 1

SÖR TRONDELAG 227

MORE 34

OPLAND 3

HEDMARK 14

Bergen 27

BUSKERUD 25

Oslo 749

AKERSHUS 134

TELEMARK 5

OSTFOLD 38

ROGALAND 10

AUST-AGDER 1

VESTFOLD 50

VEST-AGDER 4

Gulf of Bothnia

Baltic Sea

0   miles   80
0   kilometres   100

© Martin Gilbert 1982

Martin Gilbert, *Atlas of the Holocaust,* Steinmatsky's Agency Limited, Jerusalem, Tel Aviv-Haifa, 1982 (by permission).

The numbers refer to Jews living in each of Norway's *Fylker* (counties) in April 1940, but does not take into account about 200 refugees from Central Europe.

SOURCE: Odd Lindbäck-Larsen, Krigen i Norge 1940 (The War in Norway).

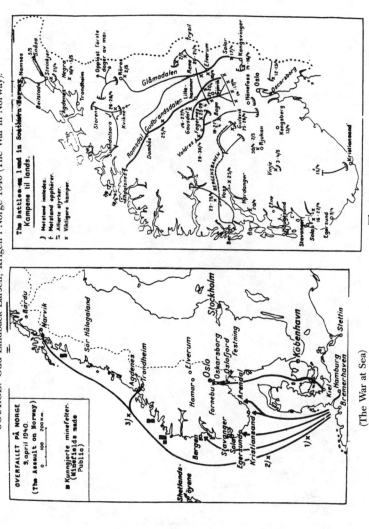

(The War at Sea)

(The War on Land in Southern Norway)

Gyldendal Norsk Forlag, 1965.

DOCUMENT 3

PROCLAMATION BY NORWAY'S SUPREME COURT.

As German army forces have taken over certain parts of Norway and thereby made it actually impossible for the Norwegian Government to maintain its administrative leadership in these parts of the country, and as it is a compelling necessity that the civil administration be in operation, the Supreme Court has found it must provide for the maintenance during the occupation of these parts of the country by German troops, of a council to preside over the civil administration thereof.

Confident that the King of Norway will approve the Supreme Court's action under the existing extraordinary conditions in seizing this necessary solution, the Supreme Court appoints as members of this temporary administrative council:

Governor of Province I.E. Christensen, Chairman,
Director J. Bache-Wiig,
Chief Medical Officer Andreas Diesen,
-District Judge O.F. Harbek,
Director Gunnar Jahn,
Lecturer R.J. Mork,
Rector of the University of Oslo Didrik Arup Seip.

Oslo, April 15, 1940.

PAAL BERG
Chief Supreme Court Justice

ANNOUNCEMENT

There has been appointed today an Administrative Council for the occupied territory.

We who have taken over this commission make an earnest appeal to organizations and private individuals in these districts to give us assistance in our difficult work.

We ask that all show calmness and self-control and at the same time assist according to ability in continuing operations and work.

Everyone in thinking the matter over will realize that sabotage and rendering difficult civil operations merely bring disaster.

Oslo, April 15, 1940.
I.E. Christensen, Gunnar Jahn,
O.F. Harbek, R. Mork, Bache-Wiig,
A. Diesen, Didrik Arup Seip.

Note: Biographical data of the Norwegian Administrative Council were forwarded with Legation's despatch No. 644 of April 30, 1940.

Kunngjøring
fra   M 22 JAN 1942
Politidepartementet

Stempling av jøders legitimasjonskort m. v.

Legitimasjonskort, grenseboerbevis, passersedler og tjenestebevis (som tilhører jøder skal for å være gyldige være stemplet med «J». Som jøde etter denne bestemmelse ansees:

1. Den som nedstammer fra minst 3 av rase fulljødiske besteforeldre, uansett hvilket statsborgerskap han måtte ha. Som fulljøde blir i ethvert tilfelle den av besteforeldrene å regne som har tilhørt det jødisk trossamfund.

2. Som jøde regnes også jødisk bastard som nedstammer fra 2 fulljødiske besteforeldre:
   a) Når han ved utferdigelsen av denne kunngjøring tilhører det jødiske trossamfund eller senere blir opptatt i dette.
   b) Når han ved utferdigelsen av denne kunngjøring er gift med jøde eller senere gifter seg med jøde.

3. Samtlige medlemmer av det mosaiske trossamfund er å anse som jøder.

Personer som i henhold til foranstående bestemmelser skal være i besiddelse av J-stemplet legitimasjonsbevis må innen 1. mars d. å. melde seg til den politimester eller lensmann som har utstedt hans legitimasjonsbevis, for å få stemplingen foretatt.

Unnlatelse herav straffes med bøter eller med fengsel inntil 3 måneder.

Oslo, 20. januar 1942.

Announcement from the Police Department of January 20, 1942, regarding stamping of "J" in Identity papers for the Jewish population in Norway as published in *Aftenposten* (Oslo) January 22, 1942.

DOCUMENT 5

Iltelegram

fra

Statspolitisjefen

den 25. oktober 1942 kl. 10,30

Alle mannlige personer over 15 år hvis legitimasjonskort er stemplet med J, skal arresteres uansett alder oppover, og transporteres til Kirkeveien 23, Oslo. Arrestasjonen skal skje mandag den 26. oktober kl. 0600. Arrestantene må medta skaffetøy, rasjoneringskort og alle legitimasjonsdokumenter. Formuen beslaglegge Oppmerksomheten henledes på verdipapirer, smykker og kontanter, og heretter må det ransakes. Bank-konti sperres og bankbokser t. Det beslaglagte beror hos Dem inntil nærmere ordre. Registrering dokumenter innsendes hertil snarest. Der må innsettes bestyrer av de arrestertes forretninger. Oppgave over de arresterte med angivelse av statsborgerforhold, spesielt om tidligere tysk borg skap, innsendes omgående hertil. Alle voksne jødinner pålegges daglig meldeplikt ved ordenspolitiets kriminalavdeling.

Statspolitisjefen.

Emergency telegram from the Chief of the State Police, Oslo, October 25, 1942 at 10:30 A.M. regarding arrests and transportations to Kirkeveien 23, Oslo of all male Jews above the age of fifteen.

"All adult women are enjoined to report daily at the Criminal Department of the Police. The arrests shall take place Monday October 26 at 6 A.M."

RECEIPT OF 532 Jews from Norway to Auschwitz, December 1, 1942.

AAPTENPOSTEN (Evening News)
Oslo, May 12,1961 ·
Fortsatt fra 1. side

Eichmann —

Konzentrationslager Auschwitz
Kommandantur / Abt. II

Auschwitz, den "1. Dezember 194 2

Az. 14 c 4 / 12,42 / St.

V.S.S.T.V.S.D.V.S.B.S.S.S.T.S.S.G.V.B.SS

Die Übernahme von -532- Juden aus Norwegen
wird hiermit bestätigt.

Der Lagerkommandant
I.A.
Obergruppenführer STARK   i.a.

1. desember 1942 kritterte leirkommandanten i Auschwitz konsentrasjonsleir for 532 jøder fra Norge. Alle-
rede ved ankomsten ble de delt i to grupper. Arbeidsdyktige menn ble satt i slavearbeide mens kvinner og
barn og de som ikke kunne arbeide ble sendt til gasskammerne. Bare 21 av de 532 overlevet deportasjonen

On December 1, 1942 the camp commander of Auschwitz Concentration Camp acknowledged receipt of 532 Jews from Norway. They were divided into two groups upon arrival.
Men capable of working were sent to work as slaves, while women and children and those
who could not work were sent to the gas chambers. Only 21 of the 532 survived the deportation.

Dødsdommer i Trondheim

Der Höhere SS- und Polizeiführer Nord meddeler: I samband med forholdsreglene for den sivile unntagelsestilstand ble følgende norske statsborgere den 6. oktober 1942 kl. 18 skutt som soning for flere sabotasjeforsøk som i den siste tid er forøvet på noen bedrifter som tjener det norske folks forsyning:

1. Advokat Otto Skirstad, Trondheim.
2. Teatersjef Henry Gleditsch, Trondheim.
3. Redaktør Harald Langhelle, Trondheim.
4. Forretningsdrivende Hirsch, kommissar (jøde), Trondheim.

5. Ingeniør Hans Konrad Ekornes, Trondheim.
6. Banksjef Birch, Trondheim.
7. Skipsmegler Per T. Lykke, Trondheim.
8. Advokat Bull Aakran, Røros.
9. Byggeleder Peder Eggen, Orkanger,
   og
10. Kaptein Finn Berg, Trondheim.

Hele formuen til de henrettede personer er beslaglagt og inndratt.

REDIESS
(sign.).

SS-Obergruppenführer und General der deutschen Polizei.

"Death Sentences in Trondheim," *Morgenbladet*, Oslo, October 7, 1942. The Murder of ten Hostages. Proclamation of Civil State of Emergency, October 6, 1942 Number 4 is "Hirsh Kommissar, (sic) Jøde," (Jew).

DOCUMENT 8

Telegram

1041 NARVIK 05006 29/27 2 1625 =

STATSPOLITISJEFEN   OSLO =

To104:

STATSPOLITISJEFENS   ORDRE 25/10 DAVID FISCHER FØDT 20/6

1899 SAMUEL FISCHER 5/10 1907 OG WULF FISCHER 12/4

1922 SENDES HERFRA IDAG STOPP DOKUMENTER FØLGER

SNAREST = POLITIKAMMERET +

25/10 20/6 1899 5/10 1907 12/4 1922 +

Telegram from Narvik police to the Chief of Police, Oslo, October 25 (1942).
Re: Arrests of Jews in Narvik of the families David Fischer, Samuel Fischer, Oscar
Bernstein, Jacob Kaplan, and Martin Fischer

Geheime Staatspolizei - Staatspolizeileitstelle Stettin

	Staatspolizeileitstelle Stettin		
30. 11. 42	Eing.: 28. 11. 42		
	Dienststelle	Gesch.	Rückfpr. erled.:
			Bericht vorgel.:

F.-S. 1842

++ OSLO FS 20089 26.11.42 2045 == FR.==

GEHEIM - DRINGEND. SOFORT VORLEGEN.-

AN DIE STL. STETTIN.-

BETR.: ABTRANSPORT DER JUDEN AUS NORWEGEN.--

VORG.: HIES. FS V. 24. 11. 42 --

HEUTE NACHMITTAG UM 14.55 UHR VERLIESS DIE '' DONAU'' M.
532 JUEDISCHEN HAEFTLINGEN DEN OSLOER HAFEN. MIT DEM
EINTREFFEN IST IN DEN FRUEHEN MORGENSTEUNDEN DES 29.11.1?
ZU RECHNEN DIE MARINEDIENSTSTELLE STETTIN, DER DIE GENAUE
ANKUNFTSZEUT FUNKTELEGRAFISCH MITGETEILT WERDEN WIRD, KA.
AUSKUNFTE UEBER DEN GENAUEN ANKUNFTSTERMIN GEBEN-- VON DE?
HIES. DIENSTSTELLE WURDE SS- U' STUF. GROSSMANN ALS --------
TRANSPORTFUEHRER EINGESETZT. ER WIRD EINE NAMENTLICHE------
AUFSTELLUNG DER JUDEN UEBERBRINGEN. DEM TRANSPORT WURDEN
BETRAECHTLICHE MENGEN LEBENSMITTEL MITGEGEBEN.- ICH BITTE,
SS- UNTERSTURMFUEHRER GROSSMANN MITZUTEILEN, DASS ER FUER
DEN RUECKTRANSPORT DER AUF DER'' DONAU'' VERBLIEBENE:
SCHREIBMASCHINE VERANTWORTLICH IST.---

BDS U. D. SD USLO - ROEM 4 B

I. A. GEZ. REINHARD, SS- S

Telex of November 26, 1942 from Norway's Gestapo Chief Sturmbannführer Hellmuth Reinhard regarding deportation of 532 Norwegian Jews from Oslo to Stettin on board the S/S/ "Donau", November 28, 1942 at 2:55 P.M.

STATSPOLITIET

Bergenskontoret

Tlf. 13 650

Bergen den 21. jan. *194* 3.

T r a n s p o r t o r d r e.

Jödinne Alice B o r i n s k y, f.15/7-92 er i henhold
til ordre fra Lederen av Statspolitiet beordret transporter‡
til Oslo.
　　　　Transporten foretas den 21/1-43 under bevoktning av
statspolitikonstablene Johannessen og Gundersen.

For avdelingslederen:

(signature) Johansen
pfm.

The State Police
The Bergen Office
Telephone 13 650

Bergen Jan. 21, 1943

TRANSPORTORDER

According to the order from the Leader of the
State Police the Jewess Alice Borinsky b. July 15,1892 is
ordered to be transported to Oslo.

The transport will take place on January 21,
1943 guarded by the 　　 State Polic e Officers
Johannesen and Gundersen.

On behalf of the Divion Leader,
Sr. Johansen
Police Officer

Document 11

Berg Interneringsleir

TØNSBERG
TELEFON 3130

D. d. mottatt jøden Hermann Ficher fra fengselsykehuset,
Oslo.

Berg Interneringsleir
TØNSBERG

Leif Lindseth
vaktsjef.

TRANSLATION

BERG INTERNMENT CAMP
Tønsberg
Telephone 3130

Tønsberg, January 26, 1944

Received under today's date the Jew Hermann Fischer
from the Prison Hospital, OSLO.

Leif Lindseth
Chief Guard

Minnegudstjenesten

i

Det Mosaiske Trossamfunds

synagoge

fredag den 31. august 1945

———— --•-— ————

22. Elul 5705

Memorial Service in the Mosaic Religious Society's Synagogue, Oslo, Friday August 31, 1945 (22 Elul 5705) containing blessings of King Haakon, Crown Prince Olav and Crown Princess Märtha and the total Royal House.

Han, som giʳ kongene seier og
de salvede makten, og hvis rike
er evighetens rike, han, som frel-
ste sin tjener David fra det tru-
ende sverd, som banet en vei
gjennem havet og en sti gjennem
de mektige vann, han velsigne og
bevare, skjærme og beskytte,
ophøie og opløfte til heder og
ære vår drott

Kong

HAAKON VII

Kronprins

OLAV

Kronprinsesse

MÄRTHA

og hele det kongelige hus!

Således være det Guds vilje!
Amen!

הַנּוֹתֵן תְּשׁוּעָה לַמְּלָכִים.
וּמֶמְשָׁלָה לַנְּסִיכִים. מַלְכוּתוֹ
מַלְכוּת כָּל־עוֹלָמִים. הַפּוֹצֶה
אֶת־דָּוִד עַבְדּוֹ מֵחֶרֶב רָעָה.
הַנּוֹתֵן בַּיָּם דָּרֶךְ וּבְמַיִם עַזִּים
נְתִיבָה. הוּא יְבָרֵךְ וְיִשְׁמֹר
וְיִנְצֹר וְיַעֲזֹר וִירוֹמֵם וְיַגְדֵּל
וִינַשֵּׂא לְמַעְלָה אֶת־אֲדוֹנֵנוּ

הַמֶּלֶךְ
הָקָאן הַשְּׁבִיעִי
יָרוּם הוֹדוֹ.

וְאֶת
יוֹרֵשׁ עֶצֶר הַמְּלוּכָה
אֹלָאף
וְאֶת
יוֹרֶשֶׁת עֶצֶר הַמְּלוּכָה
מָרְתָא
וְאֶת כָּל בֵּית הַמַּלְכוּת
יָרוּם הוֹדָם.
וְכֵן יְהִי רָצוֹן וְנֹאמַר אָמֵן:

MEMORIAL SERVICE, OSLO SYNAGOGUE, FRIDAY, AUGUST 31, 1945 (Elul 22, 5705)

DET MOSAISKE TROSSAMFUND, OSLO

Overrekkelse av medaljen fra Yad Vashem
Søndag 30. oktober 1977

1. Forstanderen for Det Mosaiske Trossamfund,
   Kai Feinberg.

2. Ernst Glaser violin
   Robert Levin klaver
   Edvard Grieg: 1. sats fra Sonate C-moll.

3. Oskar Mendelsohn
   Jødeforfølgelsene i Norge. Norsk motstand — hjelp til
   flukt.

4. Tor Stokke
   Dikt av Emil Boyson, Nelly Sachs, Gunvor Hofmoe og
   Inger Hagerup.

5. Leo Eitinger
   Fra fortvilelse til tro på mennesket.

6. Ernst Glaser og Robert Levin.
   Ernest Bloch: Simchat Torah

7. Medaljen fra Yad Vashem overrekkes.
   Israels ambassadør i Norge, David Z. Rivlin.
   Formannen i styret for Norges Hjemmefrontmuseum,
   Ole Borge.

Program for presentation of Yad Vashem Medal to the Mosaic Congregation of Oslo, October 30, 1977 by Hon. David Z. Rivlin, Israeli Ambassador to Norway.

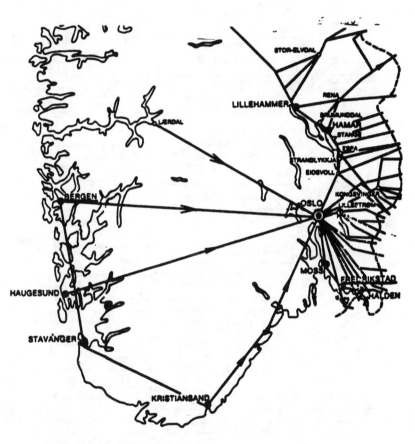

Escape Routes in Southern Norway to Sweden

Source: Ragnar Ulstein, Svensketrafikken. Flyktninger til Sverige 1940-43 (vol. 1): Det
Norske Samlaget, 1974.

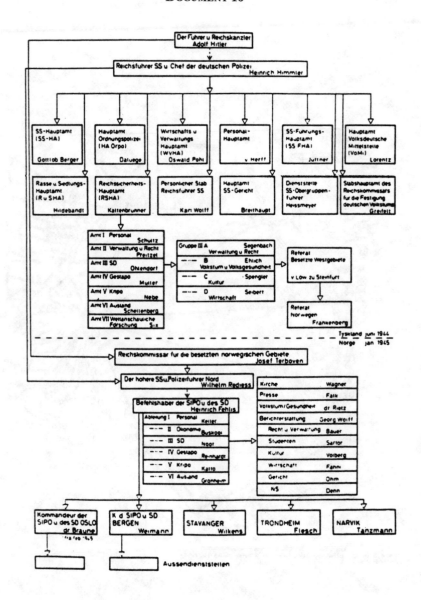

THE GERMAN POLICE ORGANIZATION IN NORWAY 1940-1945
Source: Tore Dyrhaug, *Norge Okkupert! Tysk Etteretning om Norge og Nordmenn 1942-1945*. Oslo-Bergen-Stavanger-Tromsø; Universitetsforlaget, AS, 1985, Inside Cover.

Grunnlovens prg. 2 atter i sin opprinnelige form.

„Jøder ere udelukkede fra Adgang til Riget"

I sin store tale igår i Lier offentliggjorde minister Sverre Riisnæs at ministerpresidenten samme dag på et bastemt område hadde gjenreist landets grunnlov, hvor den veke liberalismen i forrige århundre hadde skjemmet loven med et skamhugg. Nasjonal Samling bygger den nye stat med grunnloven som fundament.

Ministerpresidentens restaurering gjelder Grunnlovens paragraf 2. Han har gitt bestemmelsen tilbake det i 1851 opphevede annet ledd: «Jøder ere udelukkede fra Adgang til Riget».

På Eidsvoldsfedrenes tid hadde vi ennu bevart vårt nordiske livssyn. Vårt folk erkjente at en av de første pliktene for et folk som vil eie livets rett, er denne: Å ta vare på folkets blod. Den sunde rasebevisste tanke er også i nøye samsvar med N. S.' ideologiske syn. På meget sterkere grunn har det været for Vidkun Quisling til å gjenreise grunnlovsbestemmelsen som jødedommen idag er en ganske annen farlig fiende for vår stamme enn den var på den tid da grunnloven blev gitt.

Ministeren gav i tilknytning til sin offentliggjørelse en utredning av Nasjonal Samlings syn på de grunnverdiene som skaper et folks liv, folkets jord og blod. Det er Nasjonal Samlings første oppgave å verne disse verdiene.

Offentliggjørelsen av ministerpresidentens grunnlovsbestemmelse blev hilst med et kraftig og langvarig bifall av den store forsamling som hadde fylt herredshuset til siste plass.

Source: *Aftenposten* (Evening News), Oslo, March 14, 1942.

"Article 2 in the Constitution is again in its original wording: Jews are still excluded from admission to the Kingdom." Excerpt from a speech by Minister of Justice Sverre Riisnæs who stated that "one of the first duties for a people wanting to possess the right to live is to take care of the blood of the population." Quisling re-introduced Article 2 of the Norwegian Constitution of 1814 although it had been abolished in 1851.

Index